EVERYDAY HARM

MINDIE LAZARUS-BLACK

Everyday Harm

DOMESTIC VIOLENCE, COURT RITES, AND
CULTURES OF RECONCILIATION

UNIVERSITY OF ILLINOIS PRESS

URBANA AND CHICAGO

ISBN-13: 978-0-252-03155-7 (cloth)
ISBN-10: 0-252-03155-5 (cloth)
ISBN-13: 978-0-252-07408-0 (paper)
ISBN-10: 0-252-07408-4 (paper)

Library of Congress Cataloging-in-Publication Data
Lazarus-Black, Mindie.
Everyday harm : domestic violence, court rites,
and cultures of reconciliation / Mindie Lazarus-Black.
p. cm.
Includes bibliographical references and index.
ISBN 978-0-252-03155-7 (cloth : alk. paper)
ISBN 978-0-252-07408-0 (pbk. : alk. paper)
1. Family violence—Law and legislation—Trinidad and Tobago.
2. Domestic relations courts—Trinidad and Tobago.
3. Dispute resolution (Law)—Trinidad and Tobago.
4. Reconciliation—Social aspects—Trinidad and Tobago
I. Title.
KGX445.F36L39   2007
345.72983'02555—dc22   2007005140

This book is dedicated to my parents,
who watch carefully over
each generation

Contents

Acknowledgments   ix

Introduction: The Vanishing Complainant   1

1. Imagining and Implementing Domestic Violence Law   21

2. A Look at the Numbers   35

3. The Meaning of Success   65

4. Court Rites   91

5. Time and the Legal Process   119

6. Cultures of Reconciliation   139

Conclusion: How Law Works   159

Notes   177

Bibliography   213

Index   235

Acknowledgments

I always wanted to write, but when I was a child, I didn't realize that my decision would bear upon the lives of so many other people. This is one of those rare opportunities to say thank you and to acknowledge how grateful I am.

My thanks go first to my husband, Bill Black, for listening, engaging, seeing both sides of every story, being my tech guy, maintaining a sense of humor, and sharing the uncommon belief that we might dream and work true to our own spirits, but together. My thanks to our daughter, Lisa Lazarus-Black Matson, who has been with me on my journey for a long time and who still has the soles on her shoes, a winning wit, and a sense of the possible. It is a joy to watch you and Michael with your daughters, Rebecca and Ellie. Thank you, Jan Lee Kaplan, my sister, who sustains me in ways she probably can't imagine. This book is dedicated to my parents, Vivien and Sam Schwartz, who, as they say in the Caribbean, "grew me," and continue to grow and to guide our family.

In the summer of 1995, a grant from the Office of Social Science Research at the University of Illinois at Chicago (UIC) enabled me to become a visiting scholar at the Centre for Gender and Development at the University of the West Indies (UWI), St. Augustine, Trinidad and Tobago. That summer, and through the later periods of my fieldwork and teaching at UWI, I benefited from ongoing conversations with Bridget Brereton, Andy Caffyn, Dereck Chadee, Ramesh Deosaran, Kusha Haraksingh, Sue Perks, Rhoda Reddock, Selwyn Ryan, Dana Seetahal, and Hazel Thompson-Ahye. At the Caribbean Association for Feminist Research and Action (CAFRA), I was assisted by Cathy Shepherd. The staff at the

University of the West Indies Library, West India Collection, graciously assisted me with assembling references.

My extended research in 1997–98 and the summer of 1999 was supported by grants from the American Council of Learned Societies/Social Science Research Council and the Wenner-Gren Foundation for Anthropological Research. In addition, a Fulbright Senior Scholar award enabled me to teach at the University of the West Indies in Trinidad in the fall of 1997. While I was lecturing and holding office hours at UWI, some of the students I encountered, including Catherine Ali, Shirly Ann Hosein, Rhonda Julien, Sophia Persad, and Christine Scofield, debated and read some of my preliminary work and gave me suggestions to improve its accuracy and quality. I especially thank Raquel Sukhu for helping me collect court data in Port of Spain and for the times when we talked about this project, our lives, and life in Trinidad. Justice Arrestine Sealey, principal of the Hugh Wooding Law School, gave me permission to use the law school's collection, and June Renie was especially helpful during my research in that library. Jo-Ann Connors, Stephanie Daly, Nannette Forde-John, Sandra Ramnath, and Tracy Robinson sustained with patience my questions about law and policy.

The Humanities Institute at UIC assisted me with two grants so that Joseph Robert Targonski could conduct the painstaking labor of data entry of the court records. Thank you, Joe, for entering the data and for your sense of humor about my handwriting. In 2001, the Wenner-Gren Foundation sponsored a conference organized by Sally Engle Merry and me on "Violence against Intimates, Globalization, and the State" at Wellesley College. That conference brought us together with Madelaine Adelman, Susan F. Hirsch, James Ptacek, Sherene Razack, Rebecca Torstrick, and Sylvia Vatuk to spend three thoughtful days debating law's role—past, present, and future—in combating violence against women. Much of the draft of this book was written while I was a Fellow at the Institute for the Humanities at UIC. Director Mary Beth Rose, Linda Vavra, and my colleagues at the institute made the academic year 2001–2 an extremely rewarding experience. I thank each of these foundations, institutions, libraries, students, and scholars.

I gratefully acknowledge the women and men in Trinidad who are the heart of this book. Chief Magistrate Sherman McNichols gave me permission to observe the magistrates' courts. In each of the four magistrate's courts in which I worked, people offered me every assistance. Those who worked regularly in the court in which I spent most of my time deserve a special thanks. Lawyers and magistrates I interviewed patiently extended their time and the benefit of their experiences about how law works (or doesn't). The attorneys' offices were both places of learning and sanctuaries. Questions about what happens when a woman applies for a protection order and for what reasons needed to be answered by those who sought the courts' protection. Some of these interviewees befriended me, introduced me to their families and neighbors, and allowed me to spend precious time in their homes. (Efforts to teach me to cook were hopeless, but I am forever grateful for the experiences of sampling home-cooked meals.) The need to protect all of my interviewees' identities means that I cannot name you and thank you publicly; I thank you personally instead for your time and insights, and for believing with me that a comprehensive understanding of how law works can have useful consequences for better protecting women against violence. I'd also like to acknowledge the crew with whom I hung out on weekends and who introduced me to Trinidad's natural wonders, art, theater, music, dance, and places trendy and off the beaten tracks. These friendships are perennial.

The Department of Criminal Justice at the University of Illinois at Chicago, home to my research and teaching life, is unusual in its commitment to interdisciplinary research. I thank my colleagues for welcoming an anthropologist into territories that you refused to fence, for your support, interesting scholarship, and our debates about research and teaching, sometimes under siege conditions. Lisa Frohmann, Matthew Lippman, Mike Maltz, Greg Matoesian, and Joe Peterson spent an uncanny number of hours reading and talking about work in progress that would eventually culminate in this book. Thank you, Donna Dorney, for caring and for making the bureaucracy (and everything else) run on time. I want to acknowledge, too, those UIC students who were skeptical about having an anthropologist teach them criminal justice courses but who decided, after all, that there might be something interesting, even useful, in learning about the people of southern Africa or men who live on the streets, how people talk in courts, and why law sometimes forces impoverished women to engage in illegalities.

Both before and after meetings of the American Anthropological Association and the Law & Society Association, and sometimes just during the week, my thinking has benefited from discussions with Shellee Colen, Wendy Espeland, Marcia Farr, Leah Feldman, Bryant Garth, Carol J. Greenhouse, Susan F. Hirsch, Audie Klotz, Michael Landy, Ken Leiter, Cynthia Mahabir, Nancy Matthews, Sarah Maza, Sally Engle Merry, Elizabeth Mertz, Dennis Torreggiani, Judith Wittner, and Kevin Yelvington. Three insightful writers, my mother-in-law, Ann Black; Laura Hein; and Sydney Halpern, were especially helpful in encouraging me to frame the publication proposal. Anonymous reviewers for the two journals in which I published some of my initial findings refined my arguments. Versions of chapters 3 and 4 were published in *The American Ethnologist* (Lazarus-Black 1997, 2001), and a rendition of chapter 1 appeared in *Law & Social Inquiry* (Lazarus-Black 2003). The Centre for Gender and Development at the University of the West Indies also circulated abbreviated portions of chapter 4 as part of its *Working Papers Series* (Lazarus-Black 2002). At the University of Illinois Press, Kerry Callahan initiated this book's progress through the selection and editorial process and Anne Rogers kindly tended to the copyediting. Finally, Patricia L. McCall spent an extraordinary amount of time creating the quantitative record that comprises chapter 2 and teaching me about the possibilities and practicalities of crunching numbers (not to mention what *not* to do next time). We wrote that chapter together. Thank you, Patty.

EVERYDAY HARM

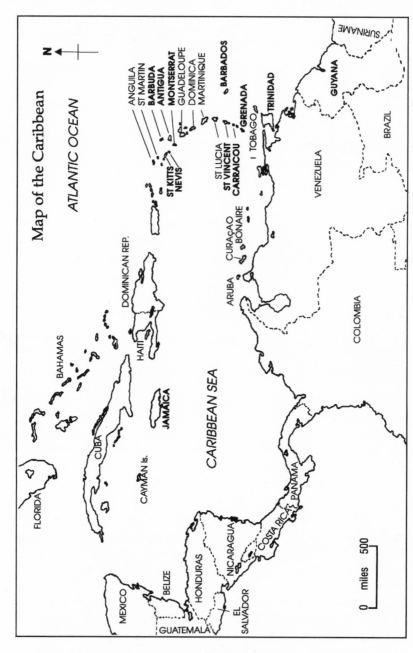

Map of the Caribbean

From Christine Barrow, Family in the Caribbean: Themes and Perspectives (Kingston: Ian Randle Publishers, 1996), ii.

Introduction:
The Vanishing Complainant

On November 13, 1990, Richard Daniel of Marabella, Trinidad, murdered his wife, Ramdaye. He followed her to her parent's house where she had gone to live following an incident three days earlier in which Richard had pulled out a knife and threatened to kill her in front of their teenage son. On the day of the murder, Ramdaye's mother overheard the couple quarreling in her daughter's room, but she had not interfered. Around noon, she observed Richard leaving the house. Not long after, someone phoned for Ramdaye. Her brother knocked at the door of her room. When she didn't answer, he went in. He found Ramdaye on the bed with her underwear stuffed into her mouth and a pillow and jersey over her face.

Meanwhile, Richard went to the village of Pointe-a-Pierre. He told two coworkers that he had just strangled his wife because she was "horning" him (having an affair) with a white man with an expensive car. Alarmed, Richard's coworkers left him at a bar near the sea and went to the police. Richard saw the police arriving and tried to commit suicide by throwing himself into the rough waters. He was rescued and taken into custody.

Initially charged with murder, Richard eventually pleaded guilty to the lesser charge of manslaughter. His lawyer told the court that Richard "had felt humiliated" and that "he was scorned by his friends and family." The judge announced that Richard would escape a life sentence because of his "relentless efforts to reconcile with a wife who brazenly admitted to her adulterous ways to him." He committed Richard to prison for fifteen years (*Trinidad Express*, December 16, 1994).[1]

The case made cultural sense to Trinidad's newspaper-reading public. Daily readers would recognize at least seven features in the account of Richard and Ramdaye that they would have read about previously.[2] First, following traditional Indo-Trinidadian custom, the couple had married at a very early age with the approval of their respective extended families. Second, Richard found his youthful bride was not up to the task of homemaking and their relationship quickly succumbed to threats of and real episodes of violence. Third, when threatened, Ramdaye sought not divorce, but refuge with her parents, since divorce remains stigmatized among conservative Trinidadian families. Fourth, Ramdaye chose to have an affair with a man whose wealth and status were exposed in the newspapers, not by naming him, but by identifying his race and his car (Miller 1994:237–45). Fifth, Richard's "honor" could not sustain his wife's adultery. Sixth, Richard attempted suicide, a common response to wife murder in the Indo-Trinidadian community.[3] Finally, the charge of wife murder was reduced to manslaughter.[4] That the judge commented in court on Ramdaye's adultery before sentencing Richard accords with the simple "truth" one hears and reads about regularly in Trinidad: "Trini man can't take horn" (Philips 2000:175).

In August 1991, just nine months after Ramdaye's murder and Richard's attempted suicide, Trinidad and Tobago became the first nation in the English-speaking Caribbean to prohibit by separate legislation domestic violence.[5] The 1991 Domestic Violence Act provided for the first time the legal right of a person who was physically or emotionally abused by a family member or an intimate or formerly intimate partner to apply to a court for a protection order. Prior to the passage of the act, incidents of domestic violence were most commonly filed as criminal matters of assault and battery—but these were infrequent filings because the police did not take seriously matters deemed to be "husband-wife business." Trinidad's Domestic Violence Act was a radical measure in that it changed the boundaries between public and private matters with respect to family life. The statute made the courts readily available to victims of abuse in a timely fashion and at little expense.[6]

Everyday Harm investigates the passage and implementation of domestic violence law and seeks to capture what law can and cannot accomplish. I address four broad questions of vital concern to social theorists, students of law and society research, gender studies, and advocates for social change. First, why and when do lawmakers write new legislation to protect victims of domestic violence? Second, why is it that, in spite of laws designed to empower subordinated people, so little results from that legislation? More specifically, what happens in and around courts that makes it so difficult for people to obtain their legally available rights and protections? Third, what can domestic violence law mean for women's empowerment, gender equity, and protection? And fourth, how do cultural norms[7] and practices intercept the law so that Richard's domestic violence and murder of Ramdaye became "understandable" to a judge? These four questions frame the narrative of this book.

Theoretical Underpinnings

I build my arguments on recent theoretical literature in anthropology and cross-cultural research on law and domestic violence that conceptualizes law and legal proceedings as discourses,[8] events, and processes that are powerful, power-laden, and subject to contest and controversy (e.g., Adelman 1997, 2000; Biolsi 1995, 1998, 2001; Comaroff and Roberts 1981; Conley and O'Barr 1990, 1998; Coutin 2000; Coutin, Maurer, and Yngvesson 2002; French 2001; Greenhouse 1986; Greenhouse, Yngvesson, and Engel 1994; Hirsch 1998; Just 2001; Lazarus-Black 1997, 2001, 2003; Lazarus-Black and Hirsch 1994; Lazarus-Black and Merry 2003; Matoesian 1993, 2001; Maurer 1997; Merry 1990, 2000, 2001a, 2001b, 2003; Moore 1986, 1992, 2001; Nader 1990, 2002; Philips 1998; Starr and Collier 1989; Yngvesson 1993). This scholarship analyzes law as an arena for oppression, examining the ways in which it engenders overt and subtle acts of domination while also acknowledging that law offers a viable place and process for protest and protection. Engaging law, litigants are able to contest hegemony (Gramsci 1971), even as law contributes to the making of a seemingly natural social order that reinforces hegemony (Hirsch and Lazarus-Black 1994).[9] Anthropologists' special, although still limited, contributions to the scholarly literature on domestic violence and their influence on policy makers and activists stem from these scholars' collective appreciation of and attention to historical context, symbols, and meaning.[10] In this study, I investigate both how law serves and undermines lawmakers, and how and why litigants' efforts to demand their rights sometimes succeed, sometimes succeed partially, and sometimes fail.

This book also contributes to the literature on law's response to domestic violence as an international phenomenon (e.g., Adelman 1997, 2000; Adelman, Erez, and Shalhoub-Kevorkian 2003; Clarke 1997, 1998; Connell 1997; Ffolkes 1997; Fischer and Rose 1995; Ford 1991; Ford and Regoli 1992; Harrell and Smith 1996; Joseph, Henriques, and Ekeh 1998;

Mahoney 1991, 1994; Martin 1976; Merry 1990, 1994, 2000, 2001a, 2001b, 2003; Pleck 1987; Ptacek 1999; Razack 1998, 1999; Reddock 1995; Red Thread 2000; Robinson 1999; Vatuk 2001, 2003; Wittner 1998). To date, the literature on domestic violence in the North is vast, but research on the criminal justice response to violence between intimates in the South is in its infancy. Although investigations of crime and victimization have emerged as critical concerns in the Caribbean, especially in the past decade, these studies mostly analyze more traditional crime categories such as murder, rape, and robbery (e.g., Harriott, Braithwaite, and Wortley 2004). Bradley (1994:25) notes the paucity of studies of domestic violence in developing countries. Ffolkes (1997), Forde (1981), and C. Mahabir (1996) find there is limited scholarly research pertaining either to women and law or to women and violence in the West Indies, although Alexander (1994) has analyzed the links between law, sexuality, and postcoloniality, and LeFranc and Rock (2001) have pointed to some "commonalities" in the causes of gender violence in the Caribbean. Studies that discuss domestic violence in the formerly British Caribbean colonies rely mainly on quantitative data or surveys of limited samples (e.g., Babb 1997; Bailey, LeFranc, and Branche 1998; Barrow et al. 1995; Creque 1995; Danns and Parsad 1989; Economic Commission for Latin America and the Caribbean 2001; Gopaul and Cain 1996; Morrow 1994; Parsad 1988, 1999; Rawlins 2000; Reddock 1995; Spooner 2001). In addition, feminist lawyers, legal scholars, and criminal justice professionals have drawn attention to similarities and differences in domestic violence statutes in the Caribbean (Boxill 1997; Clarke 1997, 1998; Ffolkes 1997; Joseph, Henriques, and Ekeh 1998; Mehrotra 2000; Pargass and Clarke 2003; Trinidad and Tobago Coalition Against Domestic Violence 2005; Robinson 1999, 2000, forthcoming). As Clarke notes: "Throughout the Caribbean, accurate estimates of the extent of violence against women are hard to obtain. . . . Anecdotal evidence indicates that legal proceedings are still agonizingly slow for women in crisis and that the judiciary, lawyers, and police must be continually challenged to fight the causes and not only the symptoms of violence against women" (1997:52, 56; see also Clarke 1998; Pargass and Clarke 2003; and Trinidad and Tobago Coalition Against Domestic Violence 2005). One study, based on sixteen in-depth interviews, examines why women in Trinidad stay in abusive relationships, the forms of abuse they experience, and what social support they need (Hadeed 2003). Efforts to create comprehensive national databases in the region to document the incidence and pervasiveness of domestic violence, and to assess the interactions between survivors and perpetrators with relevant helping agencies, are still in progress (Economic Commission for Latin America and the Caribbean 2001b, 2001c, 2003).[11] With the exception of Morrow (1994), Handwerker (1997), and James-Sebro (2001), however, none of the Caribbean studies on domestic violence relies on long-term participant observation. This study offers the first in-depth ethnographic investigation of domestic violence law in the English-speaking Caribbean and, because it draws upon analyses of anthropological and sociological studies of the processing of protection orders across a wide range of jurisdictions, provides a foundation from which to understand more generally the intersections of violence, gender, culture, and law.

Trinidad's experiences in passing and implementing domestic violence law are also interesting and relevant to historians, social scientists, and feminists because of the fascinating contradictions posed by its social and legal history. On the one hand, Trinidad is a postcolonial nation shaped by a history of imperialism, slavery, and indentureship. In passing domestic violence legislation, lawmakers understood that they were acting in a modern and progressive manner and that Trinidadians take great pride in their history, culture, and future (e.g., Barriteau 1998; Birth 1999; Bissessar 2000; Harney 1996; Lazarus-Black 2001; Miller 1994, 1997; Munasinghe 2001; Yelvington 1995). Because Trinidad set precedent in the English-speaking Caribbean with its Domestic Violence Act, it is fair to ask in what ways and to what degree the act serves the public good and in what specific ways it operationalizes law as an instrument of domination (Comaroff 2001:308).[12] Thus, this study extends our understanding of the symbolic and pragmatic roles of law in postcolonial nations as new kinship and gender relationships are legislated (Alexander 1994, 1997; Harney 1996; Maurer 1997). On the other hand, Trinidad's legal system is British-inspired; it inherited the English common-law tradition of criminal and civil codes, formal procedures, and hierarchy of courts. As a result, its litigants' experiences with domestic violence law reflect in important ways those of applicants for protection orders in other common-law traditions, such as the United States, Great Britain, and India. Commonalities in domestic violence statutes, legal procedures, and the structural organization of these courts allow me to compare and contrast the Trinidadian case with those of other nations. As I document in this book, shared features of English common-law systems influence the histories and outcomes of applications for protection orders—whether those applications are filed in the United States, England, India, Israel, Jamaica, or Trinidad. Cross-cultural analyses such as these deepen our understanding of the specific ways in which institutions shape gender violence and its legal redress, as well as the role of law in preventing violence (Counts, Brown, and Campbell 1992; Crowell and Burgess 1996).

The Form and Content of the Book

I begin by situating my research within the cross-cultural literature on the legal processing of domestic violence. Four findings appear repeatedly in this literature and also characterize the case of Trinidad: (1) the number of applications for protection orders is impressive; (2) relatively few applicants receive orders for extended protection; (3) the majority of applications are instead withdrawn or dismissed; and (4) cases take considerable time. Although other scholars have not explained why these same findings appear in different jurisdictions, this book does so by investigating how law works in and around domestic violence courts. It reveals why complainants in domestic violence cases vanish so often from the courts.

To elucidate what happens to women and men in the courts, I developed a model that I call "court rites" that describes specific events and processes that occur regularly within and around legal arenas. By "rite" I mean a repetitive, customary, formal, or ceremonial act or observance. I do not intend "rite" to substitute for "ritual," a term that for many people holds religious connotations. Court rites can occur without legal officials' conscious understanding of the fact that they are reinforcing in court dominant groups' prerogatives. By contrast, people do not perform rituals unconsciously. The descriptive term "court rites" emphasizes the repetitive quality of these events as well as their stylized, secular character.

Court rites function most often to perpetuate domination.[13] As Weber states, "domination" refers to a "situation in which the manifested will (command) of the ruler or rulers is meant to influence the conduct of one or more others (the ruled) in such a way that their conduct to a socially relevant degree occurs as if the ruled had made the content of the command the maxim of their conduct for its very own sake" (1978:2:946). Court rites include practices such as the intimidation, objectification, and humiliation of litigants by legal professionals. Another rite, silencing, makes it difficult for victims to tell their stories, and euphemism conceals the extent of a defendant's abuse. Similarly, legalizing allows judicial officials to claim legal authority that they do not actually possess, while delegalizing turns requests for legal attention into matters unworthy of the court's attention. Practices such as these are common in courts (e.g., Adelman 2000; Conley and O'Barr 1990, 1998; Coutin 2000; Emerson 1969; Feeley 1979; Hirsch 1998; Matoesian 2001; Merry 1990, 2000; Yngvesson 1993). This is the first study, however, to name and synthesize twelve widespread court rites and to show how, in various combinations and across a range of jurisdictions, they buttress class and gender hierarchies and alter dramatically the history and the consequences of any case.[14] The court rites model demonstrates how certain practices and events that operate in and around courts are shaped by and support broader social inequities, particularly class and gender inequities, in the wider society. I found that domination inheres in the unnoticed details of the formal/rational legal bureaucracy. Yet, as I also demonstrate, the complexity of court rites means that sometimes they operate in ways that challenge unacknowledged privileges associated with class, gender, and phenotypical "color" (Bartky 2002).[15]

Recognition of court rites is critical to explaining why cases take the turns they do. Discerning the operation of these rites also enables us to better understand the complexity of the nature of agency, "acting for oneself," (Mahoney 1994:59–60) in the legal process. Examining court rites makes it clear that it is too limiting to think about agency in the legal process in terms of the "atomized self-interested individual" who lies at the "core of the liberal world-view" and who informs mainstream social science, official politics and practices, and the Anglo legal system (Kabeer 1994:13; Minow 1990:193; Razack 1998:17, 157–70).[16] We must focus attention instead on the continuous interactions that comprise the legal process and on litigants' encounters with courthouse staff, police, lawyers, probation officers, and judges or—in the case of Trinidad—magistrates. Court rites reveal how and why any litigant's agency in the legal process is inherently unstable and constantly negotiated. In court, agency, like power, is fluid and dynamic, belonging less to any one individual actor than to the highly contextualized interactions between parties at different sites along a shared legal process.[17] Moreover, as scholars are learning (e.g., Trinch 2001, 2003), there is a difference between agency in practice and in its representation.[18]

Agency is, of course, a relational concept, in play with structure.[19] At the courthouse, structural constraints on litigants and the legal process include, among other variables, the contents of statutory law, contingent forms and fees, the hours the court is open, the number of police available to serve summons, and what magistrates regard as "real" domestic disputes. They also include the wider structural constraints of economy, polity, kinship, and gender organization that shape whether an abused woman knows her rights, whether she can afford to bring the case, whether there is someone to watch her children, whether she can withstand the fury of her husband, and whether she is pressured to preserve the family honor by remaining silent.[20] These empirical findings about how law works invite social theorists to reconceptualize the operation of agency and structure in other bureaucratic processes and institutions and teach us about the shape of the iron cages (Weber 1978) in which we dwell.

While paying close attention to agency and structure, my research also urges scholars, legal practitioners, and victims' advocates to examine the role that time plays in filing, processing, and trying domestic violence cases. Repeatedly, the women whose cases I followed referred in their interviews to the problem of time. By this, my interviewees referenced not just the general slowness by which legal cases proceed or overburdened court dockets, but rather multiple interactions with different actors within the wider criminal justice system. Cases take time when a clerk misfiles a form, when a police officer goes on vacation without serving a summons to a defendant, when a lawyer requests an adjournment, when a magistrate sends litigants to the probation officer, and when that officer delays writing a report. Yet sociological research has thus far missed the centrality and complexity of time's influence in the processing of domestic violence cases. Based on my ethnographic analysis, I argue that the conscious and unconscious use and abuse of time by various players in the legal system, in conjunction with the operation of court rites, often helps explain case dispositions. Time consistently works against the women who file cases for protection orders.

One additional consideration is critical to comprehend why applicants for protection orders find it difficult to secure protection. The presence and power of cultures of reconciliation pose significant barriers to a state's proclamation that family violence is a public matter subject to legal redress. Cultures of reconciliation include precepts and practices about who is included in family, what rights and duties those roles entail, and how gender is organized. They are ubiquitous, even as they vary locally. Among other tenets, Trinidad's culture of reconciliation holds that family stability is important and that family troubles are private. It makes mothers responsible for the emotional and physical care of children but also holds that fathers, even violent fathers, are essential to children's lives. The culture of reconciliation assumes that gender hierarchy is natural. It urges compromise, which often translates into women conforming to men's demands (Vatuk 2001:231). As we shall see, Trinidad's culture of reconciliation exerted a strong influence on the legislators who penned the Domestic Violence Act. At the local magistrate's court, cultures of reconciliation create a filtering process, exercising a powerful influence first on a woman's decision about whether to apply for a protection order and then on her ability to negotiate her case to trial. Cultures of reconciliation also sway people who work in courts, so sometimes the very people charged with prosecuting domestic violence legislation discourage the use of protection orders.

To summarize, this book explains why domestic violence victims vanish from the courts. It synthesizes the dynamic sway and cumulative effects of court rites, time, and cultures of reconciliation to illuminate what law can and cannot accomplish, why certain cases win a court's attention while others do not, and how statutes to protect women may simultaneously give them empowering rights and yet fail to deliver what they promise. *Everyday Harm* documents the mostly unnoticed events and encounters that alter peoples' sense of what they can accomplish in the name of justice. The study reconceptualizes the relationships between agency, structure, and time in court with obvious implications for how bureaucracies function more generally.

The Research Setting

Trinidad and Tobago won its independence from Great Britain in 1962 after a stormy colonial history that included early occupation by Spanish conquistadores; more than 150 years of domination by French and British planters "supervising" slaves into producing sugar, cotton, and cocoa; and the arrival, beginning in 1845, of an exploited labor force brought from India to continue the plantation work largely abandoned by former slaves after their gradual emancipation between 1834 and 1838. These events have made Trinidad an extremely diverse place. According to recent statistics (Republic of Trinidad and Tobago 2004), the population includes almost 1.3 million people. Approximately 38 percent identify themselves as being of "African descent" and 40 percent identify themselves as being of "East Indian descent." Twenty-one percent are "mixed" and less than 1 percent identify as "white," "Chinese," "other," or "not stated" in the census report.[21] Trinidadians practice Catholicism (26 percent), Hinduism (23 percent), Anglicanism (8 percent), Islam (6 percent), Presbyterianism (3 percent), and other religions (33 percent), including the Orisha faith, Christian fundamentalism, and Rastafarianism, but it is not uncommon for people to participate in more than one religious group. Although central and south Trinidad remain largely agricultural, much of northern Trinidad has become a bustling place, with fast cars, satellite dishes, financial institutions, daily newspapers, email and Internet, and a vibrant popular culture that culminates every year in the fantastic music and costumes of Carnival. Port of Spain, the capital, boasts a good number of shopping malls, retail stores, and restaurants.

Trinidad and Tobago became a republic in 1976 and is a parliamentary democracy. The president, who is head of state, is elected by the members of a bicameral legislature. The prime minister, the leader of the majority party in Parliament, is head of government. The prime minister appoints a cabinet of ministers, whose membership is not fixed, but which also includes by law the attorney general. Members of the House of Representatives in Trinidad and Tobago are elected in a popular vote. Members of the Senate are appointed by the president, who is advised by the prime minister and the leader of the opposition party.[22]

Trinidad and Tobago's recent economic history is unusual for the English-speaking Caribbean. Beginning in 1973, the price of oil soared and oil-rich Trinidad gained tremendous opportunities for development. Per capita income increased from U.S. $1,231 per annum in 1973 to U.S. $3,168 in 1978. Unemployment declined to less than 9 percent by 1980 (Kiely 1996:134). By 1982, however, Trinidad was experiencing an economic downturn that slid into a long recession. The crisis originated in the country's continued dependence on oil and the state revenues derived from taxation on oil and related industries (Kiely 1996:153).[23] Unemployment rose from 11 percent in 1983 to 17 percent by 1986 (Yelvington 1995:64). By 1990, approximately 18 percent of the population fell below the poverty line (Deosaran 1996:20). A 1992 survey of living conditions found almost 22 percent of the population living in poverty (Reddock 1998a:15). Women earn lower average monthly wages in every occupational category, with differences in pay in 1995 ranging from 4 percent among clerks to 64 percent among agricultural laborers (Reddock 1998a:15). More recently, however, there is some evidence of an economic turnaround. According to a 2005 Wikipedia entry on the economy of Trinidad and Tobago, the nation's GDP (purchasing power parity) was at $9.41 billion (1999 estimate); the real growth rate was at 5 percent; and per capita purchasing power parity was $8,500 (1999 estimate; Economy of Trinidad and Tobago 2005). The labor force is employed in the service sector (64 percent); manufacturing, mining, and quarrying (14 percent); construction and utilities (12 percent); and agriculture (10 percent). The unemployment rate fell from 12 percent in 2001, to 10 percent in 2002, and to 8 percent in 2004. Women consistently face higher unemployment rates than do men: 11.2 percent as opposed to 6.4 percent in 2004 (Republic of Trinidad and Tobago 2004).

Most of the people I queried regarding the composition of Trinidad's class structure told me their country had three social classes: (1) an upper class—or as one woman put it, the "ultimate" class; (2) a middle class of civil servants, teachers, shopkeepers, and the like; and (3) a lower class, including the working poor and the unemployed. Class position is determined principally by employment and income, but secondarily by education and the size and location of the family home. A female attorney described Trinidad's class structure as having shifting boundaries. She characterized the working class as comprised of persons unemployed or working occasionally. Those in the lower-middle class hold steady jobs but earn low incomes. During the oil boom, the middle class was divided into a middle-middle class and an upper-middle class. As the recession deepened, however, much of the middle-middle class slipped back into the lower-middle class. Like other interviewees, she characterized Trinidad's upper class as consisting of wealthy businesspeople and professionals.

Trinidad and Tobago's first formal legal system was the product of its Spanish settlers. Once the British arrived in 1797, they began remodeling the judicial organization according to their own understanding of the proper place and purpose of law and courts in a British colony. Today magistrates' courts hear a variety of civil and criminal matters considered less serious than other crimes, as well as preliminary inquiries into severe offenses. More sober criminal acts are tried at the High Courts. Both the magistrates' courts and the High Courts are courts of the first instance in the sense that appeals go directly to the nation's Court of Appeal. From the Court of Appeal, an attorney may ask leave to bring a case before the Privy Council in England, but few family matters muster such serious attention.[24]

The magistrate's court in which I spent most of my time is located in a town in northern Trinidad that I call "Pelau," after the popular local dish. A Trinidad and Tobago dictionary explains that *pelau* consists of a "complete meal with various ingredients all cooked at the same time in the same pot" (Mendes 1986:107). It is a fitting pseudonym for the town because Pelau's people are especially diverse in terms of race, ethnicity, religion, and class—and yet they share the same government institutions and services. In that sense, they all get "cooked in the same pot."

Described in 1851 as a "quiet village of a few hundred people with a single police constable" (*Sunday Guardian*, January 25, 1998), Pelau was first the site of large sugar estates and later was a railway hub for trains that carried that sugar away. Today it is a market town for produce and a commercial and retail center. Small shops run by family workers display randomly the clothing, shoes, and sneakers that outfit working-class families. In 2000, Pelau's population was approximately 17,000 (Republic of Trinidad and Tobago 2002), but the magistrate's court located there serves people within a wider radius of small villages. The magistrate attends to family cases such as requests for child and wife support, legal custody, access to children, adoption, and arrears of maintenance. Since 1991, the magistrate also hears applications for protection orders as outlined in the Domestic Violence Act.[25] Most of the people served by the court can be described as working class, the men giving their occupations as "construction," "mechanic," "security," "taxi driver," and the like, while the women describe themselves as "homemaker," "clerk," "sales," or "hairdresser." Evidence of their relative poverty is suggested by their other applications for maintenance for themselves and their children; most women who come to the courts accept very low stipends from their husbands or the fathers of their children. Moreover, as is true elsewhere in the Caribbean, there is a certain stigma to airing one's dirty laundry in a magistrate's court and that keeps wealthier people from these courts (Lazarus-Black 1994). Nevertheless, the applicants I interviewed at length included middle-class women employed in the civil service and a bank employee.

In short, Trinidad is an independent democracy, a member of the Commonwealth of Nations, and characterized by a capitalist economic system subject to periodic recessions and relatively high rates of unemployment. As noted earlier, it was the leader in the English-speaking Caribbean in passing comprehensive domestic violence legislation in a region in which family violence has been perceived traditionally as "husband-wife business" and not appropriate business for the state.[26] Previously, men's ability to control their women as they liked and parents' right to "mind" children as they saw fit had been unquestioned, hegemonic. In theory, the Domestic Violence Act challenged those assumptions and changed people's sense of agency and rights. My fieldwork was directed toward understanding what that would mean in practice.

Fieldwork, the Interviews, and the Court Records

This project combines historical and legal research on the postindependence era in Trinidad (1962–2002) with ethnographic fieldwork (1997–2002) in and around its magistrates' courts. Fieldwork for the first phase of the project began in August 1997, continued through August 1998, and concluded in October 1998. I conducted participant observation in Pelau on a weekly basis for ten months. In addition, I spent shorter periods in three other magistrates' courts in north Trinidad in the area commonly known locally as the "East-West Corridor," but here more broadly defined to include both Port of Spain and north-central Trinidad. My court observations were limited to Trinidad's most urban and populated areas, and do not account for how law functions in Tobago or in the rural agricultural communities that comprise most of southern Trinidad, although I did talk to interviewees about jurisdictional differences.[27] During phase one of the project, I observed seven different magistrates adjudicating cases and conducted sixty-two taped interviews with legal professionals, litigants, and other men and women in the community, some of whom who had never been to court, but who had definite ideas about domestic violence and its legal redress. The legal professionals I interviewed included twenty-two attorneys (twelve men and ten women), eight magistrates (two men and six women), and seven probation officers (three men and four women). Other persons interviewed included medical doctors, religious leaders, university students, clerks, homemakers, businessmen, a police officer, and an elementary school teacher. Depending on an interviewee's interests, experiences, and time, these open-ended discussions lasted from thirty-five minutes to more than two hours. Finally, I interviewed at length twelve women who filed charges of domestic violence at court and four persons (two men and two women) who were defendants to such suits. Most of these sixteen interviewees had working-class occupations, such as restaurant worker, homemaker, sales employee, or clerk, but they also included middle-class women. Seven persons identified themselves as having Afro-Caribbean heritage and nine claimed East Indian heritage, representing the two largest ethnic groups in Trinidad and Tobago. Of the twelve interviews with complainants, six won at least a temporary restraining order from the court, four dropped their suits, and two did not receive the protection orders they requested from the magistrate. The shortest of these case histories was approximately an hour and a half in length, but most entailed my meeting the litigant on several occasions and recording the domestic violence case history within the context of that individual's life history. In a few instances, research melted into friendship and I met the interviewee's family and friends and spent time at his or her home.[28]

During phase two of the project, June–July 1999, I increased the overall sample of interviewees to seventy-five (thirty men and forty-five women) and relocated thirteen of the sixteen litigants involved in domestic violence cases whom I had previously interviewed. In sharp contrast to most research on domestic violence law, these interviews allowed me to discern the later consequences of having brought an application for a protection order to court. Of the three parties I could not relocate in 1999, one had given me an incomplete address and I could not find him. One of the two women had died of a long-term medical condition, and the second did not return my phone calls.

I made a brief third field trip to Trinidad in May–June 2002 to observe again the court in Pelau and to finalize my collection of court records. By this time, the Trinidad government had replaced the 1991 Domestic Violence Act with the 1999 Domestic Violence Act. The new law extends further the state's power by directing the police to respond to all complaints of domestic violence, giving them more opportunity to intervene in domestic disputes without a warrant, and requiring law enforcers to complete domestic violence reports that will become part of a national domestic violence register. The statute adds the category of "financial abuse" as a form of violence, extends the duration of a protection order to three years, provides for a defendant's peace bond for good behavior as an alternative order, and changes the fines and penalties for breaching a court order. In addition, when issuing an order for protection, a magistrate can make ancillary orders with respect to residency, maintenance for children, payment of rent or mortgage, and compensation for monetary loss as a result of the violence. Perhaps most significantly, because it is highly unusual in the region, the statute clarified and broadened the parties to whom the statute applies, including offering protection to persons in visiting unions (Laws of Trinidad and Tobago 1999; Robinson 2000:116–17, 123). During my observations in Pelau in 2002, I noted the presence in court of some categories of persons who had not previously appeared. For example, a grandmother successfully charged her granddaughter with domestic violence and three brothers attempted (unsuccessfully) to sue each other. Nevertheless, the legal processes of applying for and receiving a protection order have not changed. Moreover, court rites continue to characterize legal procedures and peoples' encounters with legal officials, litigants remain subject to the ways in which legal professionals manipulate time, and the principles of Trinidad's widespread culture of reconciliation remain hegemonic. Therefore, I write in the ethnographic present.[29]

When I started this study, and quite often along the way, both men and women expressed disbelief that people would actually agree to talk to me about their experiences with domestic violence and their legal cases. Others surmised that even if people agreed, they doubted that I would hear the true story. I believe that the complainants who participated in this study did so for two principal reasons. Some were explicit about the relief they experienced in being able to talk confidentially about what had happened to them. Some had lived lives in which violence against women was common, "so common that it often goes unnoticed" (Stanko 1990:i). For many women, economic dependence, children, and the cultural emphasis on keeping the family together, whatever the daily consequences of doing so, meant that they had mostly avoided talking about the violence in their lives. A second reason women told me that they were willing to speak to me was because they hoped that the findings of this study would help other women who were also the victims of violence. I believe their honesty and altruism were genuine. Even if some interviewees left certain parts out on purpose or embellished their story, the patterns in their combined experiences with the criminal justice system are very clear and have theoretical as well as practical implications—as some of my interviewees hoped.[30]

Finally, in addition to relying on historical and legal research, participant observation, and interviews, the arguments, findings, and conclusions of this study are drawn from analyses of court records of domestic violence cases from Pelau and other courts, buttressed by local quantitative studies of case dispositions. These court records allow us to discern how many cases were filed, the sex of applicants and defendants, how often each case was continued, whether a case was dismissed, withdrawn, went to trial, or was in some other way resolved by the court, what sanctions magistrates imposed upon batterers, and how the court reacted when its orders were breached. I hope this quantitative record will be useful to social activists and policy makers for whom numbers count in ways that can make a difference (Bograd 2005:29; Urla 1993:818). As is always the case, the interpretative spin on those numbers is critical in evaluating the "success" of domestic violence legislation.

Outline of the Book

Chapter 1, "Imagining and Implementing Domestic Violence Law," asks what social, political, and economic conditions enable a people to take a stand against violence and how they can muster a successful lobby to convince lawmakers to enact legislation toward that goal. As I demonstrate, a coalescence of strategic actors and local and global influences and events made intimate violence the subject of jural debate in Trinidad. Among the most important of these factors were nationalist and more recent public narratives that encouraged pride in West Indian history, identity, and modernity, the critical expansion of education following independence, a (temporarily) booming economy, and the local and global women's movements. These historical developments enabled women's entry into the professions—especially law and politics (Colón and Reddock 2004; Reddock 1994; Ryan 1972, 1988). They would then lead the effort to combat domestic violence. I demonstrate the ways in which Trinidad's experience in writing domestic violence law resonates with that of other nations, while documenting how and why its activists and lawmakers made the local statute distinctly Trinidadian. The case of Trinidad lends support not only to Boyle and Preves's (2000) contention that international pressure for human rights significantly influences national lawmaking, but also that "new discourses, laws, and practices about gender violence between intimates develop through local, national, and global processes" (Lazarus-Black and Merry 2003:931).

Written with Dr. Patricia L. McCall, chapter 2, "A Look at the Numbers," provides an analysis of domestic violence court records from Pelau, the main site of my fieldwork, as well as comparative data from other courts. The size and broad scope of this data set is a first for the Caribbean and of interest to feminists and criminologists who ask whether protection orders protect (e.g., Belknap et al. 2001; Buzawa and Buzawa 1996; Dobash and Dobash 1979, 1992; Dobash, Dobash, and Noaks 1995; Harrell, Smith, and Newmark 1993; Hirschel and Hutchison 2001). These records reveal how many applications were filed, whether petitions were dismissed or withdrawn, how many resulted in court orders, how often those orders were breached, and what sentences magistrates imposed. We show how gender plays a part in determining case dispositions and what happens when men and women simultaneously charge each other with abuse. The chapter is peppered with ethnographic examples of how litigants behaved in court, what stories they told, and how magistrates judged. Lawyers comment on their clients and cases.[31] Readers will also meet a police constable with an unstable mental history and a defendant caught in the act of chasing his wife with "intention to wound." Trinidad's court records can help us determine whether similar criminal justice policies and procedures produce similar results locally as well as cross-culturally.

Chapter 3, "The Meaning of Success," provides a narrative explanation for the quantitative record. Ethnographic research in the courts and interviews with litigants and lawyers enable us to make sense of the numbers, which are consequences of the negotiation of agency, structure, and time in court. What kinds of cases appear regularly before the magistrates? Which cases are eligible to be heard but rarely appear before the courts? What makes a case strong enough to win a protection order? As is true of research findings about domestic violence in the United States and Great Britain, domestic violence law in Trinidad conjures up a specific cast of characters who are familiar and deemed "entitled" to relief from violence because they are victims for whom the community holds immediate empathy (e.g., Bograd 2005; Bumiller 1991; Connell 1997; Frohmann 1991; Gordon 1988; Hartley 2001; Klein 1982; Lamb 1999;

Loseke 1992; Mahoney 1991, 1994; Matoesian 1993, 1995, 2001; Maurer and Merry 1997; Merry 1994, 2000; Spohn and Holleran 2001; Stanko 1982). In Trinidad, that cast mostly includes long-suffering women with alcoholic husbands, mothers exploited by addicted sons, women in common-law relationships seeking to get men out of their homes, and women with obsessed partners. Subject to the public gaze, these victims are found worthy of relief because there is a new consensus about unacceptable behaviors in familial and gender relationships—one that also marks the nation as modern. Yet some of society's most needy victims rarely appear in court. Moreover, as I explain, who is awarded a protection order is also a function of law's literal nature and of violent men's generosity.

In chapter 4, "Court Rites," I demonstrate through the legal case of "Alena" and "John," a young couple in a common-law relationship, how court rites cause applicants for protection orders to leave court without legal remedy. On the face of it, one would have thought that Alena had an airtight case for a protection order; John had been emotionally, physically, and sexually abusive toward her on numerous occasions. During the months leading up to their trial, however, Alena encountered court rites including erroneous advice, significant delays, clerical errors, and poor lawyering. During the trial, she employed euphemistic language—language that marked her status as an educated, middle-class Trinidadian woman—but that also prevented her from using the words that would enable a magistrate to grant her a protection order. This chapter identifies twelve court rites and illustrates those rites with examples from ethnographic studies of courts in the United States, Jamaica, and Great Britain. It demonstrates the widespread occurrence of the rites and how they influence how law works.

Chapter 5, "Time and the Legal Process," provides new insights on an old problem. Complaints about the slowness of legal redress are routine; everywhere courts are understaffed and lack resources (e.g., Baumgartner 1988; Conley and O'Barr 1990; French 2001; Greenhouse, Yngvesson, and Engel 1994; Nimmer 1978). Yet as Munn notes: "Control over time is not just a strategy of interaction; it is also a medium of hierarchic power and governance" (1992:109). Time can be an instrument of power or a strategy to thwart power; different actors differently employ time and with consequences that can be subtle or dramatic. To explain how time operates in domestic violence cases, I turn to the daily practices of court clerks, police, lawyers, probation officers, and magistrates to illustrate their respective categories and deployment of time. For example, Police Time includes the time it takes for a police officer to deliver a summons to a respondent to appear in court to hear charges of alleged abuse. (That time will likely be delayed considerably if the respondent is a relative or a friend of a friend of the police officer.) Probation Time points to the time it takes a probation officer to interview parties, write a report, send it to the typist, and for it to be read by the magistrate. It is a given that Lawyer Time will include numerous adjournments. This chapter narrates seven categories of time and illuminates the complexity and consequences of the common complaint that it takes too much time to make one's case in court.

In chapter 6, "Cultures of Reconciliation," I argue that a comprehensive explanation for why domestic violence cases take the turns they do requires attention not only to law and legal processing, but also to context, cultural categories, local norms, and indigenous practices. Widely shared ideas about family, gender, and work held by the people I interviewed influenced profoundly the choices they made when they applied for a protection order and then decided whether to continue the case. Drawing on my interviews and local literature and scholarship, I illustrate that these ideas and related practices combine to form a culture of reconciliation in Trinidad that operates against the law's claim that each individual is separately entitled to protection without consideration of an alleged victim's obligations or responsibilities to children and kin. Turning to the anthropological record, I show that other historians and ethnographers have pointed to cultures of reconciliation in other locales, including the United States, Israel, and India, but without systematizing their principles.

In the conclusion, "How Law Works," I weave together the central themes of the study and reflect upon my findings. Court rites, the vagaries of time, and cultures of reconciliation color litigants' experiences in domestic violence cases across time and space. In combination, they explain why these cases are so often dismissed or withdrawn and why so many complainants vanish from the court records. They reveal, too, why some litigants succeed while others succeed only partially in the goals for which they went to court. In analyzing these "micro-physics of power" (Foucault 1979) that shape peoples' interactions in the courts, I conclude that in law, agency is endlessly negotiated, residing in the contiguous interactions of multiple players and never in any one agent. Time encourages some legal outcomes, negates others, and modifies most of them. Moreover, the structural constraints on legal cases are always processual and interpreted. Concentrating on domestic violence law, I uncovered the details of specific events and processes that accomplish domination within lower courts in Trinidad, but my findings have broader implications for how agency, time, and structure are configured in other kinds of cases and in other courts. As we shall see, vanishing complainants leave critical clues about the everyday harm they experience and how law works.

1 Imagining and Implementing Domestic Violence Law

What social, political, and economic conditions combined in 1991 to bring to the Trinidadian public's and lawmakers' attention the need for domestic violence legislation? Which actors led the movement to enact the law? What resistance did the law and its supporters meet in Parliament? To what effect? And what can we learn from the case of Trinidad about when and how women and other subordinated groups successfully negotiate new rights?

In describing the history of domestic violence law in Trinidad, I am investigating an important example of a broader, global process that I describe as "regendering the state." By "the state" I mean "the actors who control the political, economic, technological, and ideological apparatus of government, as well as their enabling institutions" (Lazarus-Black 1994:262). As Matthews points out, "the state" is "composed of numerous institutions, agencies, and organizations that have different functions acquired through processes that are social, political, and historical . . . the state is not monolithic, and its various sectors may be at odds with each other or operating in concert" (1994:5). It is marked sociologically by "the specific *means* peculiar to it . . . namely, the use of physical force" (Weber 1946:78). In the case of Trinidad, we are referring to a recently independent, postcolonial state whose lawmakers are charged with modernizing the nation.

"Regendering the state" refers to the process of bringing to public and legal consideration categories and activities that were formerly (and formally) without name, but that constituted harm to women, denied them rights, silenced them, or limited their capacity to engage in actions available to men (Lazarus-Black 2003:980). In the historical, feminist, and legal literature of the past decade or so, the concepts of "engendering history," "gendering the state," and "engendering justice" have been used widely to draw attention to the ways in which legal reforms have begun to include women and to address gendered experiences, such as rape and domestic violence. (See Leo-Rhynie, Bailey, and Barrow 1997; Mohammed 2002b; and Shepherd, Brereton, and Bailey 1995 for three Caribbean examples.) It remains commonplace, however, to continue to assume that law is "objective," "neutral," and "without gender." I use the term "regendering the state" to draw attention to the point that law and lawmaking is and always has been a gendered process. Law is a system of proclamations, procedures, and processes that has, historically, been shaped in masculine forms and language. Although it is widely defined as "objective," law often supports and protects state politics in ways that are unequal in the categorization and treatment of men and women (MacKinnon 1989).

Thus, regendering the state specifically highlights the "nonobjective" and "nonneutral" character of the English common-law tradition that formed the colonial heritage of the American legal system, as well as those of Trinidad and other nations whose domestic violence laws and procedures are analyzed in this book. Two other classic examples of the regendering process in the United States include MacKinnon's (1979) naming of sexual harassment as a crime in the workplace and the acceptance of Walker's (1984) battered woman syndrome as a legal defense. These legal formulations entail what Merry refers to as "disruptions of hegemony," involving processes in which "the hegemony of gender inequality is invaded by a new language of relationships" (1995a:67). Regendering is an example of the "legal polyphony" (Tomlins 2001) that is occurring across postcolonial states in response to global discourses and developments but also to local concerns and practices. The regendered state recognizes explicitly that some citizens are male and others are female. Barriteau's comment is insightful: "Unless the relationship between the state and women is problematized and the current assumptions of equality, neutrality, and citizenship exposed as flawed, the state will have no impetus to alter the discriminatory practices that serve to marginalize women politically, socially, and economically" (2001:23).[1] In the case of Trinidad, we must refer to the heterosexual regendering of the state because Trinidad and Tobago's Sexual Offenses Act of 1986 not only consolidated outdated legislation regarding sex crimes but also criminalized homosexuality as "serious indecency" for which conviction carries a five-year prison term (see Alexander 1994; Daly 1992; Mohammed 1991).[2] Not surprisingly, Trinidad's Domestic Violence Act did not include protection for couples in gay or lesbian relationships.

Whom did Trinidad's new law protect and from what forms of violence? The 1991 Domestic Violence Act provided for the first time the legal right of a person who was physically or emotionally abused by a family member or an intimate or formerly intimate partner to apply to a court for a protection order. Prior to the passage of the act, incidents of domestic violence were most commonly filed as criminal matters of assault and battery—but these were infrequent events because the police did not take seriously matters deemed to be "husband-wife business." Trinidad's Domestic Violence Act was a radical measure in that it changed the boundaries between public and private matters with respect to family life. The statute made the courts readily available to victims of abuse in a timely fashion and at little expense. In theory—that is, in law—the state had been regendered because it had named violence as a crime, one that overwhelmingly happens to women.[3]

In the first part of this chapter, I address the coalition of political, social, and economic forces and events that made possible the passage of the Domestic Violence Act in Trinidad at the particular historical juncture at which it became possible to imagine regendering the state. I argue that the most important of these factors were: (1) nationalist and more recent public narratives that encourage pride in West Indian history, identity, and modernity; (2) the critical expansion of education following independence and, more specifically, the unprecedented education of women and their subsequent entry into the professions; (3) a (temporarily) booming economy fueled by the oil boom; and (4) the influences of the global and local women's movements.[4] Critical to the passage of the Domestic Violence Act was the work of a small but determined and politically active group of women who wrote to the newspapers, sent petitions to lawmakers, spoke at public forums, and dressed in black to stage a "silent protest" in Parliament.[5] A voluminous literature makes clear that the advent of specific legislation to protect women from harm that is committed against them in their homes is possible only after the development of a widespread women's movement that can both focus national attention on the issue and harness enough political and economic clout to move legislators. To cite some examples, this pattern is established for the United States (e.g., Abraham 1995; Breines and Gordon 1983; Dobash and Dobash 1992; Frohmann and Mertz 1995; Gordon 1988; Loseke 1992; Matthews 1994; Pleck 1987; Ptacek 1999;

Rosen 2000; Schneider 1999, 2000; Straus and Gelles 1986), the United Kingdom (Dobash and Dobash 1979, 1992), the Republic of Ireland (Smyth 1996), Canada (Walker 1990), Brazil (Thomas and Beasley 1993), Puerto Rico (Rivera 1995; Romany 1994), Israel (Adelman 1997), Trinidad and Tobago (Alexander 1991, 1994; Bissessar 2000; James-Sebro 2001; Lazarus-Black 2003; Mohammed 2002a; Reddock 1994, 1995), the Bahamas (Alexander 1994, 1997), Barbados (Spooner 2001), the U.S. Virgin Islands (Morrow 1994), Guyana (Trotz 2004), the Anglophone and Hispanophone Caribbean more generally (Colón and Reddock 2004), Tanzania (Hirsch 2003), Spain (Miller and Barberet 1994; Valiente 1996), Hungary (Szalay 1996), and several other European nations (see Corrin 1996).

The case of Trinidad is particularly interesting to scholars and activists for several reasons: it is a postcolonial nation; heir to the British common-law tradition; and shaped by a history of imperialism, slavery, and indentureship similar to many other countries in this region. In addition, since Trinidad set precedent in the English-speaking Caribbean with its comprehensive Domestic Violence Act, it is fair to ask in what ways and to what degree the act serves those that it was intended to protect and whether it imposes unanticipated and new forms of social control (Comaroff 2001:308). As Sunder Rajan explains, postcolonial nations experience the "central role of the state; inequalities in social structures; the contrary pulls of nationalism and regionalism (or centralization and federalization); and the conflicts between 'tradition' and 'modernity'" (1993:7). In postcolonial states, Sunder Rajan continues, the state is both the guarantor of rights and, quite often, a major perpetrator of injustice. Consequently, women's movements in postcolonial nations form alliances with the state to enact laws to protect women but must also resist state power and coercion (1993:7). My case study shows this clearly. On one level, the women's movement in Trinidad was powerful in getting domestic violence law passed; on another, women who approach the courts in search of protection must resist different forms of coercion and pressure to drop their suits.

My research on the origins and implementation of domestic violence law in Trinidad also validates recent findings by Boyle and Preves (2000) who demonstrate that: (1) international pressure for universal human rights has significant influence on national lawmaking; (2) less powerful states tend to comply eventually with international standards; (3) national lawmaking is often a top-down process developed to change local attitudes; and (4) independent activists who are not dependent on local government can wield considerable influence on local lawmaking. As Boyle and Preves argue: "Looking at power struggles primarily within national boundaries reifies the nation-state and misses larger issues of control in the international system" (2000:703). One has to study, too, the "local-global interface in the creation and implementation of social reforms concerning violence against women" (Lazarus-Black and Merry 2003:931). As I will show, the passage of the Domestic Violence Act in Trinidad was a consequence of a coalition of local, national, and international events and processes. As is the case with so much of recent historical change, the language of a global discourse about domestic violence was inserted into the local debate in Trinidad, but not without the local dialogue refashioning the global discourse in interesting ways.[6] The parliamentary debates in Trinidad preceding the passage of the Domestic Violence Act, described later in this chapter, provide an excellent illustration of this process. Moreover, if in the past "cultures of legalities were constitutive of colonialism" (Comaroff 2001:309), contemporary cultures of legalities constitute postcolonial nations like Trinidad as "modern," "progressive," and "civilized" places (Bissessar 2000:66; Lazarus-Black 2003:985). As we shall see, when they passed the Domestic Violence Act, lawmakers and activists imagined a regendered state attuned to the problem of violence against women, but not without due attention to the preservation of men's rights and "the family" as these notions had evolved in the postindependence era.

Independence and the Postcolonial State

The Afro-Trinidadian middle class began the movement for independence following World War II and the breakup of the British Empire (Brereton 2004; Millette 2004). The protagonists were closely aligned by education, culture, and employment to the British colonial government, and they saw themselves as the "natural" successors. The nationalist movement, led by Dr. Eric Williams and the People's Nationalist Movement (PNM) party, won independence for Trinidad and Tobago in 1962.[7] Educated at Oxford, Williams was determined that Trinidadians study and appreciate their own history and identity. He provided them with that history in his book, *History of the People of Trinidad and Tobago* (1962). In that text, "The message to West Indians was that they were people of importance. They had played a vital role in the history of the world. . . . Williams brought West Indian history and West Indian politics together as one thing" (Campbell 1997:59–60). As Harney notes: "The rhetoric of nationalism became tied both to a discourse of anti-colonialism (William's famous 'Massa day done' phrase) and to a subterranean one of African succession. The Indo-Trinidadian population, in the 1950s still largely rural and locked out of the colonial education system and bureaucracy, saw little advantage in independence and indeed feared the unchecked power of an Afro-Trinidadian administration. Nonetheless, using the rhetoric of race and nationalism, Williams and his urban Afro-Trinidadians seized the young nation" (1996:57). This fierce pride in country and culture, a legacy of the nationalist movement, continues. Like Miller (1994, 1997), I found Trinidadians identify strongly with practices they view as specifically Trinidadian,[8] including pride in the quality and pervasiveness of schools.

Its commitment to education was one of the most important and enduring legacies of the People's Nationalist Movement.[9] The government engaged in a major program to build schools throughout the country. As Campbell notes: "Free secondary education from 1961 was perhaps the single most popular measure ever taken by Williams and the PNM government" (1997:71; see also Campbell 2004; Reddock 1998b). Meanwhile, Trinidad's economy was shifting from a heavy dependence on agriculture and blue-collar labor to reliance on the service sector and white-collar professions (Colón and Reddock 2004; Reddock 1991; Ryan 1991). Throughout the region, newly independent states instituted formal development planning intended to "control population, produce economic growth, improve living conditions, develop human resources, create higher levels of industrialization and enhance technological development" (Barriteau 1998:203). According to Barriteau, three principal features characterized Caribbean states' reconstruction of gender roles after independence: "the state's official recognition of women, retrenchment of the welfare state, expansion of private sector influence over economic policy and entrepreneurial development" (1998:203). Over time, postcolonial Caribbean governments, Trinidad among them, offered women more resources and more rights, but not always with the consequences they imagined or in ways that empowered women.[10] On the other hand, the changing economy would have a powerful impact on women's futures.

Prosperity has been found by scholars to be a significant factor in encouraging the development of women's movements. Gordon (1988: chapter 8), for example, provides a superb historical analysis of the correlation between women's claims to physical integrity and their economic independence in the United States. Writing about the development of the women's movements in Britain and the United States, Dobash and Dobash found: "The movements followed a phase of economic growth, the extension of welfare-state provisions and, for most, a social-democratic government. Reform, greater opportunism, more security, higher standards of living and more state regulation of the private sphere, usually occupied by women, formed the general backcloth to the emergence of the new women's movement" (1992:17).

Similarly, Reddock links the emergence of women's renewed consciousness of their rights and mobilization in Trinidad to prosperous post–World War II conditions: "The blossoming of women's organizations during the 1940s and 1950s reflected the awakening of women of all classes to the need to struggle for what they perceived as 'equality.' To some extent this was fueled by the improved economic position of women as a result of the war and the granting of universal suffrage in 1946" (1994:253). There were some parallel developments two decades later.

Between 1974 and 1981, oil-rich Trinidad experienced enormous economic growth because of the worldwide demand for oil (Miller 1997; Yelvington 1995). Education and economic opportunities were encouraged further by the boom (Human Rights Internet 1993:4). The government invested in social and economic services, nationalized some industries, and dramatically increased the size of the public sector. Trinidadians gained greater access to the world through trade, technology, and travel (Miller 1994:chapter 1).[11] And the world began looking to Trinidad for its literature, music, and Carnival (Harney 1996; Nurse 1999).

In Trinidad, as elsewhere, education would become a "key to women's empowerment" (Senior 1991:44; see also Seebaran-Suite 1991:239). In 1965, there were far more women than men without formal education, and five times as many men as women with university training (Campbell 1997:172). By 1987–88, 50 percent of the full-time undergraduates and almost 42 percent of the postgraduate students at the University of the West Indies in Trinidad were women (Human Rights Internet 1993:5). Moreover, women constituted 57 percent of those admitted into legal practice in 1988 (Seebaran-Suite 1991:242). These trends continued in the 1990s.[12]

During the period of the UN Decade for Women (1975–85), women began to mobilize around several issues. The Housewives Association of Trinidad and Tobago (HATT) was formed in 1975 by housewives and white-collar women to regulate food prices and other consumer items (Henderson 1988:365–66; Mohammed 1991:41). In 1980, the National Commission on the Status of Women hosted a conference on domestic violence (Bishop and Rahamut 1996). Trinidad's Concerned Women for Progress (CWP) called for equal pay for equal work, the legalization of abortion, and an end to violence against women. When it disbanded in 1983, The Group formed to continue the struggle (Henderson 1988:371;

Mohammed 1991:42–43). In 1985, The Group formed Working Women for Social Progress (Working Women) to work with and for working-class women. Two events, a seminar sponsored by professional women and a television series, brought the reality of violence between intimates to national attention (Cain 2000; Human Rights Internet 1993; Mohammed 1991). Working Women seeks to reach poor women in direct community involvement and to foster public education (Cain 2000; James-Sebro 2001). They also helped to build momentum for the passage of the 1986 Sexual Offences Act.[13] The following year, a multidisciplinary team reported to the government on child abuse (Bishop and Rahamut 1996). This was followed by government efforts to educate the public and a regional conference on child abuse hosted in Trinidad in 1989 (Creque 1995:7).

Meanwhile, activists formed a rape crisis center and began calling for shelters for survivors of domestic violence. Lobbying for the first shelter was the work of the Business and Professional Women's Club of South Trinidad under the leadership of Radica Saith. They began their efforts in 1983. Shortly thereafter, the Rape Crisis Society, led by Eunice Gittens, began providing counseling for victims of abuse and domestic violence (Babb 1997; Bishop and Rahamut 1996; Cain 2000; James-Sebro 2001). The first shelters run by nongovernmental women's organizations opened.[14]

The Trinidad and Tobago Coalition Against Domestic Violence formed in 1988. The Caribbean Association for Feminist Research and Action (CAFRA) hosted a conference on domestic violence in 1990. By now, model legislation for a domestic violence act was available from CARICOM (Caribbean Secretariat) and people were aware of the global discourse on human rights (CAFRA 1991, 1998; Clarke 1991, 1997, 1998). Newspaper articles educated the public about the passage of domestic violence laws in other countries and reported on relevant cases from abroad (e.g., *Trinidad Express* February 1, 1991; *Sunday Guardian,* April 21, 1991; Shepherd 1991). Female calypsonians sang out against violence, poverty, gender inequality, sexual harassment, and abuse in intimate relationships (Mahabir 2001). By 1991, scholar and activist Patricia Mohammed would write: "The present wave of feminism in Trinidad was clearly influenced in its early days (late 1970s) by the international struggle" (1991:40).[15] In contrast to the United States, however, Trinidad ratified many international conventions to protect women from violence.[16]

Finally, women were increasingly active in the political life of the nation and they garnered support in the new National Alliance for Reconstruction (NAR) government (Bishop and Rahamut 1996; Lazarus-Black 2003; Mohammed 1991; Shepherd 1991). Five women had been elected to the thirty-six-member House of Representatives in 1986 and four were appointed to the Senate. In 1987, there were three women in the fifteen-member cabinet. Six parliamentary seats were held by women in 1991 (Human Rights Internet 1993:5).[17] Moreover, women were extremely active in nongovernmental organizations—almost a hundred of them (Reddock 1994:326). Development-oriented NGOs within the region increasingly focused on the issue of violence (Clarke 1998; Colón and Reddock 2004).

In short, at the end of the 1980s, the people of Trinidad manifested great pride in their history, identity, and progress. The nation emerged as one of the most literate populations in the Caribbean, and women embraced opportunities to participate in education and the professions, including law and politics. It was time to take steps to stop domestic violence.

The Debate of the Domestic Violence Act

The parliamentary debate over the Domestic Violence Act, which began in January 1991, illustrates quite well the intersection of local and global discourses on domestic violence.[18] The bill was introduced to the Senate by Minister of Social Development Dr. Emmanuel Hosein. He explained the bill was a continuation of the government's commitment to "social justice and equal rights for men and women." He characterized it as continuing trends that began with the Matrimonial Proceedings and Property Amendment Act and the Maintenance Act.[19] Anticipating arguments by the opposition, and voicing his awareness of the ties among culture, gender, and law, the minister "stressed that the bill should not be interpreted as a desire on the part of the state to intervene in the home. Rather it sought to provide a mechanism for persons to avail themselves of protection against abuse and violence" (*Trinidad Express*, January 31, 1991).

The newspapers provided extensive coverage of the controversy among the mostly male members of Parliament (Shepherd 1991). Feminist attorneys and their supporters wrote of the pressing need for the bill and outlined its provisions. The main objective of the act was to enable victims of domestic violence to seek protection orders in the magistrate's court rather than having to obtain expensive and less-timely injunctions for protection at the High Court. The act protected a complainant from violence by not only a spouse, former spouse, de facto spouse, and former de facto spouse (important because of the high rate of consensual unions in Trinidad), but also parents, grandparents, children, and other dependents.[20] Both men and women could seek protection if they were subjected to actual or potential behavior of a threatening, offensive, or harassing nature and if they were fearful of injury to themselves or a dependent (Daly 1992:36–37). The statute also allowed parties other than the victim, such as police officers or social welfare officers, to act on the victim's behalf (Daly 1992:38). Once the court was satisfied with the applicant's complaint,[21] it could impose one or more sanctions, such as prohibiting the respondent from certain locations, including the respondent's own home, preventing the respondent from speaking to the person, ensuring reasonable care for dependents, or directing the parties to seek family counseling (Daly 1992:38–39).

Opponents of the measure voiced their concerns. The bill criminalized what Trinidadians refer to as "husband-wife business" (*Trinidad Guardian*, March 10, 1991), "business" that is "private" unless or until things are really out of control. The definition of "spouse" for the purposes of the act was hotly debated. Who was to count as a spouse? Some lawmakers argued that only legally married persons should be covered. One senator wanted to know: "When does a person become a de facto spouse? Is it as soon as you move in with your grip [suitcase]?" (*Trinidad Express*, March 8, 1991).

Others were troubled by the fact that the bill allowed a magistrate to order a man to stay away from the applicant, even if she resided in his house. Opponents argued that this denied individuals constitutional rights to their own property. It made "overnight vagrants" of some men, as one senator put it. And in fact the bill required a three-fifth vote in both the Senate and the House of Representatives because of its refutation of the constitutional right to property.[22]

Several lawmakers were concerned with the burden of proof required of an applicant; others argued about the technical and legal language of the statute. Empowering the police to enter a residence without a warrant was unacceptable to some lawmakers. They also expressed concerns about the discretion of the magistrates who would hear these cases. Several statesmen pointed to the lack of funding to aid victims. Finally, even two years after its passage, the Domestic Violence Act was still being criticized for its lack of "authenticity" (Maurer 1997; Yelvington 1995).[23] One prominent leader in government complained that the Domestic Violence Act had been copied "lock, stock, and barrel from other countries" (*Trinidad Express*, November 26, 1993). Moreover, he claimed the act "did not take into consideration the attitude of the Trinidadian male and his cultural predisposition to property and women . . . the Trinidadian male considers it the height of insult and provocation to be ordered out of his own home. To be made to pay maintenance for his wife and children, with the wife being free to welcome other men in his own house, on his own bed, and with his own money" (*Trinidad Express*, November 26, 1993). In a nutshell, opponents were worried about the state of a Caribbean state that would enact this legislation. They therefore began proposing amendments to limit the bill's impact, decrease the powers of the police to interfere in domestic disputes, redefine the persons who were eligible to request protection, and to alter the bill's legal terminology.

As these amendments were introduced in the Senate, several women's groups swung into action. The Coalition Against Domestic Violence, Rape Crisis Society, Caribbean Association for Feminist Research and Action, Working Women, and women from the shelter for battered women wrote letters and petitioned lawmakers. They expressed in speeches and in newspaper interviews their indignation about proposals to amend the government's bill.[24] The director of the Legal Aid Clinic at the Hugh Wooding Law School, Hazel Thompson-Ahye, argued the merits of the act in the newspaper. She objected to the notion that the bill was an affront to the constitutional protection of property by arguing that peoples' first concern should be for the protection of life. Twenty-one organizations signed petitions calling on lawmakers to reject all amendments to weaken the measure (*Trinidad Express*, March 14, 1991).[25] Finally, members from the women's groups staged a protest in which sympathizers dressed in black and sat in Parliament. A spokeswoman from the Coalition Against Domestic Violence explained that the silent protest was "based on the fact that male members of the Senate are attempting to dilute the purpose of the Bill" (*Trinidad Guardian*, March 10, 1991). The protesters wanted the bill to pass "with some teeth" (*Trinidad Guardian*, March 12, 1991). On March 13, 1991, the *Trinidad Guardian* reported:

> Women donned black outfits and made their way to Parliament yesterday. Coming from various women's organizations they sat silently to protest the amendments which threaten to dilute the Domestic Violence Bill which is before the Senate. . . . Representatives from the Coalition Against Domestic Violence, CAFRA, Working Women, Halfway House, The Shelter, Non-governmental Organization for the Advancement of Women, Rape Crisis Centre and other individuals supporting the cause filed into the public gallery. . . . There was a general feeling among the women that the powers that be are not taking the issue seriously enough, and have not yet seen domestic violence as a crime.

More than forty women had gathered in the public galleries at Parliament (*Trinidad Express*, March 13, 1991).

Pressure on the senators succeeded in winning for the women several of their goals, including retaining a broad definition of "spouse" and giving magistrates the power to put a man out of his own home. As Bartky explains, however, some compromises were probably unavoidable: "It is inevitable that movements that challenge the established order will bear its stamp. . . . Typically movements of contestation combine genuine innovation with elements that are older and more familiar" (2002:65). Of these compromises, two were especially critical for the later implementation of the law.[26] The first was the decision not to allow the police to enter a home without a warrant even if they suspected a domestic violence offense was in progress. Lawmakers were afraid that the police might abuse that right.[27] The second amendment was the provision for an "undertaking." An undertaking allows a person accused of domestic violence for the first time to sign an affidavit promising not to engage in the activities for which he or she is being charged. Signing an undertaking means there will be no formal charges against the respondent and that individual will not have a police record (*Trinidad Guardian*, March 12, 1991). Nevertheless, a breach of an undertaking carries the same penalties as a breach of an order. "Undertakings" are not described in CARICOM or other local model legislation on domestic violence (see Clarke 1998: appendix 3; Mehrotra 2000:annex 11–B); their place in the 1991 Trinidadian Domestic Violence Act was the outcome of local legislative debate.[28] As we shall see in chapter 2, undertakings play a very prominent role in the implementation of domestic violence law in Trinidad, a role more substantial than lawmakers or activists imagined at the time.

With these compromises, the Domestic Violence Act passed the Senate on April 15, 1991. Of the thirty-one voting senators, twenty-six voted for the act, one abstained, and four were absent. The law received unanimous support in the House three months later. Heralded primarily as legislation to protect individuals from abuse, the 1991 Domestic Violence Act was also about reworking crucial categories so that "the state" would intervene in family lives in a fundamentally new way. The statute produced new meanings and consequences for gender and kinship; it also regendered the state by making domestic violence a crime.

Conclusions

At least since the 1960s, there have been global and local initiatives to bring "private" violence to public attention. I have used the term "regendering" for the process by which states bring to public and legal attention categories and activities that were formerly without name, but which constitute harm to women, deny them rights, or limit their capacity to engage in actions available to men. The term acknowledges that law and lawmaking is and always has been a gendered process. Regendering the state entails naming as unacceptable language and action that previously went unnoticed or ignored, as well as the inclusion of new actors into the political and legal process. The passage of domestic violence legislation exemplifies the regendering process.

Under which conditions is regendering likely to ensue? The case of Trinidad, supported by other cross-cultural research cited earlier in the chapter, suggests that an intersection of four historical conditions—conditions that weave together local, national, and international efforts and concerns—will prove salient in regendering the state. The first is an ideology of modernity. Nationalist and more recent public narratives in Trinidad emphasize its peoples' great pride in their history, culture, and progress. Trinidadians pride themselves on being modern (e.g., Barriteau 1998; Birth 1999; Harney 1996; Miller 1994, 1997; Yelvington 1995). As Miller remarks, for example: "Being Trinidadian is increasingly linked to a sense of being global, with similar rights and expectations to those of any metropolitan country" (1997:335).[29] Not surprisingly, then, Trinidad was a leader in the English-speaking Caribbean in outlawing domestic violence. The second is education, particularly the education of women. Since shortly after independence, Trinidadian women have excelled in schools and they have entered graduate and professional training in ever-increasing numbers. The expansion of free education, high literacy rates, and women's entry into the professions, law, and politics were critical among the historical events that coalesced to enable the passage of domestic violence legislation. The third is prosperity. The oil boom of the late 1970s and early 1980s strengthened Trinidad's economy, made it an important player in the community of nations, gave people access to consumer goods and information technology, and made it possible for them to travel to other "civilized" states. And the fourth is feminist political activism. In the same period, the global and local impact of women's movements became quite significant. Building on a long history of women's activism in Trinidad (Cain 2000; Colón and Reddock 2004; Henderson 1988; James-Sebro 2001; Mohammed 1991; Ramkeesoon 1988; Reddock 1994, 1998b, 1998c), women both in and out of government united in the late 1980s to combat rape and other forms of gender violence. They succeeded in revamping a number of laws to penalize crimes that primarily happen to women. The case of Trinidad thus lends further support to the research of previous scholars that finds that domestic violence becomes a priority for the state only when women speak on their own behalf and actively garner government support. During that process, the international discourse on human rights wields considerable influence (e.g., Boyle and Preves 2000; Lazarus-Black and Merry 2003; Merry 2000, 2003). Both lawmakers and activists referred to international concerns and legislation in their efforts to parlay the domestic violence bill into law. Nonetheless, as the parliamentary debate over the domestic violence bill demonstrated, local issues and perspectives in each state are likely to modify model legislation. One Trinidadian example was the Senate's decision to include a provision in the law for an alleged abuser to give an undertaking to refrain from future violence if there has been no previous history of violence known to the court.

Trinidad's Domestic Violence Act is an important symbolic statute; it changed the boundaries between the public and the private and outlawed harm that is mostly experienced by women. After the process of naming and criminalizing domestic violence, however, comes the challenge of implementing the law. In this next stage of the regendering process, as Barriteau points out and this research confirms, "policies are not gender neutral" (1998:192), and access to justice does not necessarily create equality (Barriteau 2001:36). We turn next to the court records to see what kinds of domestic violence cases are brought to the law's attention and to investigate their fate at the courthouse. As will become clear, the case of Trinidad contributes to our understanding of under what conditions and to what degree law can operate as a liberating factor in postcolonial states at the same time that it renders visible the practical limitations of law as praxis.

MINDIE LAZARUS-BLACK AND
PATRICIA L. MCCALL

2 *A Look at the Numbers*

> There are probably few features more characteristic of modernity than the notion that we can know ourselves through numbers. . . . In the hands of the socially or politically disenfranchised, numbers may also be a language of social contestation, a way that ethnic groups, women, and minorities can make themselves visible, articulate their "differences" from the dominant society, and make claims upon the state and its services.
>
> —Jacqueline Urla, "Cultural Politics in an Age of Statistics: Numbers, Nations, and the Making of Basque Identity" (1993)

I began my fieldwork in the magistrates' courts in Trinidad six years after the passage of the Domestic Violence Act (1991). As part of my research, and partly in response to activists' concern that there was no in-depth statistical profile of domestic violence cases that litigants brought to the courts in Trinidad, I collected by hand a two-year sample (1997–98) of all applications for protection brought to the court in "Pelau," the main site of my fieldwork.[1] This chapter, written with Dr. Patricia L. McCall, provides a quantitative record of those cases and offers some comparative data from other courts.[2]

As we have seen, lawmakers and activists alike intended that the victims of domestic abuse be encouraged to speak out against violence and that they be protected through the rule of law. We should ask, therefore, of all applications for protection orders that are filed what percentage results in interim or final protection orders? How many are resolved by the defendant's agreement to refrain from future violence? And how many cases for protection orders are eventually dismissed or withdrawn?

In describing the processing of these cases, we also consider the gender of plaintiffs and respondents and whether men and women experience different treatment in court. How much time does any one case stay in the system? Does the number of times a case appears on the court docket have implications for its final disposition? What happens when men and women simultaneously file charges against each other? We survey the contents of orders and undertakings to see what forms of protection applicants receive from the court and what penalties abusers suffer when they defy a court's orders. Finally, we ask if it makes any difference which court locale one attends.

Lawmakers, lawyers, members of the Trinidadian community, and social scientists may be surprised by these numbers. Each of these groups might justifiably expect that, as a result of the Domestic Violence Act, the courts are regularly issuing formal protection orders. What our analysis reveals, however, is that a startlingly high percentage of the applications for protection orders in our sample, over 77 percent, was dismissed or withdrawn, leaving only about 23 percent of applicants receiving some form of protection from the court. The numbers reflect the phenomenon that critical legal scholars identified as a "gap" between "law on the books" and "law in action." In other words, in the interpretive space between code and practice, events and activities may operate to dissuade people from executing the rights or achieving the protections that the law affords them. What happens in that interpretive space?

Pierce has postulated that there is a standardized response "by hegemonic classes to demands, from marginalized groups, for greater inclusion in modern systems of control and resource distribution." She calls that standardized response "structural deflection," "an adroit substitution of a formal equality for a true equality that would require fundamentally changing the way things are done, or even changing the goals of the organization or both" (1996:228). The court records of domestic violence cases processed in Trinidad suggest that structural deflection is characteristic of the regendering process we have just examined. I explore the micropolitics that create and sustain structural deflection in greater depth in later chapters. This chapter gives readers a quantitative assessment of who uses the courts, for what purposes, and with what consequences. It draws on case records, interviews, and court observations to better comprehend those numbers.

We describe first the data and methods we used to analyze the court records. The analyses of those records follow. In the last section of the chapter we ask, How representative is the data set from Pelau? Can we make claims about the processing of domestic violence cases more generally from this sample? We respond to these questions by referencing the ethnographic record, investigating samples of court hearings and records from other magistrates' courts, and comparing our findings to those of a 1995 study commissioned by the Shelter for Battered Women and the Coalition Against Domestic Violence in Trinidad and to more recent tabulations of disposed cases published by the statistical unit of the judiciary of Trinidad and Tobago. Our review of these materials leads us to conclude that the findings reported for Pelau are representative of several patterns in the implementation of domestic violence law. But our analysis also reveals some evidence of a "politics of place," unique to different courts, that may influence case outcomes (Lazarus-Black and McCall 2006).

Data and Methods

Our primary sample includes all of the domestic violence cases brought to the court in Pelau from January 1997 through December 1998. During this two-year period, 1,463 protection order hearings were recorded, which represent 731 different court cases. The records also include information about 119 hearings of claims of breaches of protection orders, representing 32 breach cases.

To obtain a quantitative analysis of the domestic court cases in Pelau, a data set was created from the field notes using the SPSS statistical package.[3] Field notes were entered as codes that would facilitate tabulation of the characteristics of the cases, their participants, magistrates' orders, and case outcomes. From the 1,463 hearings for protection orders, we deleted those hearings that began toward the end of 1998 but for which we were unable to retrieve final dispositions. We deleted those cases because one of our primary interests was determining the duration of domestic violence case processing. Similarly, some of the cases recorded in January 1997 had been ongoing from 1996, but we were unable to retrieve information on the initial hearing(s) for those cases. Therefore, estimates of case-processing duration may be underestimated because some of the earliest cases omit the initial hearing(s) or represent the concluding hearing(s) of cases not included in this sample. This gives us a conservative estimate of case duration. We treated the cases of breach in a similar fashion, deleting those cases that did not come to some resolution by December 1998.

Thus, this analysis of Pelau's court records relies on a final data set of 686 closed protection order cases and twenty-five closed breach cases processed in the legal system from January 1997 through December 1998. As one would expect, the majority of the cases involve women filing against men (80 percent), but almost 11 percent represent petitions filed by men against women. Same-sex filings are far less common; 4 percent of the cases involve men filing against men, while in only 1 percent of the cases did women file against women. Of all cases, just over 9 percent involve cross-charges that occur when a female complainant comes to court only to find the alleged defendant has filed domestic violence charges against her. With regard to the family status of these litigants, more than half (55 percent) of Pelau's applicants and defendants shared the same last name. These cases mostly represent husband-and-wife conflicts, but sometimes a parent brings a son or daughter to court.[4] Interestingly, the police play an active role in the prosecution of cases of breaches of protection order: some 42 percent of breach cases in our records were filed by the police. About 33 percent of the breach cases in Pelau were brought by women who had filed for the initial protection order and a quarter (25 percent) of such applications were brought by men.

Further Research Findings and Analyses

Tables 2.1 to 2.9 display the results of our analyses of the data from Pelau. Table 2.1 summarizes five possible ways that an application for protection can be disposed. A case may be dismissed by the magistrate if he or she calls the parties before the bench and the complainant is not present to make the case. This is considered "dismissed for want of prosecution" and the case can be brought back to court at another date. A case can also be dismissed, however, if the magistrate hears the complainant's testimony and finds that there is insufficient evidence to support charges of domestic abuse. Cases in which evidence has been led cannot be brought back on the same grounds.[5] Alternatively, an application for a protection order can be withdrawn by the complainant or his attorney. A third possible case disposition occurs when the respondent offers to give an undertaking to the effect that he will not engage in future abusive behavior toward the applicant. An undertaking is an available option only in cases in which there are no former convictions of abuse. More rarely, domestic violence matters are adjudicated and formal orders for protection are rendered by the magistrate. A fifth case disposition is an interim protection order that expired after fourteen days unless otherwise continued by the magistrate.

Approximately 57 percent of the cases in Pelau were dismissed—almost half because the complainant failed to attend the court hearing. In

Table 2.1. Dispositions of Applications for Protection in Domestic
Violence Cases, Frequencies and Percentages, N = 686

	No. of Closed Cases	Percentage of Closed Cases		
Case dismissed	390	56.8		
Failure of complainant to attend hearing	(338)	(86.7)		*
Case withdrawn	141	20.6		*
Respondent's agreement to refrain from future violence (undertakings)*	130	19.0		**
Protection order granted	15	2.2		
Case ending with interim order**	10	1.4		

* In one case, both parties signed undertakings.
** In one case, the magistrate issued interim orders to both the complainant and the respondent.

Trinidad, as in other places, ethnographic research and interviews with applicants reveal that requests for protection orders fall out of the system for many different reasons.[6] Complainants may reconcile with their abusers. They are persuaded to give their partners a second—or perhaps a third or fourth chance—to change their behavior. A few find that the respondents are so surprised to have received the court summons that they (sometimes temporarily) change their abusive ways. Family, friends, and spiritual leaders also persuade women to drop their suits, convincing them not to break up their families by proceeding with litigation. Other women are intimidated or are threatened by their partners. Fearing reprisal, and perhaps adverse consequences for their children, they drop their suits. Some litigants become disillusioned by their experiences at the court because of delays, expenses, and inattention to their problems. A few will listen intently to the clerk describe what a protection order can and cannot do, and then decide it is not worth their effort. Applications are also dismissed for insufficient evidence, problems related to improper filing, or jurisdictional matters. In our sample, for example, four applications for protection and a case for a breach of a protection order were transferred to other courts.

Our analyses uncovered another common reason for the high number of dismissed cases; namely, in over 22 percent of the cases, respondents never appeared in court either because they were never located by the police or because they ignored the summons.[7] Magistrates vary in how long they retain a case before deciding there is no point in continuing it. Interestingly, only men evade the police. During my fieldwork, I encountered no cases that were dismissed because the female respondent could not be located.

An important point to make about dismissed cases is that many of them reflect women's agency and decisions to work out matters in ways that do not warrant further attention from the court. A long and rich literature in law and society research documents the creative use of law and legal procedures by men and women for purposes other than those intended by lawmakers. Researchers studying in different legal settings have found litigants "work" law and legal cases in myriad ways.[8] Therefore, the large percentage of dismissed cases should not be summarily read as evidence of the failure of the system. As we will see in the next several chapters, the system does fail some litigants—many women stop going to court because of their frustration with the endless adjournments of their cases—but the system works very well for others who find that the right to apply for a court order is an empowering experience and can lead to the extralegal outcomes they desire.

As table 2.1 also demonstrates, the second most common case disposition after case dismissals is for a case to be formally withdrawn by the applicant. Just over 20 percent of the cases in this sample were withdrawn. Cases are withdrawn for many of the same reasons they are dismissed. In addition, cases are often withdrawn when attorneys are involved. In Trinidad, lawyers work to determine the needs of their clients and to try to resolve their conflicts without recourse to formal orders. They often urge couples to drop charges. As we shall see in chapter 6, making peace and attending to the needs of children are preferred courses of action in the minds of many lawyers; they urge reconciliation rather than legal remedy. A young male attorney told me, for example, about how his attempted mediation of a family quarrel eventually failed. The parties involved in the case had lived together for a long time and had one child. His client, the man, was very much in love with the woman, but she was ready to leave the relationship. When an incident erupted between them, she hired an attorney and brought charges of domestic abuse. Both my interviewee and the woman's attorney counseled the couple to handle their conflict out of court. The application was withdrawn. Their truce lasted about six months, and then he was violent again. A new case was filed and the magistrate ordered the man to refrain from abusive and threatening behavior and to keep away from the premises—which had been his home—for one year. Ironically, the woman moved into the home of a new love, leaving the house vacant. My interviewee's client was awaiting the end of the year so he could move back into his house.

Finally, table 2.1 shows what kinds of actions and how often the court is likely to reach judgment on behalf of a complainant. An applicant is most likely to get the court to act on her behalf if the defendant agrees to an undertaking. In Pelau, 19 percent of domestic violence complaints ended with undertakings. In these cases, the parties "agree" that the respondent will refrain from future violence, as opposed to having the magistrate "order" the alleged abuser to do so. In sharp contrast, in just over 2 percent of cases the complainant received a final protection order issued by the magistrate. Ethnographic experience, supported by other tables in this chapter, suggests these represent highly contentious cases in which respondents refuse to acknowledge any verbal or physical abuse, thus sending the case eventually to trial. The last case outcome, comprising 1 percent of cases, includes those reaching their final dispositions with interim orders.[9]

Table 2.2 presents a detailed breakdown of the final dispositions of cases that included an interim order at some point during the case's history. We were interested in these cases because they represent the court's attention to victims of violence, even if, at a later date, their cases were dismissed or withdrawn. Magistrates make interim protection orders for several reasons. If a complainant convinces the magistrate that she fears for her safety, but the police have not yet served the defendant, an interim order can be put into place ex parte (without the defendant being present) for fourteen days.[10] Interim orders are also made when the magistrate is uncertain about a complainant's credibility, wants further investigation of the case, wants counseling for the parties, or chooses to give the accused party an opportunity to refrain from abusive behavior for two weeks before bringing the case back for further adjudication. Sometimes attorneys request interim orders while they work on mediating another solution. For example, on occasion I saw an application for

Table 2.2. Dispositions for Cases Involving Interim Orders (N = 21), Frequencies and Percentages

	No. of Closed Cases	Percentage of Interim Orders
Case later dismissed	7	33.3
Case later withdrawn	4	19.0
Respondent's agreement to refrain from future violence (undertaking)	3	14.3
Protection order granted	1	4.8
Case ending as interim order	6	29.2

protection withdrawn at the same time that the court ordered child and wife support. In one case, the magistrate disposed of an application by accepting undertakings from both parties, and in a second, the case was closed with both parties given interim orders.

Of twenty-one cases involving interim orders, eleven cases were eventually dismissed or withdrawn. Of the remaining ten cases, six ended as interim orders, three concluded with the respondent giving an undertaking, and one ended in a formal, final order. We can surmise the reasons that almost half of the interim order cases are later dismissed, withdrawn, or allowed to expire, ranging from the defendant's lack of further harassment of the complainant to the couple's decision to reconcile. Only a few interim orders concluded with the defendant being required to "adjust his/her behavior" in some fashion, whether by extending the interim order for additional time, granting an undertaking to desist from violence, or being formally ordered not to harm the complainant. In one case, the couple signed mutual undertakings to desist from violence. Thus the fate of a case that includes an interim order is not unlike that of other cases: structural deflection works against the parties remaining in the formal judicial process even if their cases temporarily received the court's attention.

As in all social interactions, gender plays a part in determining the dispositions of cases. These patterns can be observed in table 2.3. We consider the dispositions of cases in which: (1) the complainant is female and the respondent is male (80 percent); (2) the complainant is male and the respondent is female (11 percent); (3) the complainant and the respondent are both women (1 percent); and (4) the complainant and the respondent are both men (4 percent). Cases involving cross-charges are analyzed separately.

Women's applications against male respondents are likely to be dismissed in 58 percent of cases, but very often (in almost 30 percent of such cases) because they apply for protection orders and then later fail to appear at the courthouse. Some 17 percent of women's cases against men are withdrawn. When the court does take action to prevent violence, that action is most likely to be in the form of the respondent's undertaking (about 21 percent). Almost 3 percent of cases concluded with a formal protection order, while less than 2 percent ended with an interim order. Thus women go to court to protest the violence of their male partners but they are not very likely to pursue those cases after having initially filed them. If action is taken by the court, it is most likely to accept a man's undertaking to desist from future violence.

Table 2.3. Dispositions for Applications for Protection in Domestic Violence Cases by Sex of the Complainant and Respondent, Frequencies and Percentage of Outcome (in parentheses)

	Comp. ♀ Resp. ♂	Comp. ♂ Resp. ♀	Comp. ♀ Resp. ♀	Comp. ♂ Resp. ♂	Missing Data	Total
Case dismissed	319 (58.0)	34 (45.9)	4 (57.1)	9 (36.0)	24	390
(Case dismissed: Failure of complainant to attend hearing)	162 (29.4)	15 (20.3)	1 (14.3)	4 (32.0)	23	338
Case withdrawn	94 (17.1)	29 (39.2)	1 (14.3)	13 (52.0)	4	141
Respondent's agreement to refrain from future violence (undertaking)	114 (20.7)	10 (13.5)	2 (28.6)	3 (12.0)	1	130
(Cases involving interim order*)	19 (3.4)	1 (1.4)	0 (0)	0 (0)	1	21
Protection order	14 (2.5)	1 (1.4)	0 (0)	0 (0)	0	15
Case ending with interim order	9 (1.6)	0 (0)	0 (0)	0 (0)	1	10
Total**	550 (80.2)	74 (10.8)	7 (1.0)	25 (3.6)	29 (4.2)	686 (100)

Note: ( ) in headings denote subsets from other major disposition categories.
* Denominator equals column total plus these cases.
** Denominator for percentages.

When men take women to court, they also face high rates of dismissals: almost 46 percent of such cases are dismissed, of which 20 percent represent men's failure to attend the court hearing. On the other hand, men have a much higher rate of withdrawing their cases than do women: 39 percent as compared to women's 17 percent. In other words, although women complainants are likely to exit the system by failing to appear in court, men appear before the bench essentially to announce publicly they have no further need of law and are therefore withdrawing their cases. This behavior is in accord with two commonly held notions in the English-speaking Caribbean: (1) the idea that public space is predominantly male space and (2) the tendency to "mythologize rogues, renegades, and badmen" (Headley 1994:89) who, by definition, do not work out their differences in courts of law. On the other hand, men have almost no chance of obtaining protection from the court unless the female respondent agrees to sign an undertaking (less than 14 percent of cases).

Women's cases against other women are highly unlikely to be resolved by way of protection orders. Indeed, table 2.3 shows only three dispositions are likely in such cases. A suit by one woman against another will be dismissed in 57 percent of cases. In another 14 percent of cases, the complainant will withdraw her suit. Finally, an applicant may obtain an undertaking from the respondent (almost 29 percent of cases). There were no instances of women's cases against other women ending in the magistrate issuing interim or final protection orders. When women demand action by the court against other women, they can expect at most the respondents' agreements to sign undertakings.

In the final category, that of men bringing other men to court, we see a pattern divergent from the other three kinds of cases. A smaller percentage of men's cases against other men are dismissed (36 percent). On the other hand, as we have seen in the situation in which men took women to court, men were also likely to withdraw their cases against other men (52 percent of cases), although at a much higher percentage. As was true of the same-sex women's cases, men bringing complaints against other men were likely to receive protection from the court only if the respondent agreed to an undertaking (12 percent of cases). Apparently, the court is reluctant to process or dispose of cases involving same-sex litigants with either interim or final orders—whether those cases involve two men or two women.

In tables 2.4 and 2.5 we consider how long domestic violence cases remained in the legal process by case outcomes and the sex of the complainant and the respondent. We asked, How much time do litigants spend in court attempting to receive the court's protection before they decided either to resolve their conflicts outside the legal arena or to give up their efforts due to a negative experience in the legal system? We knew from the ethnographic data that in Pelau, on average, a protection order required at least two hearings. Commonly these involve situations in which the complainant went to court but the defendant had not yet received a summons to attend the hearing. In those cases, magistrates generally postponed the case for a second hearing in two weeks' time.

Table 2.4 describes case duration in Pelau by sex according to outcome. When the complainant is female and the respondent is male, her case is likely to reach its final disposition on average in eighteen days. If the complainant is male and the alleged abuser is female, the case averages twenty-nine days to disposition. Cases between two women average eighteen days, in contrast to thirty-eight days when the litigants are both men. In other words, once they enter the system as complainants, men are more tenacious than women about pursuing their cases. We also see, however, that when women take men to court, those cases that end in a protection order take the longest time to complete—on average fifty-two days. Withdrawn cases and those ending with interim orders take the next to the longest amount of time to final disposition—on average, about thirty-four days and twenty-three days, respectively. Dismissals and undertakings are completed most quickly—in twelve days and seventeen days, respectively. When a man charges a woman with domestic violence, cases are withdrawn after an average of forty-eight days. Men's cases against women are dismissed in about nineteen days, but they obtain undertakings in only sixteen days. In the one case when a man received a protection order against a woman, it was at the first and only hearing. When women bring other women to magistrate's court for violence, their cases last an average of thirty days before they are dismissed and ten if withdrawn, but conclude with an undertaking on the first court hearing. Finally, when men take men to court seeking protection, their cases end by being dismissed after eleven days, withdrawn in seventeen days, or resolved by undertaking in three days.

In general, then, the longest-lasting cases in the system involve women charging men with domestic violence. Table 2.4 shows that the longest

Table 2.4. Average Length of Case in Days by Sex of the Complainant and Respondent by Outcome of Application for Protection in Domestic Violence Cases

	Comp. ♀ Resp. ♂	Comp. ♂ Resp. ♀	Comp. ♀ Resp. ♀	Comp. ♂ Resp. ♂
Average length of case in days for all cases	18	29	18	38
Average length of case in days by final disposition				
Case dismissed	12	19	30	11*
Case withdrawn	34	48	10	17
Respondent's agreement to refrain from future violence (undertaking)	17	16	1	3
Protection order granted	52	1	—	—
Case ending with interim order	23	—	—	—

Note: "—" indicates no cases in these categories. "1" indicates cases ended at first hearing.

* Average length of these cases is 81 days before omitting outlier case (outlier case lasted 645 days).

of these cases are also most likely to end with a formal protection order granted by the magistrate. In contrast, case resolution by way of an undertaking happens fairly rapidly, whatever the sex of the complainant.

Whereas table 2.4 describes how long a case lasted depending on its outcome, table 2.5 presents the approximate number of days it took for cases to close based on the sex of the litigants. Forty-nine percent of the cases brought by women against men are disposed of in a single day. After that, the numbers are low and stable: 11 percent last two to seven days; 12 percent last eight to fourteen days; and 12 percent last between fifteen and twenty-eight days. Cases lasting over a month comprise over 16 percent of this sample. Cases brought by men against women show a somewhat similar pattern: 47 percent are disposed of in one day, yet over 24 percent last more than a month. Cases between two women fail to remain in the system more than one day in 43 percent of these cases, 44 percent last between eight and twenty-eight days, and 14 percent last more than forty-three days. Men's cases against other men last one day in 36 percent of the sample. Forty percent remain in court between eight and twenty-eight days and 16 percent for more than a month. In short, the largest percentage of domestic violence cases close at the first hearing, whether they involve same- or opposite-sex litigants. On the other hand, some 13 percent of applications for domestic violence involve very contentious conflicts that will demand the court's attention for over six weeks.

Table 2.5. Duration of Case by Sex of the Complainant and Respondent, Frequencies and Percentages (in parentheses), N = 686

	Comp. ♀ Resp. ♂	Comp. ♂ Resp. ♀	Comp. ♀ Resp. ♀	Comp. ♂ Resp. ♂	Missing Data	Total
1 day	271 (49.3)	35 (47.3)	3 (42.8)	9 (36.0)	25	343
2 to 7 days	59 (10.7)	6 (8.1)	0 (0)	2 (8.0)	0	67
8 to 14 days	64 (11.6)	5 (6.8)	2 (28.6)	8 (32.0)	0	79
15 to 28 days	67 (12.2)	10 (13.5)	1 (14.3)	2 (8.0)	3	83
29 to 42 days	23 (4.2)	3 (4.0)	0 (0)	0 (0)	0	26
43 days or longer	66 (12.0)	15 (20.3)	1 (14.3)	4 (16.0)	2	88
Total	550	74	7	25	30	686

Table 2.6 presents the final disposition of cases involving cross-
charges. As noted earlier, sometimes a complainant brings a case to court
only to find that the alleged abuser has brought a countersuit. There were
sixty-four such cases. Only a quarter of the cross-charges were dismissed,
a figure significantly lower than that of the more common cases involving charges by only one party. Cross-charges were also more likely to be
withdrawn than other domestic violence cases—almost 58 percent of
these cases. Participant observation in Pelau and other courts suggests
that these cases often involve attorneys who counsel their clients to mediate a solution other than that of court orders. Like other kinds of cases,
however, if the parties received protective attention from the courts, that
attention was likely to take the form of an undertaking. Undertakings
were granted in almost 16 percent of cross-charge cases while formal,
final orders were granted to less than 2 percent of the applications. These
patterns hold whether the sex of the parties involve female complainants
with male respondents or male complainants with female respondents.

The contentious nature of cases involving cross-charges is evident in
table 2.7. As we have seen, cases involving single charges are likely to be
dismissed at the first hearing in over 50 percent of cases, unless the case

Table 2.6. Dispositions for Applications for Protection In Domestic
Violence Cases Involving Cross-Charges by Sex of the Complainant and
Respondent, Frequencies and Percentage of Outcome (in parentheses),
N = 64.

	All Cases	Comp. ♀ Resp. ♂	Comp. ♂ Resp. ♀	Comp. ♂ Resp. ♂	Missing Data
Case dismissed	16 (25.0)	7 (25.0)	7 (24.1)	0 (0.0)	2
Case withdrawn	37 (57.8)	15 (53.6)	17 (58.6)	5 (100)	0
Respondent's agreement to refrain from future violence (undertaking)	10 (15.6)	5 (17.8)	5 (17.2)	0 (0.0)	0
Protection order granted	1 (1.6)	1 (3.6)	0 (0)	0 (0.0)	0
Case ending with interim order	0 (0.0)	0 (0)	0 (0)	0 (0.0)	0
Total*	64	28	29	5	7

Note: No cross-charge cases involved complainants and respondents who were both
females.
* Denominator for percentages.

involves two men. In sharp contrast, less than 24 percent of cross-charges are dismissed at first hearing; 9 percent last two to seven days; 14 percent last eight to fourteen days; 14 percent last fifteen to twenty-eight days; and a significant proportion (39 percent) last more than a month, which is in stark contrast to the overall cases that last more than four weeks. These figures demonstrate that these are cases in which reconciliation proves extremely difficult.

Table 2.8 shifts our attention from the litigants and the duration of their cases to mandates that are issued by magistrates in all hearings in which interim orders are made and cases that are closed: (1) as interim orders; (2) undertakings; and (3) final orders. As a general rule, interim orders are less detailed in their content than are undertakings and final orders. This makes sense given that many interim orders are made ex parte, before the alleged abuser has appeared in court, as opposed to undertakings and final orders, for which the accused must be present. When we turn our attention to the contents of undertakings and final orders, it is immediately clear that mostly the court provides protection to complainants against threatening language, abusive language, and assault. Seventy-six percent of undertakings and 67 percent of final orders include protection against threatening language, while 73 percent of undertakings and 40 percent of final orders preclude abusive language. Almost 59 percent of undertakings and 47 percent of final orders sanction defendants from assaulting applicants. The fourth most common mandate is protection for the complainant at her home, and particularly if the magistrate is making a final order. Almost 47 percent of final orders keep defendants away from the complainant's premises. A general directive against harassment was ordered in 16 percent of undertakings and 13 percent of final orders. Protection at the complainant's workplace is mandated in 11 percent of undertakings and 27 percent of final orders.

Table 2.7. Duration of Case When Cross-Charges Are Involved, N = 64

	Cross-Charges	
	No. of Cases	Percentage
1 day	15	23.4
2 to 7 days	6	9.4
8 to 14 days	9	14.1
15 to 28 days	9	14.1
29 to 42 days	3	4.7
43 days or more	22	34.4

Table 2.8. Percentages of Protection Orders Involving Specific Mandates by the Magistrate by Final Disposition, N = 686

Mandate	Interim Orders N = 33	Closed Interim Orders N = 10	Under-takings N = 130	Final Orders N = 15
Threatening language	36.4	50	76.2	66.7
Abusive language	27.3	50	73.1	40
Assault	21.2	30	58.5	46.7
Premises	18.2	20	20.8	46.7
Harassing	12.1	20	16.2	13.3
Business	6.1	20	10.8	26.7
Destroying property	3	0	6.2	0
Physical contact	3	0	0	0
Obscene language	0	0	8.5	0
Counseling	0	0	3.8	0
Desist phone calls	0	0	0.77	6.7
Restricted from person	0	0	1.5	6.7

Note: Less than 1 percent of the court's rulings included orders with respect to following a person, using a vehicle, deprivation of property, or hitting.

Other provisions in the Domestic Violence Act, such as provision for counseling or protection against harassment by telephone, destruction of property, obscene language, and restricted personal contact, are provided much more rarely.[11]

Finally, we present in table 2.9 the final dispositions for applications for breaches of protection orders. Such cases were infrequent and we have only twenty-five closed suits in our sample.[12] Breach cases were most likely brought by female complainants or police constables against male defendants. Of the twenty-five closed cases, eleven were brought by women and eleven were brought by the police against male defendants. In only three cases did men charge women with having breached a protection order. Fourteen cases of alleged breach were dismissed. In three of these dismissed cases, the breach was listed as having been brought by police, but the court record noted that the complainant did not want to pursue the case. Without the testimony of the complainant, police are reluctant to press charges. One breach case was "unfounded." Five defendants posted bail, one was sentenced to a week in jail, and one could not be charged with breaching a protection order because the order had expired (but he was charged with assault and fined $750 TT). In three cases there were no details as to why the suits had been dismissed.

Charges of breach of protection order were later withdrawn by com-

Table 2.9. Actions by the Court in Breaches of Domestic Violence Cases, Frequencies and Percentages of Closed Cases, N = 25 (Plus 7 Cases Not Closed)

	No. of Closed Cases	Percentage of Closed Cases
Closed Cases (N = 25)		
Case dismissed	14	56
(case brought by police, complainant did not wish to pursue case)	3	12
(unfounded)	1	4
(posted bail: BWS or OB)*	5	20
(one week in jail)	1	4
(evidence led, order expired)	1	4
(no details on dismissal)	3	12
Case withdrawn	5	20
Respondent pled guilty, fined $1,000	1	4
Respondent found guilty of assault, fined $750	1	4
Respondent reprimanded and discharged (psychiatric cases, same defendant)	2	8
Disposition unknown/Missing information	2	8
Cases Not Closed/Disposition Unknown (N = 7)		
Transferred to unknown destination	1	
Cases continued past data collection	6	

* Note that entries in parentheses are details of dismissed cases. For some of these entries, the "remark"/detail was noted during the course of the history of the case and before the final court hearing. "BWS" = Bail with surety; "OB" = Own bail.

plainants in five cases in this sample. In four of these five cases, a case against a male respondent was withdrawn by a woman; a man withdrew the fifth case against a female respondent. Only one defendant pled guilty to the charge of breaching the protection order. He was fined $1,000 TT. Two defendants escaped with reprimands from the magistrates. In two other cases, the court record did not include the case disposition. Of seven cases not closed during the sample period, one was transferred and six continued past the data collection period.[13]

Breach cases tended to be relatively long-lasting: of the twenty-five closed cases, the hearings had an average of over nine weeks until case disposition, with an average of four hearings during that period. (One very unusual case in our sample continued for ninety-one weeks and included twenty-four hearings.) Closed cases that ended in dismissals averaged almost three months and included four hearings. Cases closed by a complainant's withdrawal of a petition were shorter in duration, lasting an average of eight weeks and including three hearings.

Generalizing from the Pelau Court Records

How representative of court users, legal processes, and case outcomes are the data from Pelau? In this section, we draw upon: (1) comparative research based on fieldwork, interviews, and samples of court records from two other magistrates' courts in Trinidad; and (2) local studies by scholars and government statistics of domestic violence court cases. The records from Pelau mostly reflect patterns in court use and case processing common to other magistrates' courts throughout Trinidad, although a few interesting variations also allow us to delineate the presence of a "politics of place" that can influence case processing.

The two courts for which we offer comparative data are "Cocoa" and "Town."[14] "Cocoa," once the site of a prosperous cocoa-growing village, is today a town of approximately eleven thousand persons (Republic of Trinidad and Tobago 2002). We have not attempted to hide the identity of "Town," the magistrate court in Port of Spain, because the sheer number of cases in the sample makes that court's identity obvious. Port of Spain's population of approximately forty-nine thousand persons is about three times greater than that of Pelau and four times greater than that of Cocoa (Republic of Trinidad and Tobago 2002).

From the perspective of a participant observer, the most obvious common feature of the three courts is the sociological profile of complainants and respondents. In Pelau, Cocoa, and Port of Spain, court users are similarly situated in terms of the relationships between the parties, their ages, ethnicity, social class, and the gender of petitioners and alleged abusers.

Most litigants in each of the courts were related as husband and wife, parties to a common-law or visiting union, or those who had a child in common.[15] In a few cases, a mother or father (or both) brought an abusive child to court, especially when he was suffering from drug or alcohol addiction. As noted earlier, the courts do not entertain petitions from parties in gay or lesbian relationships. In addition to the similarity in the relationships of the parties, the courts serve similar populations with respect to the age, ethnic backgrounds, class, and gender of litigants, although they do serve different numbers and proportions of those participants.[16]

Every age cohort is represented in domestic violence cases in these courts, from young adults to the elderly. Young women complained about abusive verbal and physical maltreatment by their intimate partners, husbands, and the fathers of their children. The men they accused of violence commonly protested these charges or denied them entirely; more rarely, they admitted to bad behavior and agreed to refrain from future abuse. Working women complained of men jeopardizing their employment by harassing behavior that included excessive phone calls and inappropriate appearances at their offices. Another common scenario involved older couples in long-term partnerships who were parents to two, three, or more children. These older women came to court because the law now provided them with a forum from which to speak about the violence in their lives.

In the first major work devoted to the subject of domestic violence in the Caribbean, Danns and Parsad (1989) reported that ethnic differences in domestic violence rates in Guyana were negligible. Theirs was a study of the causes and prevalence of domestic violence and touched on court use only tangentially; however, their assertion that domestic violence crosses both ethnic and class lines finds support in more recent research in Trinidad (Cain 1996; Lazarus-Black 2001; Rawlins 2000). Court observations and interviews affirmed that both Afro-Trinidadians and East Indian–Trinidadians regularly applied for protection orders. There was no evidence to support the claims of some interviewees that one ethnic group was more violent than the other (see also Cain 1996). As we will see in chapter 6, however, certain kinship norms and practices within and between the two main ethnic groups influence how people respond to domestic violence.

The class position of litigants can be partially surmised from information they provided orally to the court, which always included occupation and place of residence, as well as by their dress and demeanor. Female applicants for protection orders in all three courts commonly gave as their occupations "homemaker," "clerk," "sales," and "domestic." The men they charged with domestic violence included taxi drivers, mechanics, construction workers, and self-described "businessmen," a euphemism for an entrepreneur who might sell a few fish from his boat, mangoes from his yard, or manage a significant business retail enterprise. During trials, litigants' levels of education, characteristics of their dwellings, domestic arrangements, neighborhoods, and previous efforts to resolve conflicts emerged as further evidence of their class affiliations. Respondents' testimonies included histories of unemployment, underemployment, their inability to support children, and substance abuse. Thus, as is true of domestic violence cases in the United States (Buzawa and Buzawa 1996; Ptacek 1999; Sokoloff 2005; Wittner 1998), abuse cases

in Trinidad were brought typically by parties from poor, working-class
or lower-middle-class backgrounds. The structural variables of poverty,
unemployment, lack of education, and (youthful) age are imminent to
explaining the pervasiveness of domestic violence (Hampton, Carrillo,
and Kim 2005; West 2005). Nevertheless, in Trinidad as in the United
States, domestic violence crosses class lines and some applicants for
protection and alleged abusers in these courts were middle class. Based
on court observations and oral testimony during trials, it is fair to say
that few litigants in the magistrates' courts represented Trinidad's most
elite families.

What about the gender of complainants and respondents? Although
we do not have a large enough sample of cases from Cocoa to address this
question by way of quantitative analysis, we have excellent comparative data on the gender of litigants from Port of Spain. As we have seen,
80 percent of domestic violence cases in Pelau were brought by women
against men. In a sample of 2,711 applications for protection orders filed
in Port of Spain in 1997–98, 78 percent were filed by women. There is
similar continuity when we check the statistics for male complainants:
close to 11 percent of cases in Pelau involved men charging women with
domestic violence, while in the capital, just under 12 percent involved
men claiming female intimates abused them. These often entailed cross-
charges in which parties accused each other of violence. In both courts,
relatively few same-sex cases appeared. Women brought charges against
other women in just 1 percent of cases in Pelau and in 3 percent of cases
in Port of Spain. Only 4 percent of cases in Pelau and 6 percent in Port
of Spain involved two men. In short, Trinidad's magistrates' courts serve
litigants in similar kinds of relationships and across a wide range of ages,
ethnicities, and classes. In the main, applicants for protection orders are
women, although the number of men bringing complaints against women
was surprising to the anthropologist and the legal practitioners.

Beyond the description of the persons who filed for protection orders and their alleged abusers, there were many other points of similarity between the courts in Pelau, Cocoa, and Town. In each place, daily
dockets were long; family cases of various kinds constituted a significant
proportion of the workload for the magistrates; most litigants were unrepresented; there were problems serving summons; domestic violence
cases were usually adjourned at their first hearing and quite often after
that; many complainants did not appear when their names were called
and therefore their cases were dismissed; few cases went to trial; formal
protection orders were granted rarely; the number of breaches brought
to court was limited; and almost no one went to prison for failure to

comply with a protection order. Excerpts from field notes from Cocoa offer a glimpse of a typical day in that court.

On February 2, 1998, the magistrate's list in Cocoa included 107 cases. There were seven applications for protection orders. Of these, three were immediately dismissed because the parties did not appear. Two cases were adjourned, one to await a probation report and the second the arrest of the defendant. Evidence was led in two cases. One entailed a middle-aged man who was bringing charges against his wife for using abusive and harassing language. The respondent admitted to using bad language when she came to the matrimonial home to see their children. (She had moved away and was involved in another relationship.) The magistrate suggested that she could give an undertaking to keep the peace and she immediately agreed to do that. The second case involved a woman who was charging her adult son with domestic violence. She alleged that on January 17, 1998, he had broken into her home, used abusive and threatening language, and "run amuck" all over the house. The magistrate asked the defendant what he had to say for himself. He kept his eyes to the floor and did not reply. The magistrate asked him if he would sign an undertaking. He agreed. The magistrate then inquired if the complainant wanted her son excluded from her home. She did not.

On this date, finally, the magistrate heard one breach of a protection order. The defendant was alleged to have broken into his ex-wife's home. The hearing began with the accused providing to the court a letter from St. Ann's, the mental hospital. The magistrate read the letter and then asked the defendant his plans for the future now that he had been released from the hospital. He replied that he planned to resume a normal life. The magistrate told him sternly that he was to "leave the lady alone," "not molest her any more," and that he "must not go back there." Turning to the complainant, he instructed her to go to the police station if she had any more trouble. The magistrate did not voice his decision in open court. After court, a clerk advised me that the defendant was a police officer with a long history of mental illness. When I checked the court records the following week, I found that the case had been dismissed. As we have seen from the records from Pelau, this is a common outcome in breach cases.

Next, we analyzed the court records from Cocoa for the month of February 1998, and these demonstrate three important resemblances to the court records from Pelau in the same time period. First, a large percentage of applications for protection in Cocoa were dismissed (72 percent) as compared to 57 percent in Pelau. Second, in both courts a great many other cases were adjourned: 44 percent in Cocoa and 55 percent in Pelau. Third, combining the number of orders and undertakings,[17] we found that the court took action to protect applicants in 27 percent of cases in Cocoa, as compared to 23 percent in Pelau.

There were two differences between the courts. The first was the lack of withdrawals of cases by applicants in Cocoa (21 percent of cases in Pelau were characterized as "withdrawn"). This difference is most likely a function of either of one of two possibilities: it may be a consequence of the small size of the sample from Cocoa or a clerical style in which any case not resulting in an active disposition from the court was marked "dismissed." Cocoa's records are also unusual in that, in a single month, the magistrate sentenced three defendants to jail for breaching protection orders and gave a fourth the option of a fine of $1,800 TT or three months' imprisonment. Nevertheless, in Cocoa, as in other jurisdictions, a defendant charged with breaching a court order is likely to be incarcerated only if the case is especially severe and/or the matter is brought along with other serious criminal charges. For example, I was in Cocoa's court when two of these four defendants were sentenced. In one case, the defendant was also charged with the crimes of "possession of a weapon" and "intention to wound." Those cases were brought against him by two police constables who were on routine patrol in a marked vehicle when they saw the defendant armed with a machete and chasing a woman who later turned out to be his wife.[18] The second case also involved police testimony, as well as medical evidence, and a determined complainant who had suffered a long history of physical abuse from the defendant. The accused, for his part, did little to aid his defense when he admitted that he had "pelted a stone" at the complainant, but then claimed it wasn't his fault if it had hit her face because "she duck[ed] into it!"

Our data from Pelau and interviews with attorneys suggest that, in general, cases for breaches of protection are relatively rare. I asked a female attorney who had been in practice for ten years at the time of the interview if she witnessed or processed breaches of protection orders. She replied, "Not very often. Well, there are breaches. But the wives are always hesitant to bring it before the court. And sometimes the breach has just been someone coming and abusing them verbally. They may be very hesitant to bring it before the court for that abuse. If it is physical, they are more anxious to come to court. In terms of my cases, I don't have any hard data, but in terms of my cases, [it is] not very often that you get breaches."

This response was typical. The attorneys also told me that they had not seen many defendants sent to jail for breaching an order. A male attorney with more than fifteen years in practice, mostly in the magistrates' court in Port of Spain, told me that between 1991 and 1998 he had witnessed just three cases in which a magistrate sent a man to jail for breaching an order.

The size of the population served by the court in Cocoa was slightly smaller than that of Pelau and their weekly court dockets were similarly organized: family matters, including domestic violence suits, were generally set for one day per week. The court in Port of Spain served a much larger population than the Pelau or Cocoa courts, and its much heavier caseload meant that family matters were heard four days per week. Although any one day spent observing cases in Town resembled days spent in Pelau and Cocoa in all of the ways delineated thus far, the court in the capital was unusual for Trinidad in its architecture, structural conditions, and workload.

For example, the spatial design and organization of Town created especially formidable obstacles for litigants. During the time of this study, nine magistrates' courts were housed in an old building in Port of Spain, but only one court was devoted to family matters, including domestic violence disputes. Although police screen and search persons entering all of Trinidad's courts, there were many more officers involved in this ritual in Port of Spain. Their uniforms, batons, aggressive manner, and sharp remarks made entry into the courts a daunting prospect. At this point, however, surveillance ended. Even after a litigant located the appropriate courtroom, there was no notice of when any one case might be called. A litigant might arrive early in the morning, stay all day, and then find the case adjourned to a new date. Moreover, although most of the courts were crowded, nothing compared to the situation in the capital. On a typical day, the court assigned to domestic matters could not accommodate all the parties. Therefore, instead of waiting inside the courtroom for their cases to be heard, parties remained in the crowded hallways but were responsible for listening to the police constable who would emerge periodically to call their names. Going to court in Port of Spain required unusual persistence and determination (Lazarus-Black and McCall 2006:149).

Town's daily docket of cases required persistence and determination on the part of its magistrates as well. On any given day in Port of Spain, some twenty-four applications appeared on the docket. In any given week, the court processed about eight times more cases than did the courts in Pelau and Cocoa. Emerson's theory of the holistic effects of organizational practices in decision making therefore partially explains what occurred in Town and, on a lesser scale, in Pelau and Cocoa, as the various legal

legal remedies. To cite another example, an attorney who specialized in criminal law, but who occasionally handled family matters, found herself representing a Hindu man who worked as a truck driver and who had been charged by his wife, a part-time maid, with domestic violence. The attorney's client convinced her that the case was "really" about his wife's wanting to leave the matrimonial home with property so that she could pursue a new relationship. My interviewee persuaded the alleged victim and her mother to come to her office, explaining to me: "I asked the girl's mother to come in so that she wouldn't feel she was being railroaded by the guy and her attorney. And she admitted the whole reason for her application before the court. She said, basically, once we talked it out, the division of property. She said, 'Ok, let's sign an agreement.' And on the next occasion she indicated to the court that she was withdrawing. So it was clear that some people have learned how to use the act to their benefit." This example is so interesting because it shows again that lawyers may keep domestic violence cases out of court, thereby contributing to the great number of cases that are either dismissed or withdrawn, and represents one of a very few examples I encountered in which a domestic violence application was not really about "abuse."[19]

In addition to participant observation in other courts, I conducted in-depth case histories with six litigants who were parties to domestic violence matters in courts other than Pelau. These interviews confirmed what I learned from litigants who had cases in Pelau; namely, that time, money, distance from the courthouse, fear of reprisal, concern for children's welfare, issues of privacy, and support (or lack thereof) from relevant third parties each play a role in persuading people to pursue or to drop their lawsuits. Indeed, few litigants have the tenacity of Rosalyn, whose case we shall follow in the next chapter. Rosalyn attended court every month for eleven months, and sometimes more than once a month, before her case was finally heard and she was issued a protection order against her drug-addicted and abusive son.

These possibilities for variation notwithstanding, the findings from the Pelau court records model general patterns and trends in court use, case processing, and case dispositions that reappear in court records from Cocoa and Town and, we suggest, these patterns likely also hold in other courts in Trinidad. Earlier independent research, to which we turn next, confirms our argument.

Trinidad's Shelter for Battered Women and Coalition Against Domestic Violence commissioned a study to "establish baseline statistics on Domestic Violence on a national level for Trinidad and Tobago" (Creque 1995:2). The report included a table provided by the office of the chief magistrate (Creque 1995:9). Data was collected from eleven magisterial districts from the inception of the act in August 1991 through April 1994. As table 2.10 makes clear, the number of protection orders granted by the courts varies in different districts.

Of the total number of applications filed in this earlier period (8,297), an average of 39 percent (3,248) resulted in some form of protection for the complainant.[20] Hence, the data from Pelau and Cocoa with, respectively, 23 and 27 percent of applications resulting in protective action, suggest these courts were conservative in issuing orders, but not unusually so. In general, the more urban courts have higher numbers of applications for protection orders filed and more court orders issued. This concurs with our findings for Town.[21]

Finally, we can compare our findings in Pelau to recent statistical tabulations of court outcomes published in 2004 by the statistical unit of the judiciary of Trinidad and Tobago. According to those data, between 1998 and 2003, the number of cases filed for domestic violence rose from 5,000 to 9,034. In that period, "the majority of cases (75.5%) were dismissed and . . . less than a quarter (21.88%) were granted Protection Orders. . . . Statistics for 2002–2003 reveal a similar situation with 75% of the cases being dismissed and 22% being granted Protection Orders" (Trinidad and Tobago Coalition Against Domestic Violence 2005:30, 31).[22] Thus we find, again, similar trends in the outcomes of domestic violence applications.

Table 2.10. Frequencies and Percentages of Domestic Violence Case Applications and Protection Orders Issued in Trinidad and Tobago Magisterial Districts between 1991 and 1994

Courts	No. of Applications Filed	No. of Protection Orders Issued	Percent
Port of Spain*	2330	1662 [sic]	71.3 [sic]
A	564	170	30.0
B	1185	184	15.5
C	1156	229	19.0
D	411	43	10.0
E	992	643 [sic]	64.8 [sic]
F	226	33	14.0
G	195	44	22.0
H	233	70	30.0
I	369	33	8.9
J	636	137	21.0

* We have identified the capital because of the obvious differences in the number of applications filed there as compared to the other courts (adapted from Creque 1995).

To summarize, ethnographic research in magistrates' courts other than Pelau, data from the courts at Cocoa and Port of Spain, and independent evaluations of applications for protection filed and orders granted in other magistrates' courts confirm that general patterns in case processing, duration, and disposition characteristic of court use in Pelau represent trends that are commonplace in other courts in Trinidad.[23]

Conclusions

Trinidad and Tobago passed the first comprehensive Domestic Violence Act in the English-speaking Caribbean. At its inception, during its revision in 1999, and regularly thereafter, the Domestic Violence Act has been publicized and scrutinized in newspapers and other media (Lazarus-Black 2001; Philips 2000; Rawlins 2000). Not surprisingly, people in Pelau and other villages and towns in Trinidad are aware of the law and their rights; they apply for protection orders to stop the violence that permeates their lives.[24] Going to court to procure rights, however, is a complicated endeavor in which claims for justice do not always receive the attention or redress that lawmakers imagined. What major patterns are revealed in our quantitative analyses of the domestic violence cases brought to Pelau?

As is true in the United States, the number of cases leaving the system without extended protection is high (Buzawa and Buzawa 1996; Fagan 1996; Fischer and Rose 1995; Ford 1991, 1993, 2003; Ford and Regoli 1992; Harrell, Smith, and Newmark 1993; Harrell and Smith 1996). Most of the complainants who file applications for protection orders in Pelau, and in other Trinidadian magistrates' courts, will eventually vanish from the court without legal redress. Over 77 percent of the cases filed for protection orders in Pelau were dismissed or withdrawn. This is not the result of any singular cause. Of cases brought by women against men, for example, 29 percent were dismissed because the applicants did not appear in court to pursue the charges. Some of these cases represent women's choices and agency. Weighing her options, a woman may decide to give a man another chance, she may be persuaded by her mother or best friend not to pursue the case, she may be worried about the court's role in the lives of her children, or her employer may not give her the time to pursue the suit. In later chapters, I identify additional reasons intrinsic to encounters with court officials in the legal process to account for the high percentages of dismissals and withdrawals of domestic violence cases uncovered in these court records.

When the court in Pelau takes action to protect a complainant, it is most likely to accept a respondent's undertaking to refrain from future violence. Undertakings constitute 19 percent of the final case dispositions there. They occur in almost 21 percent of cases brought by women against men, 14 percent of men's cases against women, 29 percent of women's cases against other women, and 12 percent of men's cases against other men. In sharp contrast, magistrates grant formal protection orders for women against men in less than 3 percent of cases and for men against women in only 1 percent of cases. There were no cases in our sample in which magistrates granted formal orders to complainants charging same-sex respondents with violence.

Gender is clearly an important variable in the processing and final disposition of domestic violence cases. Some 80 percent of Pelau's cases are filed by women, mostly against men with whom they have been intimate. Eleven percent of the applicants to the courts, however, are men protesting the violence of the women in their lives. We found that the court treats male and female applicants differently in some ways but not in others, and that when there is evidence of gender disparity, it is mostly in "gender-predictable" ways. For example, women were much more likely to receive an undertaking from the court than were men. Of the 130 undertakings, over 89 percent involved female complainants and only 10 percent involved male complainants. Of all closed cases, 17 percent of women received undertakings but less than 2 percent of men received that court disposition. Moreover, women were far more likely to win an interim order from the court. Hence, the gender-predictable notion that men do not need the court's assistance to protect them from violence is borne out in the records.

The court hardly discriminated by sex, however, when it came to issuing final orders: less than 3 percent for women and slightly over 1 percent for men. Moreover, a comparable percentage of cases by female applicants are likely to be dismissed whether the case is brought against a man or a woman: 58 percent and 57 percent, respectively. Men's cases against women were dismissed in 46 percent of cases, but in only 36 percent of cases involving another man. The disposition "case withdrawn" is proportionately most often a disposition involving a male complainant, but especially if the respondent is also male.

Case duration is an influential factor in the final disposition of a case. Fully half of the cases from Pelau last only one day, but almost 13 percent average forty-three days or longer. The cases that remain in the courts for the longest periods of time are also the cases that are most likely to receive formal protection orders. Quite often, these highly contentious cases involve cross-charges in which the parties accuse each other of violent behavior.

Whatever the duration of a case, and whether it is resolved by an undertaking or the magistrate's formal order, the protection order itself is most likely to restrain the respondent from engaging in threatening or abusive language and/or assault. In other words, the court is most often concerned with harmful words and physical abuse. The Domestic Violence Act provided for a wide array of remedies against different forms of abusive behavior, but these other protections are rarely administered by the court. We need further research to determine whether case dispositions reflect the actual complaints that are made by the applicants or whether, over time, magistrates have come to rely on formulaic decrees in rendering protection orders.

Charges of breaches of an undertaking or a protection order are fairly rare in Pelau. Our sample of closed cases consists of only twenty-five such cases in two years. Consistent with the ethnographic findings in other courts, these cases are unlikely to go to trial. Most often the complainant, whether the alleged victim or a police constable, will drop the charges. Cases were dismissed or withdrawn in nineteen of the twenty-five closed cases.

Three types of evidence support the premise that the figures from Pelau are representative of litigants, legal processes, and case outcomes in comparable courts in Trinidad. Fieldwork in other magistrates' courts revealed similarities in the sociological characteristics of the parties to domestic violence cases, including the diversity of their relationships, ages, ethnic backgrounds, and class; the gender of most complainants and respondents; how cases are handled by court personnel; the high rates of dismissals of applications; and the few cases that reached disposition by way of undertakings or formal protection orders. Some differences between the courts also came to light. In Town, the sheer number of cases processed by the court is unlike any other in Trinidad and the complexity of its organization has consequences for litigants who file their cases there. Judicial style has an influence on whether or not a case will be heard and, if heard, whether the disposition will be an undertaking or a formal order. Some lawyers are more emphatic about getting protection orders for their clients than other lawyers are, and some litigants persist in their efforts while other litigants are more easily dissuaded from pursuing their rights. Nevertheless, the trends revealed by participant observation and interviews in the courts; analyses of the court records from Pelau, Cocoa, and Town; the 1995 study commissioned by the Shelter for Battered Women and the Coalition Against Domestic Violence; and recent statistics of disposed cases published by the statistical unit of Trinidad and Tobago lend credence to our argument that litigants' experiences in Pelau's court were not unusual.

This chapter has both theoretical and practical implications. When a new law is implemented to affect social change, scholars, lawmakers, and activists must pay attention to the process that Pierce (1996) called structural deflection. Structural deflection masks pervasive underlying structural conditions that cause the subordination of some social groups or categories of persons and leaves those conditions unaltered even as these are purportedly "fixed" by law. The discrepancy between cases filed and outcomes points to the presence of structural deflection found in our case study of Pelau. Structural deflection also likely characterizes the regendering process more generally. For example, without naming the phenomenon as "structural deflection," Ptacek points to its operation in domestic violence hearings in courts in Massachusetts, where applicants for protection are empowered in law to receive compensation for injuries and spousal support but hardly ever secure those rights (1999:131–32). Additional research is therefore needed to determine if structural deflection characterizes the implementation of protective legislation across a range of times and places. I explore the micropolitics of court rites, time, and cultures of reconciliation that contribute to structural deflection in later chapters. The next chapter investigates first the configuration of ideas, events, and processes that enable applicants for protection orders to win those orders.

3   The Meaning of Success

Each year since the passage of the Domestic Violence Act in Trinidad, the number of applications for protection orders has been impressive: thousands of people go to court seeking relief from the violence in their lives. A surprising and dramatic number of these cases, as we have seen, are later dismissed or withdrawn. Who, then, beats these odds? Who are the applicants who win the court's attention and successfully negotiate protection orders? What makes an application protesting violence into a successful case?

In this chapter I describe which applicants and what kinds of cases are most likely to receive protection orders from the courts. As is true of research findings about domestic violence in the United States, England, India, and elsewhere, domestic violence law in Trinidad conjures up a specific cast of characters who are familiar, "known," and deemed "entitled" to relief from violence.[1] The litigants who succeed in obtaining protection orders fall into specific categories that are well known to the magistrates who preside over domestic violence matters. Although the Domestic Violence Act provided remedy for a variety of physical and psychological forms of violence between persons in a wide range of intimate and familial relationships, in practice it serves a more limited cohort of persons suffering more limited forms of violence.

Knowledge about the Domestic Violence Act and how the legal system functions are also critical to making a case. For example, a petitioner may not need a lawyer to pursue a protection order, but she must know what evidence is needed to convince the magistrate that domestic violence has occurred. Support from relevant third parties and the ability to withstand the time and financial burden it takes to plead one's cause are other highly relevant factors in establishing a case. Finally, as I shall explain, who is awarded a protection order in Trinidad is partly a function of law's literal nature and of violent men's generosity. I conclude this chapter with some thoughts about the "success" of the legislation, particularly about its ideological influence in reconstituting the boundaries of appropriate and inappropriate familial and gender relationships. First, however, I take the reader inside the court in Pelau and describe what it is like to spend a typical day there.

Before the Bench: Taking a Stand against Domestic Violence

During my fieldwork in Pelau, Thursdays were designated as "family day." That is when the magistrate heard most family matters, including requests for child support, maintenance for wives, variations in previous orders, adoptions, and domestic violence cases, as well as some other private and less serious criminal cases, such as assaults, using abusive and obscene language, littering, breaking and entering, and failing to leave rental quarters. Each Thursday, the court docket was remarkable for its length, averaging 139 cases each week in 1997 and 113 cases in 1998.[2] Of these, in 1997 an average of twelve were domestic violence cases, while in 1998 that number fell slightly to an average of ten domestic violence cases. Some were being called for the first time, while others had been previously adjourned. A great many were set for another date because the respondent in the case had not yet been served with a summons to come to court. But even if the respondent had arrived to hear and respond to the charges, domestic violence cases have to be heard in camera (privately).[3] The magistrate tended to them after prisoners in other cases pled to charges, the police attended to their criminal matters, lawyers pressed their clients' cases, and maintenance matters were adjudicated. Thus, although the magistrate generally worked a long day, most cases of every kind had to be adjourned to another date because the docket was so long. Only a few persons seeking protection from violence tell their story on any given day, and only a small percentage of these leave with court orders. The logistics of serving summonses and the constraints of an overburdened court clearly influence how many domestic violence cases can be heard in any week and help us in part to better understand the quantitative record. Indeed, legal professionals are most vocal about how the lack of infrastructural support undermines the state's alleged intention to combat domestic violence.[4] Other factors, however, are responsible for the kinds of cases that do come before the magistrate. I turn next to the case histories of two women who went to the court in Pelau in search of protection and who successfully negotiated the legal process.

Case One: The Wayward Son

I had seen Rosalyn in the court in Pelau on many occasions before the court granted her order for protection. When her case concluded, I asked if I could interview her for this study. I was amazed at her tenacity. A tall, portly, middle-aged woman of Afro-Caribbean descent with long gray hair, she appeared before the court again and again, mostly to find that the defendant, her son, had not been served a summons. My first interview with Rosalyn took place just a few days after the court granted her protection order. The second, follow-up interview, occurred almost a year later. Both interviews took place in the cooling breezes of the porch of her two-bedroom apartment located in a two-story concrete structure some twenty minutes' walk from Pelau's main road. On both occasions, I exchanged pleasantries with her two well-mannered teenage sons who lived with her.

Rosalyn grew up with her siblings in a working-class family. Her mother did domestic work and her father was an electrician. After her parents separated, Rosalyn's mother's mother came to live with them. Rosalyn completed her high school education and then learned hairdressing. She held a full-time job for a few years but stopped working when she became pregnant with the first of the four children she would bear for her long-term partner, Eustace. Rosalyn described their relationship as "we live common-law." Eustace had land in the country on which he grew produce, but he also earned money driving his neighbors to town and repairing cars. While their four children were young, the family resided together in a village not far from Eustace's land. Rosalyn had only recently moved to Pelau, a safer neighborhood with better schools for the two teens. Eustace remained near his land, but visited them several times a week. He always brought something with him—sometimes cash and vegetables, sometimes just one or the other. Rosalyn found various ways to supplement the household economy. For a number of years she had worked part-time as a cook. She babysat every morning for a working mother and took on other babysitting jobs when those became available. Critical to the family's welfare were the remittances and occasional gifts of clothing, shoes, and other household items sent by Rosalyn's siblings who lived and worked in the United States.

The family's troubles had begun some ten years earlier. Rosalyn's old-est son, Everett, showed little interest in school, and he left at age sixteen. A relative got him a steady job in a food processing plant, and he earned good money for seven years. Then he got involved in a prank at work for which he was immediately fired. There is very high unemployment among youth in Trinidad, so it was not surprising to learn that he could not find another job. For a while Everett worked with his father, but the two quarreled, and eventually Everett left and moved in with friends in Port of Spain. At first he spent much of his time drinking, smoking, and gambling. Later, Everett became addicted to cocaine. Strapped for cash, food, and housing, he turned regularly to his mother. Rosalyn explained that she didn't mind feeding him, but she only rarely had extra cash—and it was clear exactly where that cash was going to go. As his addiction worsened, Everett became abusive and violent. He would break into the apartment and steal items to sell to pay for drugs. Rosalyn told me it got to the point where every time she left the house for any sustained period, she would lock her cash and valuables in a safe box. Everett had stolen her costume jewelry, a cooking pot, and cloth she had purchased to make new shirts for the younger boys. Eustace couldn't prove it, but he was sure Everett had stolen some of the furniture in the small wooden house he had allowed him to stay in when Everett quarreled with his friends and they told him not to come back to the apartment in Port of Spain. In other words, Everett was constantly in need. Once he became an addict, Rosalyn told me, "He may just find a day's work. But he never go and seek a job."

Rosalyn tried desperately to get Everett help for his drug problem. He went into rehabilitation programs four times. These included church-based and state-run programs. Once he lasted for almost a year; on other occasions he stayed clean for a few weeks or months and then reverted to taking drugs. Rosalyn begged for and borrowed money from her fam-ily and, once, an employer to get Everett into these programs. One year, a kind counselor helped her to find a sponsor to partially defray the fi-nancial burden she accrued in trying to keep Everett in rehabilitation programs. It was many years before she finally decided she could do no more and that she had to protect her two youngest sons against Everett's unpredictable behavior.

Rosalyn's first encounter with the criminal justice system involved a theft. She came home from an errand one afternoon to find her son sleeping it off on the couch. She immediately noticed that her living room lamp was missing. She surmised that Everett stole the lamp to buy drugs. She went to the police station and reported the theft and the thief. Two police officers followed her back to the house to take Everett into custody. Rudely awakened, a stunned Everett inquired: "Mommy, you went and got the police for the lamp? I borrowed it!" The officers told Everett that he needed to take them to the party to whom he had sold the lamp. According to Rosalyn, the police told Everett, "'Once they get back the lamp, everything will be all right. They didn't tell him they were going to lock him up. Because if they had told him that, maybe he would not go for the lamp. So they just said come, we will go for the lamp. And when we come back, we will let you go." At her wit's end, Rosalyn allowed the deception.

Some time later the police returned with a lamp—but not Rosalyn's lamp. They went back to the station and questioned Everett again. The second time he led them to the person to whom he had sold his mother's lamp. The police took the lamp as evidence and told Rosalyn they would prosecute the case and that there was no need for her to appear in court. Then they informed Everett that they were locking him up until his court appearance. The officer told him, "Your mother told me that she is fed up with you!"

During the case involving the stolen lamp, which happened to be heard on a Thursday when I was in the court in Pelau but before I had met Rosalyn or knew of her relationship to Everett, Everett pleaded to the magistrate that he had only borrowed his mother's lamp because the place where he was sleeping had no light. After hearing Everett's and a police officer's testimony, the magistrate asked the constable to make sure that Rosalyn's lamp was returned to her and then dismissed the case. This decision initially surprised me, but later I would learn from the court records and Rosalyn's testimony that Everett was no stranger to this magistrate. He had other cases pending against him in Pelau for shoplifting produce and for larceny of a carpenter's tool. Everett had also been convicted on an earlier shoplifting charge.[5]

Like many victims of domestic violence, Rosalyn sought advice from family, friends, various drug counselors, her pastor, and members of her church's congregation. She also spoke on several occasions with a female neighbor who was a police constable. This neighbor helped her understand her rights, urged her to get a protection order, and later supported and advised her as she proceeded with the case. On the other hand, Rosalyn had contradictory responses from other officers when she went to the police station to complain of Everett's continuing harassment. One officer admonished her: "Madame, if your son is on drugs, take him to rehab. We are not here for that." Angered by this response, she started to leave the station. Another officer, however, overheard the remark and advised her to check on whether an arrest warrant had been issued. (It had been issued, but no one had taken any action on it.) This officer eventually found Everett months later and served him the summons. Rosalyn chose not to have Everett immediately arrested, even though the arrest warrant made that possible.

For the first several months after she had filed her application, Rosalyn's case was adjourned because Everett, unemployed and without a residence of his own, drifted from place to place for shelter and the police had trouble finding him. The scenario in court was always the same; Rosalyn would appear for the hearing and the magistrate would adjourn the case because there was no evidence that Everett had been served to appear in court. My review of the court records showed Rosalyn was in court nine times between February 1998, when this case began, and August 1998, when it was resolved.[6]

When he was finally served with the summons, Everett was outraged. He tried several times, sometimes nicely and sometimes using intimidating language, to get Rosalyn to drop the charge. Once when he was verbally abusive and she thought he was about to hit her, she fainted. Hours later, when her youngest son returned from school, he found her unconscious on the floor.

Rosalyn suffers some chronic health problems and shortly before her case was to go to trial she was hospitalized. Everett knew of his mother's hospitalization. Therefore, he was stunned when she appeared in court as a witness against him. Everett told Rosalyn that he went to court because he had to face shoplifting charges, but he never imagined that on that date he would have to defend himself in the domestic violence matter.[7] Rosalyn explained to Everett, and later to me, that her doctor had released her the day before the trial. This was good timing. Rosalyn already knew from her neighbor, the police officer, that it was likely that the case would be dismissed if she didn't appear in court. She told me: "At times I just get fed up. Every time going back to the court and just put off, put off. I felt I was just wasting time. But she [the neighbor] said, 'No! Continue to go! And one day it will come. Because if a day you don't go, they are going to throw it out. Because you are the one who laid the matter.' And I kept going. I said to Constable R—, 'I'll continue going.'"

The trial was brief and held in camera in the magistrate's chambers, although I was permitted to observe the proceedings. Rosalyn explained that Everett was a drug addict, that he continually stole things from her home, and that he came and went from the house at all hours, unpredictably. She said, "I'm tired and fed up and I can't take it any more." She explained that she had tried to help him, that she had seen Everett through four unsuccessful attempts of rehabilitation and treatment. Moreover, she had promised the landlord when she signed her new lease that only she and her other two children would reside there. Everett knew that she had rented the apartment in Pelau with no intention of housing or supporting him. He was supposed to reside in the country, in the small house provided by his father.

When he took the stand, Everett concurred that he was supposed to live in the country, but his father had recently rented the house to a cousin, leaving him with no permanent home. He complained that his father should be providing him with building materials so that he could construct another abode. He offered to leave his mother alone if the magistrate would help him get the money he needed to buy construction materials. The magistrate responded that she would not go into that issue; it was "not a matter before me today." Turning to the matter at hand, she inquired whether Everett would agree to give an undertaking to keep away from his mother. His initial response was to agree, but only if the magistrate would help him with the building materials. Obviously annoyed, the magistrate told Everett that she could take the evidence and make the order herself. Everett relented. He agreed to sign an undertaking. He then asked if he could collect his clothes from the house. The magistrate told him he could and started to write that he was permitted to collect them the following morning. He asked if his mother would please wash them for him when she did her Sunday washing. He could pick up the clothes on Sunday afternoon. The magistrate asked Rosalyn whether "she would grant her son this one last favor." She agreed, but asked that thereafter Everett not be allowed to come to the house.[8] The magistrate explained the penalties he could incur for breaching the undertaking: "Did he understand that it is a serious thing and that the police can come and pick him up?" Everett said he did. Did he realize that "this is to stop you from how you normally get on? To give your mother some peace of mind. Because you don't go near her, you are not to be assaulting her with words. 'Cause she has minded you long enough. . . . Your mother and father can only do so much for you. In the end, it is up to you. It is your life." The magistrate instructed her clerk to record: "Defendant undertakes and is prohibited from being within 500 meters of [Rosalyn's address]. Defendant undertakes to desist from using obscene and threatening language against [Rosalyn] with effect from [court date]." The parties were then sent to complete the paperwork.

Rosalyn told me that after the case, Everett spoke briefly to her:

He tell [me] he is not annoyed with me, he is not vexed with me. If he meet me on the road, he will still talk to me. He ask me if I will still talk to him. I say, "Well, yes. If I meet you on the road and you talk to me politely, I will answer. 'Cause [you know] the magistrate told him to stay—that he have to keep away—500 meters away from his mother's premises and if he meet me on the street anywhere. . . ." [The magistrate told him] "I don't want you abusing her." He say, "No, your honor. I love my mother. And I won't do her those things. I will meet her and talk to her casually."

In July 1999, I found Rosalyn in better health. She was willing to discuss what had happened in the months following the court order. We talked uninterrupted except for the presence of a young girl who, along with her working mother, now shared the apartment with Rosalyn and her two sons. Rosalyn took them in because they needed a place to live and because she welcomed assistance with the rent. The older teen had just finished school—he was sixteen—and he was looking for work. Rosalyn's youngest son, age fifteen, hoped to enter a vocational program. Eustace visits, as he always has, and "is still maintaining" [providing some child support]. One sister visited Trinidad for Carnival, bringing gifts of clothing for the boys; other relatives send assistance when they can.

Rosalyn was very pleased with how things turned out following her court case. In the beginning, Everett came around on occasion begging only for food but not cash or to spend the night. Rosalyn said she always warned him that he could not stay, but at the same time she would pack some food for him to carry away. There had been only one unpleasant incident since the court order. Everett had arrived at the apartment one evening high on cocaine and in a foul mood. Rosalyn was out. An argument started between Everett and one of his brothers and the situation became tense. The younger brother said he would go get the police. By the time the police arrived, however, Everett had fled the scene. Except for that incident, Everett has left them alone. As a result, Rosalyn and the boys are under much less stress. She no longer worries about locking things up when she leaves her home, and she has saved money because she has not constantly had to replace items that Everett pilfered. The neighbors have commented to her about what a relief it is not to have to hear and watch him behave abusively. When, on occasion, they meet in town, Everett has kept his promise to speak politely to her. She is saddened by the fact that he is unable to kick his drug habit. Earlier in the year he had once again unsuccessfully tried another rehabilitation program. At the end of our interview I asked Rosalyn if she planned to return to the court to get another protection order, since it would soon expire. She said that that depended on Everett's future behavior. She hoped she didn't have to go back to court, but she was not averse to doing so if necessary. She told me that she would strongly recommend to others that they apply for protection if they were experiencing violence. This same recommendation came from Karrene, the complainant in my next case study.

Case Two: The Obsessed Lover

Karrene's case was unusual in that her relationship to Mohan, the respondent, was relatively brief (they had lived together for only three months), they were not living together when she filed charges against him, they did not have a child, and there was no financial dependency between them. From the perspective of at least some magistrates I interviewed, those facts would have precluded charges of domestic violence although, as we shall see, Karrene had grounds for charging Mohan with assault, harassment, and abusive and threatening language. The case was also unusual in three other ways. First was the rapidity with which it captured the attention of the court—going to trial the first day that the parties appeared in court. Second, the vast majority of domestic violence cases I observed involved only the complainant and the defendant. This case, in contrast, included testimony by two witnesses. Finally, Karrene was unusually articulate in framing her case and in cross-examining the respondent and her witnesses. Karrene's case was typical of domestic violence cases more generally, however, in all of the following ways: (1) the charges included both verbal and physical abuse; (2) the abuse had been ongoing for a long time; (3) various efforts had been made to stop the harassment before the complainant finally turned to the court; (4) the police had been contacted; (5) the parties represented themselves instead of hiring attorneys; and (6) the respondent refused to accept the fact that his relationship with the complainant was over.

I was sitting at the lawyers' table when the case was called. A woman dressed in a white blouse, a blue skirt and blazer, and navy pumps stepped to the front of the court. She appeared to me to be of Indo-Caribbean heritage, her long, shiny black hair pulled back neatly in a ponytail. I guessed she was in her mid-twenties. A moment later, the respondent, a tall, thin man about thirty years old whose name and phenotype suggested mixed European and Indo-Caribbean ancestry, took his place in the front of the courtroom. He wore slacks, a T-shirt, and sneakers. He was scowling and playing with his cap. His demeanor irritated the magistrate who told him "not to take that attitude" in court. She then read the charges. First, on [date in 1998] he was alleged to have assaulted the complainant, causing her bodily harm. The respondent denied the charge. Next, between the dates of [a two-month period in 1998 following the first alleged offense] he was charged with using abusive and intimidating language. The respondent also denied those charges. The magistrate inquired if either party had witnesses. Karrene said she had two. Mohan didn't have any witnesses and, besides, he "didn't know what she was talking about so why should he need witnesses?" The magistrate asked Karrene when she could get her witnesses to come to court. (I was sure at this point that the case would be adjourned for trial on another date.) Karrene surprised the court, however, by informing the magistrate that she could get her witnesses to court that day and then by asking the magistrate to hear her case immediately because she felt that her life was threatened. The magistrate inquired if either party wanted time to obtain counsel. They did not. The parties were instructed to return after the lunch recess.

When the court reconvened, the magistrate took care of a few expeditious matters and then cleared the courtroom to hear the case. Karrene took the stand testifying that she worked at a local bank and that the respondent was formerly her boyfriend. The magistrate asked her a crucial question: "Would she describe their relationship as common-law?" Karrene responded positively, thereby qualifying the relationship as one covered by the Domestic Violence Act. The magistrate next instructed Karrene to tell the court what had transpired on the night of the first alleged offense and about the incidents that followed.[9]

One Saturday night two months earlier, after Karrene had already moved out of the apartment she shared with Mohan, he had waited for her near her parents' home. He knew she often slept there on Saturday night so that she could enjoy Sunday lunch with her family. That evening, Karrene's friends had dropped her off some distance from her parents' home because the road was not paved all the way up to the house. Therefore, no one knew Mohan was waiting in the shadows. She wasn't certain of the exact time, but it was after 1:00 A.M. when she headed up the hill from the road. She was shaken when Mohan called out to her. He was angry that she had gone out without him, he became verbally abusive, and then he slapped her nine or ten times and dragged her down the hill farther from the house to ensure that no one would hear them quarreling. She called out, "Oh please, God! Stop! Stop!" He demanded to know what was going on and she said, "Nothing!" He accused her of lying. He said he wanted to kill her. She told him she was sorry and that she didn't mean to hurt him. When she finally got him to calm down, they talked for about two hours. He told her how much she had hurt him and that he didn't think there was anything wrong with their relationship. He told her not to tell her parents what had happened and to blame her bruised and swollen face on her having accidentally bumped into a wall. By now it was very late and there was no public transportation still running. Therefore, Karrene allowed him to sleep over in her room. The next morning, they quarreled again and Mohan left the house. When Karrene finally left her room, her mother took one look at her and knew she had been abused. A few hours later, Mohan began calling, asking to speak to Karrene. She refused to speak with him. His incessant phone calls caused a lot of stress for the whole family.

Over the next few weeks, Mohan repeatedly harassed Karrene. He called the bank where she worked and demanded to speak to her. Karrene confided in a few coworkers who were responsible for answering outside calls. They would put him on hold and eventually disconnect the calls without even mentioning them to Karrene. When Mohan realized that the receptionists were not passing on his messages, he became abusive to them. In addition to the stressful phone calls, Mohan would wait outside the bank at closing time. Karrene testified he told her "that if she did anything about his hitting her or involved the police, things would get worse." He also told her that "if she had any intentions of leaving him, she would end up in a wheelchair." The day he threatened her life she went to the police station and filed the first of three reports. Karrene was terrified and so was her family. Family members escorted her to and from work.

Karrene began to keep a record of Mohan's behavior. She read in court excerpts of incidents that had occurred between them. She also had records of the reports she had made to the police. She told the magistrate about the day that Mohan had worn her down and she had agreed to talk to him—but only at the police station. He met her outside the station and they talked briefly. He apologized and said again that he wanted to continue the relationship. She responded that she couldn't continue the relationship because she was afraid of him. He wanted to know if she was leaving him for another man "because he was not going to allow that." He also claimed that he had filed police reports against her. At that point, one of the officers to whom Karrene had filed a complaint saw them and headed toward them. Mohan saw the officer and walked in the opposite direction to try to avoid him.

The magistrate inquired if Karrene had any intention of continuing the relationship with Mohan. She did not. The magistrate excused her from the witness stand. There was no doubt in my mind that Karrene had made a strong case against Mohan. Her story was clear and consistent, she had the dates, times, and places where and when the alleged abusive incidents had occurred, members of her family were well-informed of her situation, and she had reported the events to the police.

The magistrate asked Mohan if he wanted to cross-examine Karrene. He seemed confused. She asked again: "Didn't he want to challenge any of her story?" He replied, "About 25 percent of what Karrene said is true." He then inquired whether he would have the opportunity to tell his side of the story. The magistrate said he would, but she urged him again to cross-examine Karrene. She reviewed each of the incidents that Karrene had alleged had happened. (In other words, the magistrate bent over backward to give Mohan the opportunity to challenge Karrene's testimony.) Thereafter, Mohan asked a few questions. Karrene admitted that she had no proof that he had "lashed" her and that she had no medical evidence.

The magistrate then called Karrene's first witness, a woman who worked at the same bank. She testified that she had received phone calls for the complainant from the same man on many occasions. She told the court that she had not met the defendant in person, but that she recognized his voice from having talked to him so often. She said he called so frequently that she "had lost track of the number of phone calls. He would always ask for Miss [last name] but he did not give his name." The magistrate registered concern after hearing this, noting that it was possible that the phone calls were from more than one man. The witness then explained that last week when this man phoned she called the complainant and asked her directly if the person on the other end was "the gentleman she had spoken to her about." Karrene had said "yes," and "to tell him she was unable to come to the phone." The witness had followed Karrene's instructions, whereupon the caller became abusive. He was "loud and aggressive to me on the phone," so she had hung up. In short, the witness established that she knew it was the respondent because she had come to know his voice very well over time. Mohan had no questions for the witness.

Karrene's second witness was her stepfather, a man I'll call "Saisnarine." He had last seen the defendant on [date]. He had walked his daughter to work, and when they arrived he saw Mohan standing across the street. Karrene went into the bank, and he went over to speak to Mohan. They talked calmly at first, and Saisnarine told him that he did not want him phoning his daughter or making threats to her. He advised Mohan that he was aware of the abusive incident outside his home. After that, things heated up and the two men got into an argument. Saisnarine claimed that Mohan admitted that he had hit Karrene, told him he was sorry about it, and that it would not happen again. During this same conversation Saisnarine learned that Mohan had done military service, that he was currently employed in a temporary part-time job as a casual laborer, and that he very much wanted to continue his relationship with Karrene. He admitted that he could not recall other details of that conversation.

On cross-examination, Mohan wanted to know where, when, and on how many other occasions he and the witness had entered into conversations. Saisnarine responded that they had had another conversation one evening when they met by chance on the road. He couldn't recall much of that encounter, except that the defendant had admitted that he had "raised his hands to Karrene" and that Saisnarine had told Mohan to leave his daughter alone.

When he took the stand to testify on his own behalf, Mohan described his occupation as "casual laborer." He said he had gone to Karrene's family home on [date] just to talk to her. He arrived at 9:30 P.M. and waited until 1:45 A.M. for her to get home. He acknowledged that they had an argument but he denied slapping her or dragging her down the hill. They had slept together in her room that night, but quarreled the next morning. Mohan said he had called the home the following day and left a message with her brother for Karrene to call him. By evening, when she hadn't called back, he called again.

The magistrate carefully questioned Mohan about each of Karrene's accusations. Had he threatened her? Had he demanded that she not tell her parents anything? Had he told her the "situation would get ugly"? Did he say "that if she left him she would end up in a wheelchair"? Mohan denied each of these queries. He admitted calling the bank, but not as often as Karrene or the bank employee claimed. Mohan concurred that he had a conversation with Saisnarine one morning after he had walked Karrene to the bank. Mohan described it as a "friendly conversation." He told Saisnarine that he was frequently in the vicinity of Karrene's workplace because he practiced nearby with his band. Karrene was correct when she stated that they had met to talk about their relationship near the police station and that their conversation was brief. As he was walking away, the officer served him with the summons to appear in court.

Karrene next cross-examined Mohan. Did he admit he had waited at her house for hours without their having previously agreed to meet that evening? He had. Had he hit her that night and then warned her not to tell her parents? Mohan claimed neither of those accusations was true. He admitted he called her at work, "sometimes twice a day, but sometimes I don't call for three or four days." Mohan testified that he never threatened her; he only "requests to meet you." The cross-examination continued in this vein for about ten minutes, with Mohan denying that he had ever hit, threatened, or used abusive or threatening language to Karrene.

The magistrate's decision was immediate. She told the parties that she had no doubt that Mohan had engaged in inappropriate behavior and language and that Karrene was afraid of him. She was concerned that Mohan had waited for hours outside Karrene's home when the couple had no prearranged plans for that evening. She was also concerned about his constant phone harassment. She noted that Saisnarine testified that Mohan had admitted slapping Karrene. She found Mohan's conduct "harassing, abusive, and threatening." It seemed clear to her that the complainant did not want the relationship to continue and that she was afraid of the defendant. "Otherwise, why would she make these constant trips to the police station?" Therefore, she granted Karrene an order for protection. The court records state: "Evidence led. Order that the respondent desist from the vicinity of [location of complainant's home] and to desist from [location of complainant's workplace]. To desist from calling applicant at her workplace, and to desist from using abusive and threatening language. With effect from [court date] [for one year]."

I approached Karrene after the trial, and she agreed to participate in this project. Karrene was twenty-four years old. She had taken several advanced courses in high school and later completed a two-year program in secretarial and computing skills. After receiving her certificate, she was hired as a bank teller. Later she was promoted to a more prestigious job at another branch bank. Karrene was a busy woman, working full time at the bank and occasionally catering church and social events with her aunt. How, I asked, had she become involved with Mohan?

Karrene met Mohan through mutual friends on a weekend "lime."[10] They began dating and at first she had no reason to believe that Mohan was aggressive. In fact, she first began to have doubts about their relationship because he seemed to lack ambition and not because of any hostile behavior. Mohan drifted from one unskilled laborer's job to another. Karrene and her mother discussed the fact that he was five years her senior and should be acting more maturely. Karrene began finding excuses not to see him. Annoyed at her rebuffs, Mohan called her obsessively, both at home and at work. Karrene eventually met him for a soft drink and told him the relationship was over. His behavior became more aggressive after that; he would not accept that she was breaking up with him. One day he called the bank eleven times. At first sympathetic, the management began to have doubts about the effect of his abuse on other staff and customers. Called to a meeting, Karrene's employer told her that she had strong support at the bank but that they would have to let her go if Mohan's harassment continued.

Karrene sought advice first from her family and a girlfriend at the bank who had had a similar experience years ago. Next she contacted an acquaintance who was a police constable. The constable counseled her to go to her local police station for assistance. Like Rosalyn, Karrene discovered there were some officers who were supportive and others who were not. The first time she went to the station she talked with a female constable whom she described as "very reluctant to write a report." Karrene insisted. Some weeks later she spoke with an officer who told her the police were there to enforce the law and "there really wasn't much they could do" unless she filed a formal complaint. One officer offered to find Mohan and "warn" him but, according to Karrene, "up to now, he hasn't been warned."

When I asked Karrene how she had learned about the Domestic Violence Act, she looked at me inquisitively and replied that "everybody knew." She had read about it in the newspapers and heard it discussed on radio and television. She was also aware that there were services available for victims, including counseling and shelters. Once she visited the probation officer at the courthouse for advice and information. She described that visit as "helpful." The probation officer counseled her to find a "community-designated" police officer who would be sympathetic to her situation,[11] encouraged her to apply for a protection order, and gave Karrene her phone number which she could use "at any time." When I asked her whether she thought about getting an attorney to represent her, Karrene told me she had an acquaintance who was an attorney but she felt too embarrassed to contact him. She wanted as few people as possible to know about her situation.

The first time Karrene went to the court in Pelau to file for a protection order she told her story to a justice of the peace, who politely advised her that he didn't think she had a case because of the nature of her relationship with Mohan. Discouraged, she left the court without filing any paperwork. However, Mohan's aggressive behavior continued over the next month. Something had to be done, so she went back to the courthouse. This time she talked to another justice of the peace who filed the case. Karrene and Mohan were in court a few days later.

I caught up with Karrene just over a year after our first interview. She was struggling financially. Because of the recession in Trinidad, the bank had cut back on her hours of employment. Karrene was happy, however, in her new relationship. She had met a wonderful man, "David," and they had moved in together. David was a secondary school teacher with ambition to study for a master's degree. He encouraged Karrene to get a college degree. David had family in the United States, and together they planned to attend schools in Miami. Both had already taken the appropriate exams and had been admitted into schools. In fact, I had found Karrene just in time because they were departing for the United States three weeks later!

The legal story of what had transpired since the day Karrene's protection order went into effect is less happy. Immediately after the trial, Karrene had been instructed to take a copy of the protection order to the police station so that the officers would have it if Mohan breached the order. She did that, and observed an officer posting it on the bulletin board in the station. Over the next months, she carried her copy of the order in her handbag wherever she went. As she told me, "I never walk without that paper!" It comforted her and reminded her that the law was on her side. For almost ten months, Mohan did not come near her and he did not call. Early in January 1999, however, he had one of his friends call her "just to see how she was doing." The call upset Karrene, and she told the man never to call her again. Subsequently, she got an unlisted phone number, but the incident continued to unnerve her and she decided to tell the police. She wanted a record in case Mohan tried to contact her again. Karrene and David went together to the station to inform the police. Much to their astonishment, the police told them that they had no record of Karrene's protection order. Shown her copy, the officers claimed it was too faded and they couldn't read it. One accused her of never having delivered the order to the station. Karrene told me the experience was completely unsettling. She realized she had been living with a false sense of security. They went back to the courthouse, obtained a new copy of the original order, and carried it back to the police.

Karrene was angered by the way some of the officers had treated her and by their bureaucratic incompetence. With the exception of the justice of the peace who first discouraged her from applying for a protection order, however, she had only positive things to say about her court experience. She praised highly the magistrate who heard and sympathized with her fear of Mohan, gave her time to find her witnesses, conducted an immediate trial, and took action to protect her from Mohan's abuse. Because she was leaving the country, she decided not to pursue another protection order when hers expired. Nevertheless, Karrene told me she would recommend that other victims of domestic violence file for protection orders.

A Typology of Successful Domestic Violence Applications

The Domestic Violence Act included protection for persons in several relationships: parents and children, guardians and dependents, husbands and wives, and persons in intimate and formerly intimate relationships. The law also enabled the police, social workers, and other interested citizens to bring applications on behalf of adults or children who were abused or neglected. In practice, however, only a few types of cases appeared regularly before the courts. These categories were deftly and succinctly explained by one magistrate I interviewed. They accord with my own observations in Pelau and in other courts in Trinidad in which I conducted research, and were also substantiated in interviews with other magistrates. Here are the magistrate's words:

> I would say the average case is a wife complaining of assault and beating by a husband. And I would say in most instances, it is related to drug or alcohol abuse. . . . Older couples I think, it is usually alcohol. And when he's under the influence, he hits. . . . And now they—they come to court. Longtime, [in the past] they would take the abuse. But now that they have the act—you see these older couples come to court. . . .
>
> And . . . with mothers and sons, it is narcotics abuse. Their sons are addicts, and they demand that the mothers, usually it is the mothers, help them with money. And when the mothers cannot, they either beat them into doing it, or they break up their homes. The mothers find it very difficult to deal with, and the police just don't help. I categorize them, and these are the categories I see coming to court. Right? Alcoholic husbands, the addict sons, and once in a while you get people who use it for ejectment purposes. . . . [T]here are a lot of common-law relationships also where the couple—both of them—build a home. And they have either fallen out of love, for one reason or another, and the wife decides that it is time for him to get out. But, I mean, both of them shared in the building of the home and the easiest way for her to get him out is with a domestic order and ask for him to be thrown out of the premises. . . .
>
> And what else? Oh . . . guys who can't deal with breakups. They have a child together, and he can't deal with the fact that the mother decides to move on with her life. To get on with other guys, and he turns to violence. And she has to come to the court to say look, I want him to stay away from me, I don't want him to come home. . . . And he still feels that this is the only woman for him. That's another group of people who come to the court.

In other words, although the statute provided relief for parties in a wide range of relationships, persons in four types of domestic violence matters were regularly heard in court: (1) older women with alcoholic husbands; (2) mothers with addicted sons; (3) women in common-law relationships seeking to get men out of their homes; and (4) women with obsessed partners. To this list, other magistrates added: (1) women whose own mothers were abused, who married young, and who grew up accepting that husbands beat their wives but who have now "reached the end of the line" and (2) women with mentally ill partners or children.

Why do these particular kinds of cases come most often to the courts?[12] In part, they are an index of gender hierarchy.[13] Overwhelmingly, the cases involve men who physically and psychologically abuse women. As we have seen, men do bring cases of domestic violence but these are more rare. Domestic violence cases also point to Trinidad's broader social problems, especially the poverty and economic dependence of women with young children who remain with violent men because they have nowhere else to go and who hope a protection order will bring some relief to the chaos of their households. The drug and alcohol addictions or mental illnesses of their partners or children also bring women to the courts. Although some rehabilitation programs are available, these cannot meet demand. Therefore, for some women, a letter for free counseling provided by the court's probation officer, or the magistrate's order to send an abuser to the local mental hospital for observation and diagnosis, brings welcome temporary relief. It is likely, too, that the public has limited knowledge of the parties and situations that are covered by the statute. Several legal professionals pointed out to me, for example, that although the act covered abused and neglected children, hardly any child abuse cases come before the magistrates as domestic violence cases. Finally, in the ethnography of the modern state, these women are "known," but also "entitled" to recourse from violence because Trinidad is a "modern," "progressive," and "civilized" place. Subject to the public gaze (Burchell, Gordon, and Miller 1991; Escobar 1995:155; Foucault 1978, 1980; Razack 1998:20, 92, 131), exploited mothers with addicted sons, like Rosalyn and Everett, young women tortured by obsessed men, like Karrene and Mohan, and long-suffering wives with abusive husbands who "longtime [long ago] would take the abuse" exemplify the new consensus about familial and gender relationships.[14]

Even if the courts are now open to listening to certain women who have suffered domestic abuse, it is nevertheless true, as we have seen, that a great many applications for restraining orders drop out of the legal system. What do the interviews and participant observation reveal about why that occurs? And what other types of cases are likely to result in orders?

From the Bench: Dismissals, Withdrawals, Orders, and Undertakings

As we saw in chapter 2, between January 1997 and December 1998, 686 cases for domestic violence in Pelau were disposed of, 77 percent of which were dismissed or withdrawn. Most commonly, the complainant did not return to court and the matter was dismissed. Sometimes the case was withdrawn by the applicant or her attorney. Asked why that is the case, the lawyers, magistrates, and probation officers I interviewed responded similarly: complainants do not appear because the parties have reconciled. As one magistrate put it, "things settle up." The interviews in Trinidad confirmed what earlier research has recorded as the reasons that women drop charges.[15] In some cases, applicants become disgusted with the continuous adjournment of the case. As we will see in greater detail in chapter 5, going to court means paying to get there, waiting for hours for the case to be called, and sometimes losing a day's wages. Fear of losing maintenance keeps other women away. Another magistrate commented: "A lot of women are dependent upon male support and the males threaten to withhold funding from the family. And I think as a result of that, a number of people do not come back." Pressure from either the wife's or the husband's family may cause a woman to drop her claim. Some women are intimidated into dropping the suit. Three people told me they had personal knowledge of situations in which women were offered financial compensation if they agreed to withdraw the case. Cases also fall out of the legal process because once the applicant begins to tell her story, the magistrate realizes that the dispute does not involve persons to whom the act applies.[16] Moreover, occasionally a magistrate decides a case is not "really" about domestic violence, but some other form of dispute, such as a claim to half a house, a piece of land, or other property. Also dismissed are a few cases in which the magistrate suspects the applicant is bringing charges of domestic violence in order to remove her partner from the premises—and perhaps to move another lover in. Initially, I rejected such assertions as "backlash." However, because the charge came up regularly in the interviews and in all the jurisdictions in which I worked, I had to consider that there must be at least some basis to the claim that some women fabricated domestic violence in order to gain sole use of the matrimonial home. After further inquiries, I concluded that, in the lower courts, those cases are rare.[17] A magistrate who suspects a complainant's ulterior motives, however, can transform a request for a protection order into some other legal or extralegal conflict (e.g., Cobb 1997; Frohmann 1991; Frohmann and Mertz 1995; Lazarus-Black 1997;

Mather and Yngvesson 1980/81; Merry 1990, 1994; Yngvesson 1988). All of these efforts are, of course, expressions of negotiated agency.

If there are occasional abuses of the system, it is nevertheless true that the overwhelming number of cases are legitimate cries for assistance against abuse. My analysis reveals two types of cases are likely to result in protection orders in Trinidad. The first type includes cases that result in court orders because law is literal. That is, an applicant wins a protection order when she satisfies precisely the law's understanding of domestic violence as behavior: (1) affecting parties in specific relationships; (2) of a persistent and harassing nature; and (3) instilling in the applicant fear of mental or physical injury. Attorneys for men charged with domestic violence regularly quote the legal prescriptive in court: "to the extent that the spouse . . . is fearful of injury, physical or mental, to herself" (Laws of Trinidad and Tobago 1991:92).

The requirements in the statute that domestic violence both persist over time and provoke fear in the victim alert us to why some protection orders are not granted. Eruptions of violence in intimate or familial relationships are often spontaneous and occasional, rather than persistent. Magistrates do not interpret the statute as providing relief from a "cuff," struck in the heat of passion; however, the general public is unaware of this.[18] Moreover, when magistrates face couples who agree readily to go for counseling to deal with their problems, they are very reluctant to make protection orders. Reconciliation rather than legal restraint is preferable, in magistrates' opinions, particularly because so many couples have dependent children.[19] Orders will almost always be granted, however, when there are multiple charges, evidence of frightening and persistent abuse, and it is clear that the applicant does not intend to reconcile with the respondent.

In the second kind of domestic violence case, an applicant gets a protection order because her abuser "allows her" to have one. As we have seen, in Trinidad's Domestic Violence Act, a defendant may give an undertaking. By this, it is meant that he undertakes to cease and desist from certain future behaviors related to the allegations made against him. For example, a complainant charges that on January 29, 1998, the respondent used obscene language against her, and that on February 6, 1998, he used threatening language and also beat her with his fist. In response, he may admit his conduct and undertake to refrain from using abusive language or assaulting her. The magistrate then explains that an undertaking, like a court order, lasts for one year, and a breach of an undertaking has the same consequence as a breach of an order; namely, a custodial sentence of up to six months and/or a fine of up to $5,000 TT (U.S. $835).[20] The court clerk then records something to the following effect in the official documents: "With consent. Respondent undertakes to refrain from [the admitted conduct] in the future. With effect from today and for a period of one year." As we have seen, of 686 closed cases in Pelau in 1997 and 1998, about 23 percent received some form of attention from the court. Nineteen percent of those cases were disposed with undertakings; in just 2 percent of cases did the complainant receive a formal protection order. Thus, the court is much more likely to give protection to a complainant whose alleged abuser agrees to mend his ways.

Why do abusers agree to give undertakings? One reason is that they are committed to the relationships and do not wish to lose their partners. A respondent who is convinced that his partner is at the point of leaving him may come to court as a way to convince her not to leave. A second reason respondents give undertakings is because their lawyers advise them to do so. A female attorney with more than eight years of experience in practice explained: "The hardest thing, I think, is to represent a man in a domestic violence application. You are bound to lose. I mean, if I suspect that something is actually going on—that there is some merit to the woman's claim—I will try to convince the man to sign an undertaking. To put the whole situation to rest. And give him strong advice that he has to be very careful because if he breaches the undertaking, certain consequences are coming."

Giving an undertaking both speeds up the processing of the case and saves legal fees. It also has another useful purpose from the point of view of the defense: the evidence of the respondent's abuse is kept private. No testimony will be given in court. In other words, an ironic state of affairs is established in which an abusive party manages to set the terms both of the day in court and his own future behavior. Undertakings help men to continue the relationships they want to continue, and protect them from having to make public their private business.

Nevertheless, undertakings can and do empower women. In one case, an abused wife used an undertaking to get her husband to leave the matrimonial home. Her attorney explained: "I learned that he would sexually abuse her. . . . And in addition to that . . . there was the usual physical abuse. . . . So we got the order. And without giving evidence. Because she told him that if the matter did go to trial, she would tell exactly what he used to do in terms of sexual abuse and all that. And if he wanted that to be taken on record, she was willing to do that. . . . He consented to the order to be made against him and he was excluded from the matrimonial home."

Undertakings also empower women by preventing men from committing future violence—in large part because of men's fear of being picked up by the police and of going to jail. Rumor has it that some police constables are quite willing to impose a few "licks" on men they pick up for defying court orders. Hence, men's fear of other men—men in uniform—may keep some women safe from further violence. Moreover, everyone in the country knows the jails are seriously overcrowded and unhappy places (Hagley 1995). One litigant who won her case for a protection order told me her husband was terrified of the police. She believed the order worked because of that fear. And an attorney in Port of Spain explained her clients follow her advice to give an undertaking where one seems warranted: "Because usually men who are brought before the court on domestic violence charges, I have found, at least the ones that have come to me, are people who are going before the court for the first time. They have these images in their heads about the magistrate's powers, about the things that she can do to them. And I think that they actually believe that the act is more draconian than it is. So they are just totally riddled with fear. And I find them to be very receptive to advising."

In short, experience has taught legal professionals that undertakings are as effective as court orders. Breaches do occur on occasion, but relatively few cases return to court. One magistrate told me he has processed more than a thousand protection orders and undertakings since the inception of the act and, of these, he recalls only four men returning for breaking the order. Other magistrates told me they were fairly rare, but there might be one or two a month. In any case, as is true in the United States,[21] the magistrates I interviewed have sent few persons to jail for breaching protection orders. More commonly, such defendants are fined; however, this fact is not known in the community and men fear greatly the possibility of jail time. In this situation, lack of information protects women.

Finally, other factors contributing to a complainant's success in winning a protection order include whether she has the time, money, and determination to sustain the case's almost inevitable adjournments and whether there is support for the complainant from others—whether family members, friends, or legal professionals, including the police, probation officers, or lawyers—to prosecute. One probation officer I interviewed, for example, explained that once she became involved in a case, she would see it through the legal process. Yet this probation officer also conceded that different magistrates make more or less use of the probation officers attached to their courts. She explained magistrates evaluate probation officers' work and then either rely on them heavily for reports that influence their judgments, or not. As we saw in our two case studies, family, friends, and neighbors can have real influence in sustaining a complainant through the legal process. Rosalyn had ongoing advice from her neighbor, a police constable, who urged her never to miss a court date. Karrene mustered her stepfather and a fellow bank worker to come to court as witnesses on her behalf. Each of these parties played essential contributory roles in the eventual outcome of these cases.

Conclusion

In conclusion, I reflect on three questions. First, given the statistics provided in chapter 2 and these narratives, can we say that Trinidad's Domestic Violence Act is a "success"? Second, what does this study of domestic violence law reveal about litigants' agency as they turn to law seeking the right to protection from violence and in the face of processes of structural deflection that operate to dissuade people from using the courts? Finally, are the experiences of these litigants in Trinidad similar to those in other common-law legal systems?

Whether the Domestic Violence Act is considered a "success" depends, of course, on what is meant by "success." If we measure "success" in terms of the number of relationships that are regularly protected by the courts, the statute succeeds only moderately. As I have shown, in Trinidad, a specific group of women involved in certain kinds of abusive relationships regularly gained the court's attention: wives with alcoholic husbands, mothers with addicted children, women who are beaten in the homes they have helped to pay for, and the former partners of obsessed men. Persons facing violence in other kinds of relationships and experiencing other forms of familial abuse, however, appeared only occasionally in the courts. Abused children, persons with disabilities, and the elderly appeared infrequently. Thus, some of the most vulnerable members of society remain hidden from the court's attention.

The Domestic Violence Act also appears only marginally successful when the number of applications for protection is compared to the number of orders granted by the courts. There is a popular belief that prevails among lawyers and litigants alike—the belief that most women who go to court for protection orders get the orders they apply for. One young male attorney, for example, estimated that women who apply for court orders get those orders 80 percent of the time. A seasoned female attorney told me: "Well, wives usually get their protection orders." It was a very common response in my sample. In reality, however, most applications for protection are dismissed because the complainants fail to pursue their cases. Moreover, many complainants who do get court orders get those orders because their abusers consent to them by signing undertakings.

I suggest that a simplistic quantitative comparison of applications for protection and formal orders granted, however, gives an entirely false impression of the law's impact. Much of the success of the Domestic Violence Act lies in its undeniable ideological impact in the nation. Public awareness of domestic violence is extremely high. The issue receives extensive coverage in newspapers and on television and radio (Mohammed 1989, 1991). I asked an interviewee who was responsible for public awareness of domestic violence and the law. He responded: "The government. And news coverage. Look at today's newspaper. [He shuffled through some newspapers.] Look at the newspapers. And see if you don't see in the headlines something about women's rights in Trinidad and Tobago. I have noticed for the past several months there is inevitably, in one of the daily newspapers, you will find something about that."[22]

Following this lead, I asked a woman with more than twenty years of experience in Trinidad's legal system if she thought Trinidadians were knowledgeable about the domestic violence law. She replied: "I think so. I think now and it has a lot to do with the media and education as well. The opportunity for education, [and] adult education. You have a lot of courses, that sort of thing. . . . Twenty-five years ago, domestic violence in Trinidad was accepted as part of the culture and it was from people who had the education, had the training, and spoke about it as something not to be accepted. That's when you had the Domestic Violence Act."

Beyond regular discussion of domestic violence in the media and special programs, government officials held four public forums in 1997 to discuss the strengths and limitations of the Domestic Violence Act.[23] A domestic violence hotline has been established, several halfway houses opened, schoolchildren attend plays that teach that domestic violence is wrong, and almost everyone I interviewed commented on the changing attitudes of the police toward perpetrators and victims. As Merry suggests in her work on domestic violence in Hawaii, "gender is being redefined" and "a new cultural understanding is emerging" (1995b:23, 19). Not surprisingly, then, Trinidadians go to court to stop abuse. For most, their domestic violence petition represents their first encounter with the courts. They have accepted a new way to think about themselves and their relationships, adopting the language of the law and reinforcing and expanding its legitimacy. The flood of applications for protection under the act is a critical index of social, cultural, and political transformation and an important measure of the law's "success."[24]

The Domestic Violence Act rendered public what formerly had been private familial behavior. The state wrote new boundaries for legal and illegal behavior in familial relationships. Most certainly, surveillance by the state has been dramatically extended in the realm of quotidian practice. The law also shifted relations of domination and subordination and realigned issues of agency and structure in Trinidadian society. Yet Rosalyn's and Karrene's experiences demonstrate how complicated agency is as it is constructed in the legal process. As I have shown, their efforts to obtain protection orders were deeply influenced by their ability to retain agency over the process of negotiating with disparate actors and legal processes, including contending with the police, filing charges, sustaining adjournments, telling their stories to clerks and magistrates, and mustering the evidence that makes a case worthy of legal redress. These cases demonstrate the inaccuracy of thinking about battered women as either victims or as only having agency when they "exit." They illustrate the pragmatic and symbolic performance and negotiation of agency and its structural constraints in and around the courthouse. Importantly, these case histories also disclose how law empowers marginalized people. These women were both adamant about their right to exercise agency at court and to be included in law. The ability to make a case, as well as its outcome, lays at the core of their own sense of agency. In Rosalyn's case, the matter of agency also included protecting her other children. For Karrene, agency and justice were inseparable.

Criminalization of domestic violence in Trinidad has undoubtedly changed peoples' minds about what is permissible in the "discipline" of women (Bartky 1988; Foucault 1979). Yet, as I have demonstrated, in practice, Trinidad's domestic violence law does not provide relief for anyone who suffers familial abuse; it protects only certain categories of women and far fewer of them than most citizens imagine. Importantly, this kind of categorizing of victims is not uncommon in other common-law courts. The process of dividing persons and cases into deserving and undeserving categories has been documented in a variety of different kinds of legal cases, including rape (e.g., Bumiller 1991; Frohmann 1991; Matoesian 1993, 2001; Stanko 1982), hearings for political asylum (Coutin 2000; Razack 1998, 1999), and domestic violence (e.g., Crocker 2005; Ford 1991; Loseke 1992; Ptacek 1999). In the United States, for example, "The 'ideal victim profile' of a woman seeking protection from battering would describe a white woman who speaks English and has no material needs or who has the means to hire an attorney to seek financial support through probate court" (Ptacek 1999:133). Thus, although the characterization of who is worthy of protection may differ in different nations, the process that creates worthy and unworthy victims is common across different jurisdictions.

Finally, like the "poor," the "malnourished," "landless peasants," or "lactating women" who were "brought into the domain of international development" as target groups to be "assisted," but in ways "consistent with the creation and reproduction of modern capitalist relations" (Escobar 1995:89, 106–7), the women in Pelau who were granted protection orders, like their counterparts in the United States, Great Britain, and elsewhere in Commonwealth nations, were protected according to certain rules and under certain circumstances that do not radically challenge the fundamental structures of economic and gender domination. In fact, by claiming to protect a wide array of persons in need of protection, the state buttresses its own legitimacy—and that of the political elite—and contributes to the hegemony of law. Understanding commonalities in institutional practices and processes reveals the magnitude of the project of transforming them, of implementing domestic violence law, and of making a future free of domestic violence. In the next chapter, I demonstrate why, when, and how cases for protection orders fall through the cracks of the legal system.

4 Court Rites

In "Notes on the Difficulty of Studying the State," Abrams reminds us that "the most important single characteristic of the state is that it constitutes the 'illusory common interest' of a society; the crucial word there being 'illusory'" (Marx and Engels as cited in Abrams 1988:64). This chapter investigates specifically how a state creates the illusion that it is representing the common interest by passing legislation to protect persons who experience domestic abuse while in reality it provides them very little protection. How and why is that possible?

To explain how states are able to project such illusions to citizens and why legal reform is so difficult to implement in practice, I developed a model of certain practices and processes that operate not only in and around the magistrates' courts in Trinidad, but also in other British and British-inspired court systems. The model explains how the noncoercive form of power that Gramsci named hegemony is advanced at court. Hegemony is power that "naturalizes" a social order, an institution, or even an everyday practice so that 'how things are' seems inevitable and not the consequence of particular historical actors, classes, and events. Hegemony enables everyday harm. It sustains the interests of a society's dominant groups, while generally obscuring those interests in the eyes of subordinates (Hirsch and Lazarus-Black 1994:7).

Thus, although Trinidadian lawmakers succeeded in their efforts to secure legal reform on behalf of victims of domestic violence and believed that they had accomplished that goal, I will argue that everyday activities in the magistrates' courts mostly reproduce—instead of eliminate—inequities and buttress structures of domination that characterize

91

the wider social contexts of which these courts are a part. Legal reform, in other words, can be undermined by the legal process.

Courts are integral to the systems of "legal-rational domination" (Weber 1978) that characterize modern nation-states. In Trinidad, as we have seen, courts are organized bureaucratically, arranged in terms of hierarchical "offices," and occupied by professionals educated to the task. The bureaucratic administration of the courts promotes specialization, predictability, calculability, and legality. As Weber observed, there is, however, a critical relationship between bureaucratic administration and domination: "Every domination both expresses itself and functions through administration. Every administration, on the other hand, needs domination, because it is always necessary that some powers of command be in the hands of somebody" (1978:2:948). Weber's discussion of the relationship between domination and administration, however, was mainly concerned with hierarchical structural organization, and less so with the details of the specific processes that accomplish domination within an administration.[1]

Those processes concern us here. As I will demonstrate, courts are complicated places in which legal procedures, processes, and officers mainly support the class and gender hierarchies that prevail in the wider society and hinder legal reform designed to redress social injustice. My work builds on earlier research that has shown that even when socially subordinated people gain formal access to legal hearings and to courts, they are often negatively perceived and sometimes feel compelled to speak and act in ways that invite dominant speakers to devalue or ignore them (e.g., Conley and O'Barr 1990, 1998; Coutin 2000; Hirsch 1998; Hirsch and Lazarus-Black 1994; Lazarus-Black 1997; Matoesian 1993, 2001; Merry 1990, 2000; Razack 1998, 1999; Trinch 2003; White 1991; Yngvesson 1993). Moreover, the "rules" and the available resources for resistance differ for men and women.[2]

To illuminate how class and gender hierarchies are accomplished in the courts, I synthesize certain practices and processes into a model I refer to as "court rites." Court rites are secularly stylized events and processes that occur regularly in the legal processing and enforcement of court orders and that preserve and promote class and gender hierarchies. Individually, the rites are generated in the interactions between legal officials and ordinary citizens; each rite reveals how people's commonsense understanding of class, family, and gender mediates activity at the courthouse. As a composite, the model provides a useful theoretical tool for: (1) making sense of how a society's wider relations of domination and subordination are perpetuated in legal arenas; (2) explaining why certain legal reforms that potentially upset prevailing class and gender hierarchies are difficult to implement; and (3) illustrating the problematic relationship between agency and structure, particularly as it affects how men and women sometimes successfully plead parts of their cases but are constrained or even suppressed by legal officials in other matters before the courts.

Readers will recognize many of the rites I define; they are identifiable in courts in contemporary Britain, the United States, and elsewhere in the English-speaking Caribbean. This is not surprising because each of these societies shares the British common-law tradition, has a comparable hierarchical organization of "lower" courts to contend with "petty" matters and "higher" courts to hear "serious" matters, and is comparable in its bureaucratic organization of courts, legal personnel, and legal discourse. I identify and explain court rites that occur in Trinidad's magistrates' courts, establish their symbolic and pragmatic consequences, and reveal how they operate to support prevailing class and gender hierarchies. The critical issues of how the rites articulate with each other in different times and places, and how they are marked in culturally specific ways, become apparent in the course of my analysis.

My central purpose is to reveal precisely how practices in legal arenas support and are shaped by structures of domination in the wider society; a second concern is to illuminate when and why legal arenas sometimes empower subordinated people, enabling them to resist domination and, occasionally, to achieve aspirations lawmakers never intended or even imagined. I begin with "Alena's" story. Her story portrays many of the common characteristics of abusive relationships and the hegemonic response to domestic violence by victims, family, and neighbors, as well as by criminal justice officials. It is in many respects typical of the domestic violence case histories that I encountered during my fieldwork. For example, as in Alena's case, there are often no warning signs of potential abuse at the beginning of the romantic relationship. Almost without thinking, the woman leaves her family and friends in favor of her newfound romantic love. Family and friends respect the intimate partnership and refrain from "interfering" in any way. The abuser then further isolates his partner by denying her the right to work or even to use the phone. When the abuse begins, therefore, there is no one to turn to. Instead, the survivor spends her time trying not to anger in any way the abusive partner. Emotionally and economically dependent, she sees no way out of her troubles and she blames herself for her own limitations as a partner, homemaker, and mother. People become aware of the abuse, but they "mind their own business." Alena's story is unusual only insofar that she was younger than most of the litigants I observed in court and because she eventually escaped from her abusive partner and returned to school and a caring, middle-class family. Otherwise, her story reveals common patterns in abusive relationships, why women decide to go to court, and events and processes that characterize their case histories.

I then use Alena's case and other ethnographic research conducted in courts in the United States, Great Britain, Jamaica, and Antigua (all heir to the British common-law tradition) to define and give examples of court rites that mark different moments in the legal process.[3] Taken separately, each rite allows us to see the specific points at which either the reforming legislators' intentions have been thwarted (often unintentionally) by courthouse officials.[4] Considered together, the rites offer a more comprehensive perspective on the making and advancement of hegemony in legal institutions. Less frequently, but with important consequences, rites can sometimes operate to the benefit of otherwise subordinated litigants (Lazarus-Black 1997). In the last section of this chapter, I reiterate this point with some examples from my fieldwork. More commonly, as I demonstrate in Alena's case, court rites undermine the protective capacity of law.

Alena's Story

"Alena" met her future common-law husband, "John," accidentally—they were both waiting to use a public telephone. She was in high school with a year to go before graduation and working part time at a hotel. He was impressive in her eyes; he had a new, expensive motorcycle and a full-time job making deliveries. They began dating. Alena's mother, Pauline, disapproved of the relationship. She worried that John was too old for Alena, that he had little education, and that he was an unskilled laborer. Alena would not listen. She dropped out of school and went to live with John.

At first Alena was proud of the fact that John didn't want her to work. She busied herself with keeping their apartment clean and cooking. John didn't seem to like any of her girlfriends, so she slowly let go of those relationships. But she grew worried when bill collectors began sending letters. She thought she ought to get a job. John agreed, although he insisted on driving her back and forth from the retail store where she had obtained work as a sales clerk. Just a month later, however, he announced that he had seen her interact "inappropriately" with a male customer and that he would not tolerate that from "his woman." He beat her for her "misconduct" and forced her to resign. That was the beginning of the abuse.

Living with John meant moving often. He would pay a deposit and the month's rent and then remain in an apartment until the landlord realized he would have to evict them through the courts. Then he lost his job, after which he was employed only intermittently. Sometimes there was food and sometimes Alena went to bed hungry. John was verbally, physically, and sexually abusive. One time when he had been drinking he threatened to break her foot so she would never be able to walk properly again. He would not allow a phone in the apartment. Alena called her younger siblings on occasion from a public phone, but begged them not to tell their mother where she was living. She was ashamed of her situation. After their fourth eviction, the couple went to live with John's mother.

Alena was four months pregnant before she realized she was having a baby. She was thin and depressed. The news pleased John and he was excited when Alena delivered a baby boy who would be his namesake. He was not happy when the baby woke him up at night. His abusive behavior escalated. John's mother would not comment on or interfere with her son's behavior. When John would start to yell at and hit Alena, his mother would retreat to her bedroom and close the door.

Another four months passed. John was mostly unemployed and spent his time with his friends. One day, extremely depressed, Alena called her mother. She burst into tears when she heard Pauline's voice and hung up. Pauline was frightened. She questioned her other children and got a phone number from which she traced Alena's whereabouts. Pauline contacted the police and with their assistance she found her daughter. Two police officers accompanied her to the house. John was not at home. Pauline was shocked at her daughter's appearance and at the fact that she was now a grandmother. She took her daughter and grandson home with her.

Alena slowly regained her emotional and physical health and returned to school. On occasion, however, John appeared outside her school or at the baby's preschool. He would threaten her and demand to see their son. Alena told me she did not want her son to grow up without a father so initially she agreed to visitation. But John abused the situation, failing to return the boy at the agreed-upon time. One evening, Alena met John by chance on the street. He was drunk. He followed her, forced her into an alley, and cursed and beat her. She decided to apply for a protection order.

On their first day in court, the magistrate read the charges to John and inquired if he wanted an attorney. He said he did, so the magistrate adjourned the case for a week. Pauline had already secured an attorney on Alena's behalf. The next time the parties appeared, John was alone and the magistrate inquired if he had obtained an attorney. He told her that he had been to see a lawyer, but the attorney wanted $500 TT (about U.S. $85), which he found "a little steep." He had decided to proceed on his own. Alena did not know why her attorney was not in court that day. She told the magistrate that John had come by her house that week and they got into a fight. He complained that the fight was as much her fault as his. Alena said she wanted John to sign a paper to leave her alone. The magistrate advised John that she would not have him sign anything if he wanted an attorney present. John did not respond, complaining instead that Alena was not allowing him to see his son. The magistrate asked him if he had applied to the court for visitation rights. He had not. The magistrate turned to Alena and asked her if she wanted to proceed with the case. Alena replied that she would prefer not to; she had paid her lawyer and she wanted him to be with her in court. She also told the court that John smoked "weed," cursed her, and committed adultery. The magistrate ignored the first two of these three comments and informed Alena that John could not be accused of committing adultery because they were not married. She suggested to John that he should keep away from Alena's residence, her school, and workplace, as well as from the day care center. At this point, John suddenly said that this was all too confusing and that he would sign the paper. The magistrate explained to him the nature of an undertaking and what penalties follow if the un-dertaking is breached. She then turned to Alena and said that John was willing to sign the undertaking, but did she want her attorney present? Alena said she did. The case was adjourned again.

At the next hearing, three weeks later, Alena's attorney told the magistrate that "things were going very badly between the couple" and that John had "flogged" her the previous week. A report had been filed with the police in another jurisdiction. John was not in court when the case was called. The attorney asked the magistrate for a warrant for his arrest. The magistrate noted that John was usually in court. She put the case aside temporarily, but he did not appear before the noon recess. The magistrate then issued a warrant for his arrest. Around 1:00 P.M. that afternoon, while I was working on court records, I saw John at the back of the court. He had been under the impression that he was due in court at 1:00 P.M. A clerk informed him that there was a warrant out for his arrest and he was advised to go to the police station. After that day, a mix-up in serving a summons to John caused the case to be delayed another three weeks.

Both Alena and John appeared in court on what was to be the last day of Alena's attempt to win a protection order. She told me later in our interview that her attorney had only told her that John would probably sign an undertaking that he would leave her alone. Therefore, she was entirely unprepared when John failed to make that offer and the magistrate called her to testify.

Alena's testimony was confusing. She was unable to recall specifically when John had allegedly abused her, the exact nature of the abuse, or the words with which he had threatened her. Asked to cite an example of the abuse she had suffered when they lived together, she told the court that he once told her when she was pregnant that he would not "take the child if there was anything wrong with it." She said she was applying for a protection order because John harassed her about seeing their child. Once, when he was really angry, he threatened to kill her. He called her "a little girl who had to stay by her mother" and said she was "old-fashioned" and that "that was why he had to have a real woman, not a girl like you." She testified that she was "annoyed, angry, and very hurt" by his words and actions. Alena also testified that John showed up unexpectedly at the preschool, that he called her home persistently, and that he told her "he knows he can talk his way out of anything." She failed to mention the incident in the alley. Her attorney rested the case.

The magistrate put down her pen and spoke directly to the attorney. She explained that there seemed to have been some harassment when John went to the preschool and when he telephoned. "But there is really nothing here that qualifies for domestic violence. He calls her a child; he says he has to have a woman?" She explained that an application for a protection order is "a serious thing for preventing suffering and threatening of life." The magistrate found that the testimony she had heard amounted to some abusive language, but not something that would come under the Domestic Violence Act. She alluded to the fact that the attorney "might have an issue elsewhere," but she could only be concerned with events that happened in her jurisdiction.[5]

Alena's attorney made a feeble attempt to protest this decision. He noted that John made abusive remarks to Alena and had threatened to kill her. The magistrate took a copy of the Domestic Violence Act and proceeded to read from a section of the statute. She then told the attorney that he had not brought evidence that "reached that far." The attorney reiterated that John had threatened to kill Alena. The magistrate countered, "Well, yes, but that was on one occasion when clearly the two of them were quarreling over their son." She stated again that for a protection order she must have admissible evidence that the person is really fearful of injury and that she had to go by "a fear of life or limb sort of thing . . . by a certain standard. Because this is a severe thing to do to someone. It means the police will be looking over his shoulder for a year." In this case, the evidence presented "fell short, very short, of what is required in the act." The case was dismissed.

John asked if he could say something. The magistrate said no. Alena and Pauline both looked shocked. They left the courtroom immediately. The attorney slowly gathered up his papers, bowed to the magistrate, and departed. I remained in court to listen to the final cases of the day.

When I interviewed Alena a short time later, she mostly blamed herself for the outcome of the case.[6] She told me she had not testified properly and that John was smart and often able to get away with things. She did not blame the magistrate, whom she imagined had been outwitted by John. Nor did she blame her attorney for failing to prepare her for the case or its outcome. In fact, she had retained him for the criminal cases she later brought against John in another jurisdiction.

What happened in Alena's case, and in so many other cases I observed during my fieldwork, is that specific court rites combined in ways that disempowered the complainants and made it unlikely that they would win orders for protection. In the next section, I define twelve such rites, providing comparative examples from earlier research in courts that pointed to the existence of these practices, but which did not synthesize them systematically as I do. Of the court rites described here, some are associated with pretrial activities, others configure trials, and a few shape the enforcement process. Because different cases involve different parties and have separate histories, they include different combinations and numbers of rites. As we analyze how the rites interconnect, we are able to explain how an abusive man like John can leave the court without so much as a reprimand, without a record, and having avoided the expense of paying for an attorney.

Court Rites

Courts are "complex sites of resistance" (Hirsch 1994:208) because although they allow certain forms of protest and acts of empowerment, other words, actions, activities, and inactivities by legal personnel within the system create constraints and forms of coercion. To explain how this occurs, I developed a model to describe how combinations of rites mostly promote and protect prevailing class and gender hierarchies, as well as the pervasive belief that the state should not interfere in relationships between intimate parties.[7] I define each rite briefly and then provide comparative examples from research in other English common-law jurisdictions. My analysis is thus based on Alena's case and dozens of others I observed during fieldwork, interviews with legal professionals, analyses of magistrates' court records, and accounts of lower courts from other times and places. The model includes twelve rites: giving instructions, intimidation, delegalizing, legalizing, humiliation, euphemism, objectification, extraprofessional and erroneous professional advice and ill-treatment, silencing, judicial discretion, second chances, and unenforced enforcement. Identifying the rites and observing how they articulate with each other make it possible to discern why legal reform, in this case to assist victims of domestic violence, succeeds only partially. It also demonstrates how the courthouse is so powerfully influenced by, even as it influences, prevailing social hierarchies. Finally, I point to evidence to show that when a magistrate consciously manipulates a rite on behalf of a subordinated person or, alternatively, when economically and socially disadvantaged litigants speak out on their own behalf, the consequences can be empowerment and success against the odds. I begin with "giving instructions."

GIVING INSTRUCTIONS: SHARP INSTRUCTIONS TO SUBORDINATE THE MIND, VOICE, AND BODY TO AUTHORITY

In Trinidad, as is true in American, Jamaican, and British courts (e.g., Conley and O'Barr 1990; Eaton 1986; Emerson 1969; Feeley 1979; LaFont 1996; Merry 1990, 2000; Ptacek 1999), one must have good manners in court. Instructions given to litigants and witnesses in the courts may include orders to be quiet, bow, sit, stand, pray, or remove one's hat. Instructions set the tone of the court and establish its authority. Various officers of the court give such instructions. I regularly observed Trinidadian police constables, for example, ordering parties to behave in certain ways. On just one court date in August 1998, I listened to them instruct litigants to "Button up your shirt," "Take your hands out of your pockets," "Stand properly," and "Take the gum out of your mouth" (see also Purdy 1997:118–20).

Litigants are also regularly admonished by magistrates about the inappropriateness of their attire for court. Magistrates derided T-shirts, cutoff jeans, and shorts—the clothing of working-class youth. The forms of appropriate court attire are, of course, culturally constituted. For example, when I began my first research project in the magistrate's court in Antigua, I remarked to a clerk that I found it amusing that so many people wore American baseball caps to court. She explained to me that what I was seeing as informality was actually a symbol of respect for the court—wearing a hat that would then be removed by the litigant in the presence of the magistrate. That the hat was a baseball cap was utterly beside the point.

Giving instructions is a common practice in English magistrates' courts: "All defendants are escorted into the courtroom by the policeman calling the cases. Once the defendant is in the docket the escort acts as a kind of personal choreographer to him. He tells him when to stand up and when to sit down . . . when to speak and when to be quiet, when to leave the docket at the end of the hearing. During the hearing the policeman can tell the defendant to take his hands out of his pockets, chewing-gum out of his mouth, his hat off his head and the smile off his face" (Carlen 1976b:29).[8]

A similar situation exists in the Family Court in Jamaica: "A sign outside of the courtroom informs its users to wear their best clothes. The result, with the women, is a colorful fashion show of Sunday best mixed with black and gold evening attire. The men are less influenced by the posted message and usually arrive in shirt and trousers. Courtroom behavior is formal and the guards are quick to order participants to tuck in their shirt tails, stop chewing gum, take their hands out of their pockets and stand up straight" (LaFont 1996:70).

Armed sheriffs do much of the directing in American courts. For example, Ptacek found: "In both Dorchester and Quincy [two courts near Boston], police officers wearing revolvers routinely walk in and out of the courtrooms; bailiffs wear handcuffs and enforce order by hushing spectators and even forbidding the reading of newspapers; and all are instructed to rise when the judge enters and departs" (1999:147). In Chicago, Wittner found: "The armed sheriffs who bark commands to be quiet, order people out of the courtroom, and stand guard over the courthouse can be intimidating" (1998:87).[9]

Giving instructions flows in one direction: from the powerful to the subordinated. We saw several incidents of this in Alena's case. The magistrate gave instructions to John when she asked him if he wanted to seek the services of an attorney and then postponed the case so he would have time to secure one. She gave instructions to Alena when she chided her for not allowing John to see his son. She also postponed the case at the convenience of Alena's lawyer. As other researchers have noted, "giving instructions" and "intimidation" are often linked (LaFont 1996; Wittner 1998).

INTIMIDATION: CREATING AN ENVIRONMENT IN WHICH INDIVIDUALS FEEL THAT THEY CANNOT SPEAK FREELY BECAUSE THE LISTENER(S) HOLD(S) PHYSICAL, SOCIAL, PSYCHOLOGICAL, OR ECONOMIC POWER OVER THEM

Intimidation is a regular part of people's experience in small claims and juvenile courts in the United States and Great Britain (e.g., Conley and O'Barr 1990; Emerson 1969; Feeley 1979). For example, White (1991) discusses in detail the intimidation of Mrs. G, a black mother, at her hearing to determine welfare fraud. Because of intimidation, people in courts in England and the United States wait hours for their cases to be called, often without any official explanation (Carlen 1976a:52; Mileski 1971:489), while juvenile delinquents in America suffer threatening and moralistic lecturing (Emerson 1969:173–83). Feeley provides another example of intimidation in American courts: "A prosecutor is . . . speaking very rapidly and forcibly, asking the defendant, 'Why do you want to go to trial? Don't fuck around. Take a small fine. Why come back again or perhaps two or three times? Why miss a few days' work and end up with a stiffer sentence than you would get from me? If you go to trial, you may go to jail'" (1979:183).

Women applying to domestic violence court in Chicago complained of feeling "intimidated, overpowered, and uncertain in their interviews with court staff, much as they had felt in the violent situations that brought them to court in the first place" (Wittner 1998:85). In Massachusetts, three women described their first hearing in domestic violence court as very frightening:

> First applicant: I was absolutely positively petrified. I was by myself too. . . . All these men and then there was me.

> Second applicant: Real, real scary. I get scared in courts and in hospitals. . . . The [woman from the restraining order office] told them to give me a restraining order. I didn't understand everything they said. It went so fast. Judge talked to the lady. . . . I was crying.

> Third applicant: Scary, shaky. . . . I've never been in front of a judge before, and I wanted to walk out. . . . It was very intimidating, and there were a lot of people there, which made it hard to talk. (Ptacek 1999:146)

Similarly, in Jamaica, "the average court user is duly intimidated by the process" (LaFont 1996:70).

In magistrates' courts in Trinidad moments of intimidation expose the tensions people experience when they must speak about domestic violence and contend publicly with what is for them an unusual exposure of their private lives.[10] There is little doubt, for example, that Alena felt intimidated in the witness stand. That was obvious by her words and demeanor. In sharp contrast, John did not have to address any of the alleged violence; rules of evidence protected him from having to testify. One would expect that learning there was a warrant out for his arrest would have caused John some feelings of intimidation. The matter of the warrant, however, was never again addressed by the court. That fact brings us to the third court rite, "delegalizing."

DELEGALIZING: CONVERTING A DISCOURSE ABOUT LEGAL RIGHTS INTO A COMPLAINT THAT IS NOT WORTHY OF LEGAL REDRESS

Delegalizing is common in American courts. For example, "gatekeeper" clerks (Yngvesson 1988, 1993, 1994) discourage people from bringing to court what they define as trivial matters, unworthy of legal redress. In addition, knowledge about how much time, effort, and expenses are involved in processing a suit often discourages people from pursuing their cases (e.g., Feeley 1979; Merry 1990; Yngvesson 1993, 1994). This was true of some of the women I interviewed in Trinidad and it has been documented in Jamaica (Jackson 1982; LaFont 1996).

Delegalizing also occurs through changes in the discourse through which a case is defined and transformed. Merry (1990:ix) points out, for example, that lower-class litigants in New England find that court officials redefine litigants' troubles as moral or therapeutic problems, requiring counseling or mediation but not legal remedy. These litigants are turned away from the courthouse and denied the opportunity to present their cases. Yngvesson provides another example of delegalizing:

> . . . a young woman described the "violent actions" of her former boyfriend, and her fear "that he will kill or hurt me in some way when I'm not expecting it." The defendant did not appear for the hearing, but the clerk dismissed her complaint, again on grounds that there is "no such crime" as harassment. He counseled her, however, that "if he bothers you again, file the right complaint and we'll issue it quick"; and he suggested that she might bring a complaint of trespassing, if the defendant was on her property. Appalled, the woman exclaimed, "You mean, because I used the wrong word?. . . . He didn't show up, and nothing happens?" (1993:57)

Judges in Massachusetts practice delegalizing when they ignore domestic violence victims' requests for maintenance for their children: "Despite the acknowledgment of the material dimensions of women's victimization by most of the judges interviewed, however, in the case of the Dorchester District Court, where the women seeking orders are mostly African American or Afro-Caribbean, women's requests for child support and compensation were generally ignored" (Ptacek 1999:128).

Delegalizing also occurs when police tell battered women that they can do nothing to protect them unless they already have a restraining order (Ptacek 1999:163). Several women I interviewed in Trinidad had been told this when they sought police protection from violent men. Delegalizing is exactly what happened to Alena's case. After hearing her testimony, the magistrate concluded that what was before her was a quarreling couple who could not get along, but not cause for ordering a protection order that would place John under restraint for a year. Alena's case "reproduced the gender inequality within which the conflict was structured, intensifying, rather than diminishing, the complainant's sense of disempowerment" (Yngvesson 1993:58). In short, delegalizing is commonplace in courts. Its opposite, "legalizing," has been less frequently observed.

LEGALIZING: ADDRESSING PARTIES AND MAKING ARRANGEMENTS AS THOUGH JUDICIAL POWER EXISTS, WHEN IN FACT NO LEGAL BASIS EXISTS FOR THOSE ACTIONS

Legalizing is a process in which officials assume powers that are not legally theirs (Carlen 1975:363–64). For example, in 1987, when I was conducting research on family law in Antigua, I only rarely heard magistrates discuss men's access to their children. On occasion, a magistrate lectured a party on the necessity of allowing children to visit with the noncustodial parent. By 1994, however, a new cohort of magistrates regularly took it upon themselves not only to lecture about children's needs for access to both parents but also to work out very specific child visitation arrangements. In fact, there is no statute that grants magistrates any legal authority to make these arrangements. Several lawyers pointed this out to me; but no one tells the parents.

As Coutin recognizes, legalizing can also take the form of accusatory questions designed to elicit information that is none of the business of legal officials. Excerpts from hearings in which immigrants to the United States hope to regularize their legal papers provide examples: "In one suspension hearing, the judge not only asked an applicant whether he planned to marry the mother of his child but also questioned his answer that he was 'not yet ready' for marriage. When this applicant's girlfriend (whose legal status was not an issue in this case) took the stand, the judge explored her financial and living arrangements, even asking if she was entitled to receive welfare if she was working" (2000:124).

Legalizing was not a part of Alena's case, but it has been observed in U.S. domestic violence courts by Ptacek: "Although neither this observer nor the volunteer advocate assisting the woman heard the defendant ask for visitation, the judge struck out the part of the order barring the defendant from contacting the children and stated that visitation should be set up through an intermediary. According to the Supreme Judicial Court, district court judges have no jurisdiction to order visitation in restraining order hearings" (Ptacek 1999:105). In another case Ptacek followed, the complainant experienced both delegalizing and legalizing: "At the first hearing, a different judge had asked this woman why the defendant had not been arrested, given his threats to kill her and his previous conviction for violence against her. Yet the judge at the second hearing denied the restraining order, dismissing the threats as a 'lover's quarrel' and pressing the woman to arrange visitation by the defendant with the children—which goes beyond a judge's legal authority, as established in a 1986 Supreme Court decision" (Ptacek 1999:160).

Redefining violence as a "lover's quarrel" also occurred in Alena and John's case. As we see next, Alena and her attorney, but not John, experienced "humiliation" at her trial.

HUMILIATION: CREATING AN ENVIRONMENT IN WHICH CERTAIN LANGUAGES, SPEECH STYLES, INDIVIDUALS, SOCIAL GROUPS, OR FORMS OF BEHAVIOR ARE "AUTOMATICALLY," "NATURALLY," "HEGEMONICALLY" POSITIONED AS SUBORDINATE

This is sometimes the process of creating "stigma" (Goffman 1963). Throughout the English-speaking Caribbean, a woman who seeks support for a child whose paternity is denied by the alleged father must prove her case through corroborating evidence (Lazarus-Black 1994, 2001). Such proof usually comes in the form of witnesses who can testify to the parties' relationship, but in the past there were lawyers who dragged children into court and demanded of the magistrate whether it was not obvious whose "picknee" this was! Men's humiliation at being brought to court is also clear. One man I interviewed specifically characterized his trial as a "degradation of character" (Lazarus-Black 1994:202). A case to determine paternity affiliation and child support indicates that a man is not a good father and that he has lost control of his woman. He experiences in court what Garfinkel (1956) calls a "degradation ceremony" (see also Emerson 1969:172–215).

The practice of humiliation is an ordinary part of peoples' experiences in juvenile courts in the United States (e.g., Cicourel 1968:124, 166–67,

315–16; Emerson 1969:174) and in magistrates' courts throughout the English-speaking Caribbean (LaFont 1996; Lazarus-Black 1994; Senior 1991:136). I once heard a magistrate lecture a woman who had requested a protection order "not to use the child against him because at the end of the day he is the daddy. And a child needs to see the daddy in the best possible light. Her dad is part of her roots. So live positively for her sake." In American small claims courts, women who complain about assault and battery by their former husbands are sometimes themselves admonished about their behavior and parenting skills. Yngvesson, for example, describes a lecture on fathers' rights by a New England clerk to a woman who complained about her former husband's abusive treatment of her (1993:56–57; see also Wan 2000:625). Defendants brought to lower criminal courts are also stigmatized (e.g., Mileski 1971:496–97, 530, 536). Humiliation was not a factor affecting Alena's initial attempt to win a protection order, but it was certainly present at the verdict. Alena and Pauline were both humiliated by the judge's decision that no real violence had occurred. The magistrate also humiliated their attorney who had clearly failed to prepare his client and his case. Humiliation is often a swift and blatant event. More subtle in character is "euphemism."

EUPHEMISM: REPLACING A WORD OR WORDS WITH OTHERS THOUGHT TO BE LESS BLUNT OR HARSH, WHICH MAKES CERTAIN PRACTICES VAGUE AND LESS SUBJECT TO QUESTION. EUPHEMISM IS USED BY DOMINANT GROUPS TO MASK POWER AND TO CONCEAL CERTAIN CONDITIONS AND ACTIVITIES

As Thompson correctly points out, in our everyday lives we are all constantly engaged in euphemisms of one form or another:

> Individuals implicitly and routinely modify their expressions in anticipation of their likely reception—in the way, for instance, that adults alter their vocabulary and tone of voice when speaking to children. Hence all linguistic expressions are, to some extent, "euphemized": they are modified by a certain kind of censorship which stems from the structure of the market, but which is transformed into self-censorship through the process of anticipation. Viewed from this perspective, phenomena of politeness and tactfulness, of choosing the right word for the right occasion, are not exceptional phenomena but are simply the most obvious manifestation of a situation common to all linguistic production. Tact is nothing other than the capacity of a speaker to assess market conditions accurately and to produce linguistic expressions which are appropriate to them, that is, expressions which are suitably euphemized. (Thompson 1991:19–20)

In characterizing the rite of euphemism, I have in mind practices that deliberately distort in order to conceal power. In Great Britain (Carlen 1976a:53–54) and throughout the English-speaking Caribbean, for example, magistrates become "Your Worship" and "Your Honour," lawyers are "learned friends," police are "public servants," and probation officers are "knowledgeable experts." Such titles perpetuate the hierarchical relationships between the agents of the state and ordinary citizens who bring grievances to court. Euphemism in courts also occurs when legal officials speak about a defendant's prehearing imprisonment as "detention" (Feeley 1979:205–6), when defendants are sentenced to "time served" (Feeley 1979:171), when suits are deliberately delayed to give the accused time to pay for his mistake (Feeley 1979:175), and when juveniles are "helped" by placing them under "probation" (Cicourel 1968:64; Emerson 1969:219–45).

Like the other rites, euphemism is constituted in interesting and culturally specific ways. For example, euphemism allows conflicts that are "really" about a regionally recognized practice known as "sharing a man" to be brought to court under charges of "failure to keep the peace." Senior explains: "A significant number of women in the Caribbean are in 'sharing relationships,' that is, they knowingly or unknowingly share a man with whom they have a steady relationship with another woman (or other women). Children by the various women are frequently the outcome. Such sharing relationships exist at all levels; it is not uncommon in middle- and upper-class families for there to be a set of 'inside' children of the 'real' or legal family and 'outside' children with another woman. Sometimes these parallel families exist unknown to each other, or at least unknown to the 'inside' family; others might be aware but turn a blind eye" (1991:175–76).

"Sharing a man" cases involve women of all ages and social classes. In these cases, a man's disreputable behavior to two or more families is ignored, while the mothers of his children are recast as troublesome characters under the guise of the euphemism "failure to keep the peace." Court cases involving "sharing a man" occur throughout the English-speaking Caribbean, but to the best of my knowledge, scholars have not analyzed their frequency or implications. Certainly "sharing a man" is difficult; jealousy and frustration occur, sometimes accompanied by intimidation and violence (Senior 1991:175–79). When the dispute escalates, "sharing a man" goes to court under the euphemism of "keeping the peace." The case brings to court two women whose source of tension arises from their common partner's unfaithfulness—a "crime" for which there is no name in law. Ironically, the man not only remains outside the case but also watches the state scold his women to behave themselves and command them to keep away from each other—precisely as he prefers.

Alena applied euphemism in her testimony to the court. She told me that she thought she should be "polite" on the stand. She was too embarrassed to use the actual words John used against her. She had no idea that the magistrate would not "read into her words" what had actually transpired on numerous occasions between herself and John. Her case demonstrates the literal quality of the law and its insistence that certain words and deeds constitute crime while others do not. Alena whitewashed her language to the point that the magistrate heard nothing to justify issuing a protection order; Alena's testimony amounted to a case of annoying language. Trinch describes a similar phenomenon among Latina women in the United States who mask the violence of rape as "having sex," "private relations," "making love," or being "intimate." They do so "because this type of language keeps them from violating sociocultural restrictions of speaking the unspeakable" (2001:572–73). An unwillingness to speak the unspeakable also prevents South Asian immigrant women in the United States from making public the marital violence in their lives (Abraham 2000). Euphemism sometimes incorporates the next rite, "objectification."

OBJECTIFICATION: CREATING AN ENVIRONMENT IN WHICH PERSONS ARE TREATED AS OBJECTS

This rite includes activities such as talking about individuals as though they were without rights, not present, or were children. Legal officials objectify litigants by assigning them to socially subordinated categories. This occurs with stunning regularity in English and American courts. Carlen explained the process in this way: "The objectification of people as defendants begins when they are charged with an offense. Thereafter objectification processes are systematically crystallized throughout the court hearing, so that by the time the magistrate asks for reports the defendant has already been transformed into client, prisoner, or patient" (1975:375).

Juvenile delinquents in the United States are similarly treated: "Officials frequently discuss details of a delinquent's life and behavior as if he were not there, making no acknowledgment of his presence either by word or by glancing in his direction" (Emerson 1969:179). During immigration status hearings, Central American immigrants are discussed as if they are not present and are often identified only by such legalisms as "male respondent" or "adult female respondent" (Coutin 2000:116).

Women who apply for protection orders in Massachusetts complain of being reduced to the category of "victim" (Ptacek 1999:148).

Attorneys sometimes objectify their clients and make fun of litigants in ways that amuse the court but also suggest that domestic violence cases do not warrant serious legal attention. On one occasion when I was in court in Pelau, for example, a woman who filed for a protection order asked her attorney to appear in court for her. He told the magistrate that he had earlier spoken to the parties whom he described as being "in a little huddle downstairs this morning." The attorney for the accused piped in: "I would say a little cuddle! Yes, sir, so it seems as though the parties have worked things out!" The case was dismissed.

The magistrate who presided over Alena's case provides us with another example of objectification. After hearing Alena's testimony, the magistrate put down her pen and spoke directly to the attorney, carefully avoiding eye contact with Alena. She explained her decision to dismiss the case by reading to the attorney a section of the Domestic Violence Act. The verdict rested on precise rules of evidence but in this case it denied the experiences of violence in Alena's life.

EXTRAPROFESSIONAL AND PROFESSIONAL ERRONEOUS LEGAL ADVICE AND ILL-TREATMENT: CONSCIOUSLY OR UNCONSCIOUSLY PROVIDING BAD DIRECTIONS OR INADEQUATE ADVICE

Feeley notes that much of the free legal advice given by courthouse personnel to litigants in the United States is sound (1979:184). One could say the same of the free counsel offered by lawyers and clerks in the magistrates' courts in which I've conducted research in the Caribbean. Occasionally, however, I have overheard instances of inept lawyering and of erroneous advice. Clerks, for example, regularly provide information about lawyers. They have a working knowledge of the abilities and conscientiousness of the attorneys and regularly provide information or shape laypersons' opinions when asked. The problem is that some of the most popular lawyers are not necessarily the best advocates. One lawyer I interviewed in Trinidad complained to me about the misinformation given to the public by justices of the peace who screen domestic violence cases before they reach the attention of the magistrate.

The problem of erroneous and inadequate legal advice was documented in a report prepared by an American Battered Women's Working Group and published in Boston in 1985. Troubled by women's treatment at the hands of court personnel and the police, the group began interviewing complainants. They found "widespread patterns of noncompliance" with the domestic violence law by the police and clerks. Moreover, judges incorrectly applied the law, exhibited biased attitudes to litigants, and sometimes gave inaccurate legal advice (Ptacek 1999:52). Analyzing cases of battered women who killed abusive partners, Schneider discovered: "Cases involving claims of ineffective assistance based on counsel's failure to offer jury instructions on battering suggest that many attorneys lack knowledge about the particular complexities of representing battered women" (2000:145).

As we have seen, Alena's attorney had not prepared her to testify. He had assumed incorrectly that John would give an undertaking. As a consequence, when Alena took the stand, she was embarrassed, intimidated, and ill-prepared to give the testimony she needed to give to win a protection order. The next rite, the practice of "silencing"—a practice that is a regular and important part of the adversarial system of justice—operated with important consequences in Alena's case.

SILENCING: CREATING AN ENVIRONMENT IN WHICH CERTAIN VOICES ARE HEARD BUT OTHERS ARE NOT

Silencing also occurs when a person is given the opportunity to speak but the content of the message is ignored. It is the power to control both speech and silence.

Silencing regularly characterizes domestic violence and its legal redress. Many women initially avoid telling anyone about the abuse they suffer. In the Caribbean, where the temperature is warm and peoples' windows are open, neighbors know about violence but remain silent because there is cultural sanction against interfering with "husband-wife business." Women in Trinidad have been humiliated and silenced by police officers who trivialize their cases. As one recounted: "I called the police so many times when my husband came to harass me! And when I go to the station they would just turn up their face and say, 'She? Don't take she on. She's always here!' And I would not get any help from them. They say they're going to warn him but he would still come and harass me. I'd go to the police station and he would still harass me in front of them and they would just sit down and watch and not say anything."

Silencing is a pervasive phenomenon in courts. In the American context, O'Barr looked at "certain specifically legal aspects of silence: the right to remain silent, the consequences of refusing to obey the usual rules regarding silence in courts, and the matter of 'silencing' the official record," as well as lawyer-witness interactions, means for resolving the ambiguities of silence, and strategies for managing its interpretation in the courtroom (1982:98). Among other things, O'Barr concluded that "there are, in fact, a great many rules regarding silence in court. They operate for the most part at the level of public, shared understandings. But there is another aspect of silence that deserves recognition. It is that in many of these instances variable meanings might be assigned to silences. In these situations, the court—usually in the person of the judge—usually goes to great length to attempt to *interpret* the silences" (1982:103–4).

Being unable to tell one's story, or to tell it only partially, is a common experience for litigants in courts (e.g., Conley and O'Barr 1990, 1998; Ewick and Silbey 1998; Matoesian 1993, 2001; Merry 1990, 2000; Schneider 2000; Yngvesson 1993) and in hearings to establish immigrants' legal status (Coutin 2000). Chicagoans who file for protection orders are regularly admonished by judges, lawyers, and other court personnel to just "stick to the facts" (Wittner 1998:86).[11]

In the case of Alena and John, the person who was most obviously silenced was John. As we have seen, the magistrate directly denied him the opportunity to speak. Ironically, this silencing prevented him from giving potentially incriminating evidence. The silencing of Alena was a more subtle and complicated process. Alena's attorney had not prepared her for the possibility that she might have to testify. She went to court, therefore, without understanding what words and events constituted domestic violence. Alena had the opportunity to tell her story, but she spoke in language that betrayed her socialization as a young, educated, middle-class Trinidadian woman who was also a mother. In other words, she avoided cursing and mentioning specific behaviors that are considered inappropriate for a woman of her status. Surprised and intimidated at being called to the witness stand, Alena used euphemisms to describe what John had said and done. Alena expected the magistrate to respect and appreciate her decorum in the witness stand. The consequence of these assumptions was that her testimony was an illustration of what Conley and O'Barr have characterized as "powerless" speech, speech that the legal system devalues and finds lacking in credibility (1998:65).[12] The magistrate also silenced Alena's attorney by reading out loud the clause in the Domestic Violence Act describing what constitutes evidence of domestic violence. Dismissal of the case, of course, was silencing writ large. Judges and magistrates often exercise the next court rite, that of "judicial discretion," in ways that support already privileged groups.

JUDICIAL DISCRETION TO SUPPORT PRIVILEGED GROUPS:
THE CONSCIOUS AND UNCONSCIOUS USE OF THE POWER
OF THE BENCH TO SUPPORT THE OPTIONS AND PRIVILEGES
OF DOMINANT GROUPS

Judicial discretion that supports privileged groups has been documented
qualitatively and quantitatively in Merry's historical and legal research
on Hilo, Hawaii. Investigating court records from the 1870s, she found
that the most frequent type of case prosecuted was plantation laborers'
desertion from work (2000:171) and that "courts generally favored the
more powerful, but were careful to examine evidence and sometimes
acquitted the workers" (2000:173). Twenty years later, in the 1890s, the
men who controlled the plantations continued to find support in legal
arenas. Workers were "generally disadvantaged," while the courts were
a "much more amenable forum for employers" (2000:185, 186).

Scholars are well aware of the difficulties subordinated people face
when they attempt to speak to power (Scott 1985). In the case of domestic violence, applicants for protection orders must prove to the court's
satisfaction that words and deeds constituting violent behavior were
committed at specific times and places, and in ways that caused the applicant to be fearful of future harm. Judicial discretion is also influenced
by the process of judicial appeal. Knowing that a case can be appealed
places pressure on magistrates to render verdicts with which their senior
colleagues can agree. Not surprisingly, they are often conservative in
their reading of statutes and in deciding how much evidence is enough
evidence to support a decision.[13] As we saw in Alena's case, her lack of
coherency in testifying and use of polite speech left the magistrate in
doubt about whether the offense of domestic violence had occurred. In
sharp contrast, John never took the stand. He was privileged in the sense
that he did not have to explain his words or actions. Instead, John was a
participant in the rite I call "second chances."

SECOND CHANCES: PROVIDING INDIVIDUALS WHO
ARE UNDER COURT ORDERS WITH OPPORTUNITIES TO
POSTPONE OR AVOID THOSE ORDERS

The rite "second chances" is illustrated most readily in the case of men
who fail to pay court-ordered child support. "Deadbeat dads" are as commonplace in the Caribbean as they are in the United States. For example,
in both Antigua and Trinidad, a man is always allowed to fall into arrears
for some weeks after a magistrate makes an order for child maintenance.
Then a summons is issued directing him to explain in court why he has

failed to pay. If the man pays after receiving the summons, the case is marked "withdrawn" and the process starts all over again. If he ignores the summons, an arrest warrant is issued. It will be delivered to him by the police—eventually. The man must then pay the officer or go to jail. Thus a man's "first" second chance is the summons; his "second" second chance is the warrant.

The most salient example of "second chances" with respect to Trinidad's Domestic Violence Act was the provision in the law for undertakings. As we have seen, undertakings give men the opportunity to avoid a trial, public evidence of their abusive behavior, and a criminal record by undertaking to refrain in the future from violence they are alleged to have committed in the past. On the other hand, some complainants and officers of the court prefer undertakings because they sanction men from future violence in a timely fashion and with the same penalties for breaching the court's directive that occur when the court makes a formal order. One of the great ironies of Alena's case was that early on John offered to give an undertaking but Alena rejected his offer because she wanted her attorney to be present before she made any agreement with him. Abusive men's options are protected further by the twelfth rite, "unenforced enforcement."

UNENFORCED ENFORCEMENT: FAILURE TO ENSURE THAT THE COURT'S ORDERS WILL BE EFFECTED

This may take several forms, including failure to provide manpower or funding to carry out the court's directives or a waning of supervisory powers so that a defendant adheres to court orders with decreasing frequency over time. Unenforced enforcement reinforces a defendant's ability to postpone or even avoid entirely the state's demands. Unenforced enforcement of child support orders is pervasive in the United States (e.g., Blankenhorn 1995; Fineman 1995; McLindon 1987; Weitzman 1985, 1987), in Jamaica (e.g., Jackson 1982; LaFont 1996), in Antigua (Lazarus-Black 1994, 1997), and in Muslim kadhi's courts in coastal Kenya (Hirsch 1998).

Unenforced enforcement influences domestic violence cases in Trinidad in two ways. First, there is the matter of summoning persons to court. When a person files a charge of domestic violence, the alleged assailant must be notified to appear in court within seven days. Very commonly, however, the officer entrusted with serving the summons will not be able to deliver it in the timely fashion the law commands. Therefore, after they hear their name in court, complainants most commonly hear the magistrate state "fresh service," followed by a date that is usually two weeks later. Some litigants understand what is meant by this, but others are clearly confused and have to be instructed by their attorney, a police constable, or a court clerk to return to court two weeks later. Hopefully the alleged offender will have received the summons by the next court date. If a defendant has not been located after several weeks, the magistrate asks the complainant if she wishes to swear out a summons for his arrest. Unenforced enforcement of summoning defendants and witnesses thus undermines lawmakers' intentions that domestic violence cases be heard in a timely fashion, the subject of the next chapter.

Second, unenforced enforcement characterizes the processing of cases of breaches of protection orders. The attorneys I interviewed told me their clients were unlikely to return to them to prosecute breaches of protection orders. Obtaining the evidence to win breach cases is often difficult; it might be a matter of his word against hers. Verbal assaults are ignored; only cases of continued physical abuse are likely to return to court. Even if the case reenters the legal process, however, it is unlikely to remain in the courts. As we saw in chapter 2, of twenty-five breach cases disposed in Pelau in 1997–98, 56 percent were eventually dismissed and another 20 percent were withdrawn. Only occasionally was a respondent found guilty of breaching a protection order and, if he was, the likely penalty was a reprimand.

In short, court rites most often combine in ways that keep already subordinated people in their place and reduce their probability of attaining rights. Moreover, court rites operate, for the most part, without notice or comment. Nevertheless, as the following incidents suggest, on occasion, court rites contribute to the making of social justice.

Rites and Rights

During previous fieldwork in a magistrate's court in Antigua, I witnessed a case in which court rites combined in ways that mostly promoted class and gender hierarchies, but that also empowered a married woman and granted her the autonomy for which she had really gone to court. An antiquated Antiguan law required a married man to sign his child's passport. In the case in question, the husband had continually refused his wife's request to sign the document. Without his signature, the complainant was unable to take their two children on vacation to the United States. All of her efforts to secure his signature, which included speaking to his boss and hiring a lawyer to send a letter, had previously failed. The complainant then filed cases at the magistrate's court for maintenance for the children, even though she had been supporting them herself, with the help of her mother, for some years. Since the children's father had a monthly

salary as a police constable, the magistrate awarded maintenance. During
the case, however, the magistrate also used the authority of the bench to
command the defendant to sign the passport. The magistrate thus used
the rite I've called "legalizing" to reverse the gender hierarchy that made
it impossible for a married woman to obtain a passport for a child without
her husband's signature (Lazarus-Black 1997). As was true in this case,
women in the English-speaking Caribbean are commonly misperceived
as going to magistrates' courts only for money, while in reality many
have other motives and goals for themselves and their children (LaFont
1996; Lazarus-Black 1991, 1994). Litigants employ euphemisms that get
their cases into the courts, even if their real goal is not the award of a
pittance of maintenance. Two other illustrations from my fieldwork in
Trinidad also remind us that court rites sometimes operate in ways that
challenge hegemonic structures of power.

A case I observed in Trinidad in March 1998 involved "delegalizing"
to protect children. The matter involved an older couple. The woman
had brought four cases for child support against her former common-law
husband. Their children had been born in 1981, 1982, 1985, and 1986. The
father accepted paternity for each child. He then informed the magistrate
that he couldn't pay any child support because he was not working and
he needed a minor operation. The magistrate told him she "understood
his situation, but that he must pay something to help support the children. What could he offer on a weekly basis?" He repeated that he was
not working, that he was scheduled for surgery, and that he couldn't pay
child support. He added: "She knows I give her when I working." The
magistrate asked him, "How are you living if you are not working?" He
explained that he was staying with his married children from an earlier
union. The magistrate inquired if they could help. He said, "No, they have
to see about their own families." The magistrate turned to the woman.
She established the ages of the children and that they were all attending
school. What did she have in mind with respect to child support? The
woman said she needed at least $100 TT per week per child (about U.S.
$17). The magistrate noted that the father was currently unemployed
and then made an interim order (which could be revisited when the man
became employed) in the amount of $200 TT per week to begin in two
weeks' time. She warned the man that if he didn't pay he could be arrested. She repeated that she "understood that you are now unemployed,
but your children must eat. Two hundred dollars is reasonable. You must
make some effort." The case was adjourned for six weeks.

How, you may ask, could this magistrate make an order for child support when the father in question was unemployed? Shouldn't the magistrate have engaged in a more detailed interrogation to determine the father's means?

By the time of this court hearing, I had spent enough time in Trinidad to understand the magistrate's decision. Trinidadians pride themselves on their entrepreneurship. In numerous ways, people creatively earn a little cash. Men get day jobs, fix appliances, sell produce from their land or fruit trees, help neighbors with projects, go fishing and then sell their catch, and so on. Similarly, women babysit, braid hair, sew, and sell baked items. Moreover, extended families, friends, and neighbors help each other out. Magistrates know that fathers have access to some cash—and believe their children have a right to a portion of it. They may use the power of the bench against the prevailing Caribbean custom that men give child support when and if they have a mind to (Lazarus-Black 1995).

Finally, I observed in court on several occasions the court rites I call "intimidation" and "humiliation" used by magistrates against men charged with domestic violence. One such case involved a middle-aged couple who were in a long-term, common-law relationship and who resided together with their children. The defendant was charged with having assaulted the complainant on one date in December 1997 and again in February 1998. He immediately denied both charges. The complainant told the magistrate she had two witnesses, but only one was in court. The magistrate asked the accused if he had witnesses, to which he replied "my kids." Learning that the children were six, eight, and eleven years old, the magistrate advised him that "surely he didn't want to bring small children like that into court." He agreed, thereby depriving his case of witnesses who could testify on his behalf. The complainant then requested that the case be heard immediately. Without formally going to trial, the magistrate decided to hear a little of what they each had to say. The woman claimed he regularly slapped her, pushed her, pulled her by her hair, and used threatening and abusive language. The complainant's mother, her witness, could attest to that; she had observed his violent behavior in the December incident. The respondent countered that the complainant was guilty of domestic violence against him and that her mother was generally a nuisance. The magistrate focused on the first incident charged in the complaint. He admitted that they argued on the date in question and that he had slapped and pushed her, but he denied that he did any "damage" to her. That comment led to the following exchange:

Magistrate: Did you cuff her to her mouth?
Respondent: No, I just touch her.
Magistrate: Look at me. You are talking to a big woman and you are
    telling me you "touched" her? Did you slap her?
Respondent: [sheepishly] Yes, I did.
Magistrate: Right!

By the end of her discussion with these litigants, the magistrate had
turned denials of charges of violence into admissions of abuse. He also
admitted he had a drinking problem. His entire demeanor had changed
dramatically. The magistrate lectured him about being violent in front
of their children "because then the children grow up and they are violent
to other women." She inquired if he would go to Alcoholics Anonymous
or to family counseling. He agreed to counseling. The magistrate decided
to have the probation officer prepare a report. She adjourned the case to
wait for the report, explaining to the complainant that she would see
about orders when she had additional information about their situation
and instructing the respondent that he was leaving the court "with a
stern warning." Thus while this complainant did not on that date obtain
a protection order, legal intervention on her behalf had been set in motion
and the abuser had confessed to the charges of violence. Two weeks later,
the probation officer issued her report, and the man gave an undertaking
to attend counseling and to refrain from assaulting his common-law wife
or using abusive or threatening language.

As these examples demonstrate, court rites can operate to empower
those who are disadvantaged by gender, class, or the violence in their
lives. Moments occur in legal proceedings when rules are stretched, terms
are broadly interpreted, and power is invoked in the interests of justice
and not according to the letter of the law. Most commonly, however,
court rites combine in ways that undermine the protective capacity of
law and make it difficult, if not impossible, for the law to function as
lawmakers' intended and members of the community expected.

Conclusions

Litigants who bring domestic violence cases to magistrate's court in
Trinidad are sometimes empowered in ways that are not always evident
to lawmakers. Yet if there are moments when the court enables rights,
cases for protection orders are most often stories about the pervasiveness
of prevailing class and gender hierarchies. In Trinidad and other British
and British-inspired legal traditions, litigants who apply for protection
orders encounter court rites that impinge upon their ability to secure the

protection they seek. In Alena's case, bad advice, intimidation, silencing, objectification, humiliation, euphemistic language, judicial discretion, delegalizing, and second chances each contributed to her failure to win a protection order. Before, during, and after her court appearances, rites combined to limit the effectiveness of Alena's testimony and her case. She was ill-prepared to give evidence and the language she used—language that marked her social identity as an educated and polite woman and mother—worked against her. Her case is emblematic of an important point Hirsch has drawn to our attention:

> It is precisely around the use of language that the category "battered woman" becomes problematic. The designation itself often implies that the victim has been silenced over an extended period of time. This serves to explain why she failed to speak to authorities or, more generally, why she did not leave a relationship that exposed her to violence. Yet these assumptions conflict with the expectations placed on her in the context of the courtroom, where she is supposed to not only tell her story publicly but also speak authoritatively. This example alone shows that only a theory of discourse that understands subjectivity as encompassing the notion of subjects as speakers will begin to illuminate how gender is constructed in legal processes. (1998:289–90)

In sharp contrast to Alena, John did not testify in court. Following the rules of evidence, the magistrate denied him the right to speak. We can only surmise whether his words might have incriminated him.

What is revealed in Alena and John's case is that which goes unnoticed most of the time: an articulation of practices that principally reinforce prevailing class and gender hierarchies and the pervasive notions that the state should not interfere in domestic matters or subject men to the indignity of court orders or police surveillance unless the court is absolutely convinced that each tenet of the Domestic Violence Act has been breached. The literal quality of the practice of law, and the operation of court rites, undermine women's ability to secure sufficient and timely protection. When examined as a collection of independent but interactive and mutually reinforcing phenomena, the rites show us how the legal process is shaped by, and advances, the structures of domination that prevail in the wider social order. We can demonstrate specifically how legal procedures and members of the court contribute to the maintenance of those structures. Courts reproduce the power relations of the wider society because, quite simply, they are designed, organized, and run by persons for whom "order" references the existing class and gender hierarchies. We can also point to moments in the legal process, however, when the status quo is momentarily disrupted.

Finally, court rites reveal an important irony, one that deserves the attention of legal reformers. Through lawmakers, the state can pass laws designed to improve the lives of victims of domestic violence. Through officers of the court and in the legal process, however, that same state participates in court rites that ensure the perpetuation of class and gender hierarchies, undermine women's use of the court as a forum for rights, and make achieving protection from violence a difficult task. In this way, the state creates the impression that it is protecting the victims of violence while in reality it maintains hegemony. In the next chapter, I deconstruct the ways in which "time," operating in tandem with court rites, mediates agency and structure in legal processes.

5 Time and the Legal Process

Trinidad and Tobago's Domestic Violence Act was designed to ensure speedy hearings and remedies for persons who experienced domestic abuse. Nevertheless, as we have seen, a great number of applications for protection are dismissed or withdrawn and few protective orders are granted. Thus far I have accounted for these numbers in part by the prevalence of twelve court rites that, in various combinations, dissuade litigants from pursuing protection orders or result in magistrates denying them. In this chapter, I examine time as another factor that operates with critical consequence in legal cases generally, but that in two specific ways can have especially profound results in the matter of domestic violence. First, the cliché that "time heals all wounds" has special meaning in the context of understanding peoples' willingness to make public the violence in their lives. Time unravels the immediacy of an emotional or physical attack, especially if the abuser is subsequently apologetic. Second, alleged abusers, court clerks, police, lawyers, and other criminal justice professionals manipulate time in ways that cause victims to change their decisions to pursue their legal rights. My research reveals that the witting and unwitting use and abuse of time by various actors in the criminal justice process, like their participation in court rites, erodes the sense of rights that initially brings people to court. More specifically, my project in this chapter is to explain concretely how time figures into and transforms domestic violence cases.

As French points out, there have been few studies of how time works in law (2001:663) despite the fact that time functions in a variety of important ways in legal practice:

As a *measuring device*, it determines trial deadlines, or the period of a time-share. As a *value unit*, it tells us how many billable hours have accrued, the length of a prison sentence, the unit for which one is hired, or the proper time for a notification clause. Time functions as a *delineator of rights* that are initiated and terminated at certain times such as a statute of limitations on suits. Time is a great *organizer* for telling us when we are supposed to go to lunch and how to order those chronological charts that we make for presentation at trial. Time can often determine what is *reasonable* or not, such as reasonable response time for police or when a trial has been "speedy." It is a *power* that can be withdrawn or held over one's head, such as when the other side threatens to delay the time of a trial or a murder prosecution awaits the impending death of the victim under the federal year-and-a-day rule. Time is part of the *professional duties* of a lawyer who must make timely filings and complete contracts in which "time is of the essence," and it *resolves conflicts*, such as when the IRS does not file for a claim within the ten-year period and the action is lost. Finally, it is an *intrinsic part of basic legal concepts*, such as precedent and stare decisis (French 2001:664–67; italics in original).[1]

If there has been too little attention by scholars to the myriad ways in which time functions in the legal process, that is not true of criticism of that process. Complaints about the slowness of legal redress are commonplace—and not just in Trinidad. Ethnographers working in American, English, and other Caribbean courts, for example, also attest to the delays that litigants face.[2] Moreover, the reasons people in Trinidad gave me for the delays in the courts are the same reasons that people in Great Britain, the United States, India, and Jamaica give for the delays in their courts: everywhere courts are understaffed and lack resources. Yet, as Munn points out, "'being slow' is not a neutral state. . . . Control over time is not just a strategy of interaction; it is also a medium of hierarchic power and governance" (1992:104, 109). The matter of time, therefore, should not be dismissed only as a simple matter of too few actors working with too few resources.[3] Time is sometimes an instrument of power and sometimes a strategy to thwart power. As we shall see, time is often specifically "about" agency (Greenhouse 1996:7).

To explore how time functions in domestic violence cases, I describe in the first part of this chapter the everyday course of events and the kinds of interactions with legal professionals that a typical complainant in Trinidad encounters at the courthouse. I turn to the seven actors most commonly involved in domestic violence matters and to their respective categories and uses of time that figure so importantly in the processing of protection cases. These include: (1) Applicant Time; (2) Courthouse Time;

(3) Police Time; (4) Respondent Time; (5) Lawyer Time; (6) Probation Time; and (7) Magistrate Time. Both individually and in combination, the typical encounters between complainants and courthouse officials alert us to the multiple ways in which control over time challenges peoples' agency and modifies the structural constraints of law and legal procedures.[4] As is true of court rites, there is much evidence that time functions with sometimes dramatic consequences in domestic violence cases not only in Trinidad, but also in other British-inspired courts.[5] I draw from this ethnographic literature to synthesize and explain why litigants across a range of common-law courts are often dissuaded from seeking or obtaining the remedies that law provides. I found that pressures from various parties for more time, and subsequent delays in handling applications for protection, reconfigure domestic violence cases in ways that contribute to structural deflection, mitigating the alleged equality of the parties before the bench and diluting the seriousness of complaints of abuse.

I then describe three cases from my fieldwork to illustrate empirically how matters of agency, structure, and time intersect in law. In two instances, the complainants filed for protection orders but subsequently decided not to pursue their cases. One litigant eventually gained a protection order—but only after her second attempt to win the court's attention. The cases reveal covert forms of coercion that occur during the legal process that applicants for protection orders often describe as the "problem of time." Importantly, by this my interviewees referenced a variety of different responses and circumstances they encountered as they engaged with law. Like Alena, whose case was described in the previous chapter, these women regarded their experiences as idiosyncratic events. As was true in Alena's case, analysis of the patterns that characterize the hearings, trials, and outcomes of domestic violence cases suggests otherwise.

Speed and its inverse, delay, are functions of time, and time can compel a complainant to change her mind, give a defendant the chance to change it for her, allow the parties to reconcile, or teach a litigant that sheer determination has an important role to play in the legal system. In that case, time can result in a litigant's decision to try the court again. Ironically, Trinidad's Domestic Violence Act promises speedy redress for victims of abuse but, in practice, speed is hardly ever characteristic of domestic violence suits. The point is especially relevant when we examine Applicant Time.

Applicant Time

Applicant Time involves the matter of how long a woman waits before filing a case, whether she represents herself or obtains an attorney, and how long it takes before the initial and subsequent hearings. As is true in other countries, including Great Britain (Dobash and Dobash 1979, 1992), Guyana (Danns and Parsad 1989; Parsad 1988, 1999), India (Sitaraman 2002, Vatuk 2001, 2003), Israel (Adelman 1997, 2000), Jamaica (LaFont 1996), St. Kitts and Nevis (Spooner 2001), Barbados (Spooner 2001, 2004), and the United States (Ford 1991, Martin 1976; Merry 1990; Ptacek 1999; Wittner 1998), Trinidadians go to court only after having tried a variety of other methods to stop violence: they try reasoning with the abuser; seek the assistance of family members, friends, and ministers; call the police; move away; and contact shelters. In most cases, therefore, a lot of time passes before a woman files for a protection order.[6] If she files the application herself, she will learn that, by law, the case must appear before the magistrate within seven days. If she goes to an attorney, she must give counsel time to prepare for and file the paperwork. Thereafter, an unpredictable amount of time passes as a result of adjournments. Requests for adjournments can come from the applicant, the defendant, either of their attorneys, the probation officer, the police, or the magistrate. In my experience, magistrates in Trinidad rarely denied such requests.

Ptacek found that most of the women interviewed in his study in Massachusetts had talked with family and friends about the violence they were experiencing before they approached the courts. Women also sought protection from the police, mental health institutions, counselors, shelters, and hotlines (1999:141, 143–44).[7] Wittner cites another example of the complexities of Applicant Time from her fieldwork in Chicago's Domestic Violence Court: "Erica Chase, a secretary, had come to court because her ex-husband, Patrick, had shouted threats at her in family court the day before. Erica had gone to family court to force Patrick to pay their son's Catholic-school tuition. . . . Most of the court workers who heard Erica's story told her they didn't think the judge would issue her an order of protection. These discouraging assessments reinforced her discomfort with the court. When court recessed for lunch hour before her case was called, she walked out, not wanting to miss another full day of work for nothing" (1998:92). In short, Applicant Time very quickly becomes a journey of negotiating other peoples' time—that of family, friends, and employers—and then with the court staff.

Courthouse Time

Courthouse Time refers to the time litigants engage with the staff at the court. The courthouse in Pelau opens at 8:00 A.M., closes for lunch from noon to 1:00 P.M., and closes for the day at 4:00 P.M. As in Barbados (Spooner 2001:191), women in Trinidad can only file for and obtain a protection order during the business day. When an incident happens in the evening or during the weekend, a woman must wait considerable time before pressing her case. In the magistrates' courts in Trinidad, legal forms, notices for and about hearings, and court testimony are handwritten and all of the paperwork must be physically filed.

Applicants for protection orders are first sent to speak to the court's justice of the peace. The justice listens carefully to the applicant's story and asks the alleged victim to state precisely what events unfolded on what date(s). In the court in Pelau, the justice of the peace regularly took brief notes that he gave to the applicant to show to the clerk, who would then process the correct forms. Thus, the justice of the peace functioned as a "gatekeeper" (e.g., Merry 1990; Yngvesson 1988, 1993), filtering from the court's docket cases that seemed inappropriate in some way or causing any particular case further delays should the justice urge the complainant to return to court on another date with evidence or witnesses.[8] Other components of courthouse time involve how many courts are available to hear domestic violence matters and how many cases can be heard each day. In Pelau, one magistrate heard an average of 139 cases on Thursdays, the day set aside to hear family and domestic violence complaints. At the very end of my research, a second magistrate was appointed, which undoubtedly quickened the pace at which cases could be heard.

LaFont's (1996) work on the Family Court in Jamaica contains numerous references to complaints about the problem of courthouse time in child support, wife maintenance, paternity affiliation, and child custody cases. The problem of "time as money" emerged explicitly as women complained about taking time off work, spending bus fare to get to the court, and waiting hours for their cases to be heard. Moreover, as LaFont points out, class differences can have a profound impact on litigants' interactions with court personnel: "The court staff is predominantly middle class, with the top of the court hierarchy being upper-middle or upper class, so a class difference is operative in the interactions between court users and court employees, who think little of asking someone to wait for an hour or more or to return the following day. Disgruntled patrons have no options except to accept the system" (1996:71–72). To cite an American example: "In Massachusetts, access to the court is controlled by the clerk, who has discretionary power to allow or deny applications by citizens or by police for the issuance of a warrant or summons" (Yngvesson 1994:139). In other words, Courthouse Time can sometimes mean there will be no court time.[9]

Women who take their troubles to the courts in India find much to complain about with respect to Courthouse Time. Vatuk points out, "I have ample evidence that the women with whom I spoke are impatient with the way counseling is carried out in the courts, that they resent the time and money spent coming to court month after month, sitting for hours, on the floor, without water or toilet facilities, while they wait, often only in order to hear that they should come back again next month. They often distrust the intentions of the police, lawyers, judges and other staff of the family court who hold such power over their lives" (2001:242). In short, Courthouse Time references multiple persons, processes, and procedures. It begins with the filing of a case and continues when the police issue summons to alleged abusers.

Police Time

Once a request for a protection order is filed, the respondent must be notified to appear to answer the charges. This involves Police Time, which begins when a constable searches for the named party to give him a summons. In my experience, Police Time causes major delays in the processing of domestic violence cases (see also Trinidad and Tobago Coalition Against Domestic Violence 2005:59). Some of this is not their fault. As is the case in rural Kentucky (Websdale 1998:xxix), the police are overworked and underpaid—and sometimes they are working without adequate transportation and with bad addresses. On the other hand, the situation in Trinidad is not unlike that of Jamaica, where complainants often have trouble getting defendants served for reasons other than a faulty address: "If the baby-father [child's father] has friends at the local police station (and this is not rare) the police often 'misplace' his summons or insure that he is short-served, meaning if he does not show up he is not in disobedience because the proper prior notice was not given. Policemen are notoriously difficult to bring affiliation or maintenance suits against because of police force solidarity" (LaFont 1996:85; see also Economic Commission for Latin America and the Caribbean 2003:5; Hadeed 2003:189–90). In the United States, Websdale has referred to this practice as "knowing the man" (1998:105).

One result of the police "knowing the man" is that when a complainant appears for the first hearing of her case, she will very likely find it is adjourned—and generally for two weeks. Thus, Police Time regularly results in applicants' first appearances in court being a waste of time. Police Time also gives defendants time to continue their harassment and to try to talk applicants into dropping the charges.

In the United States, some police urge victims of domestic violence to go to court to obtain a restraining order, but others avoid taking action against perpetrators of domestic violence *until* victims have obtained an order (Ptacek 1999:161). Dissatisfaction with the police because of their unwillingness to arrest, victim blaming, and minimization of abuse were common complaints by court users in Ptacek's study of two urban courts in Massachusetts (1999:162) and in Websdale's study of the justice system in rural Kentucky (1998:chapter 4). On occasion, however, Police Time may include the time during which an officer decides to take a matter into his own hands, generally in an offer to find the alleged abuser and to warn him that his actions have the attention of the authorities. I heard about this practice from several interviewees and the same practice has been documented in Chennai, India.[10]

Finally, a component of Police Time has to do with their appearances as witnesses. Some constables show up for hearings and trials, but matters in other courts, vacations, and sick days are causes for further delays. In all of these ways, Police Time has also been a problem for victims of domestic abuse in Great Britain (Dobash and Dobash 1979:98), St. Kitts and Nevis, and Barbados (Spooner 2001:174). Respondent Time both precedes and follows Police Time.

Respondent Time

Respondent Time, as I have already noted, is partially constructed by Police Time because alleged abusers need not respond to charges until they receive an official summons. Trinidadian men successfully avoid summonses in very creative ways: they move, they go off island, they don't show up at work, and they work deals with the officers who are supposed to serve them. Moreover, like their counterparts in Jamaica: "Young men often have several places they can 'cotch' (stay temporarily). Once they hear that a summons is going to be served they can simply 'cotch' with someone else for awhile. Male solidarity at the work place often means if the man realizes he is going to be served, he can deny his identity and no one is likely to come forward and say otherwise" (LaFont 1996:84–85).

If the accused is a police officer, there will undoubtedly be problems—first trying to get him served and later prosecuting the case. Women complained to me about this in Trinidad and in Antigua, but it is also common in Chicago. Wittner's description of the plight of "Bonnie Jordan" is not unusual:

> Bonnie was the former wife of Don Jordan, a suburban police officer. She had come to court to charge Don with a violation of an order for protection. Twice before, despite an order of protection already in force, her husband had threatened her, slashed her tires, and once, in front of two police officers, he had pushed Bonnie in the chest as she was coming out of the courtroom.
>
> Each of these times Bonnie had brought and then dropped charges. Now she was here again because Don had threatened her with a gun. This time there were no witnesses and Tom Klein, the assistant state's attorney assigned to her case, wanted Bonnie to drop the charges. Bonnie reported, "He said it's hard because [my husband] is a police officer." (1998:97)

Like some defendants called to appear in the lower criminal courts in the United States, some Trinidadians accused of domestic violence decide not to appear in court because prior knowledge about how the court operates has taught them that the chances that the police will come after them are slim. As we have seen, the police in Pelau failed to locate quite a few men. Others forget the court date, leave the court before their cases are called, or misunderstand that the lunch hour is simply a recess. Finally, defendants are encouraged not to appear by the court's general leniency toward nonappearance itself (Feeley 1979:226–27, 232).

While they are waiting for their hearings, respondents to charges of domestic violence in Trinidad plead with their partners to drop the case. They promise the violence will never happen again, ask for second chances, and declare their love for their families. Sometimes they threaten to or actually physically harm the applicant or her children if she proceeds, a phenomenon Mahoney (1991) named "separation assault." Once they appear in court, respondents employ tactics to postpone cases, such as asking for time to obtain counsel, offering doctors' and lawyers' notes requesting adjournments, and pleading not guilty so that the magistrate will set a date for trial, only then to confess their guilt. As Ewick and Silbey argue, taking time, or taking *one's time,* operate as forms of resistance: ". . . foot-dragging is less of a refusal (to pay, or act, or work) than it is an assertion of some level of autonomy in the course of complying" (1998:215, 216). In this situation, taking time provides alleged abusers with considerable control of the case. If one or both parties obtain counsel, the dialectics of agency shifts again and the case entails Lawyer Time.

Lawyer Time

Lawyer Time can sometimes result in speeding up the time it takes to process a case. For example, one of my interviewees told me that she first went to court alone but when her case was postponed on two occasions, she hired an attorney. Having done so, her case proceeded quickly and she obtained a protection order. Moreover, on any given day, as a matter of professional courtesy, magistrates call first the cases involving attorneys. That allows the lawyers to attend to their clients and then frees them to go on to other business. Litigants who are unrepresented, in contrast, await their turn on the list. A host of competing factors and interests, however, complicates Lawyer Time. Attorneys request adjournments in domestic violence cases for several reasons. First, most lawyers practice in both the magistrates' courts and the High Courts, which hear "serious" matters. Cases at the High Courts always take priority. Therefore, if there is a conflict in his schedule, an attorney obtains an adjournment of the matter in the magistrate's court. Attorneys also ask for adjournments to take time to prepare the case, to find witnesses, and to try to resolve the matter outside the court. It is considered "good form" by both attorneys and magistrates to give both sides adjournments for reasonable excuses such as the failure of a witness to appear, a death in the complainant's family, or a lawyer's scheduled vacation.

Moreover, as Blumberg pointed out for the American case, a lawyer "has far greater professional, economic, intellectual and other ties to the various elements of the court system than he does to his own client" (1967:21). Members of any court depend on each other's reliability. And because so much of a lawyer's work is intangible, judges and other attorneys permit performances in the courtroom and delays in case processing that convince clients of their need for their attorneys and of the value of their fees (Blumberg 1967:25).[11] In the case of an attorney whose client has been charged with domestic violence, delay can be a deliberate strategy: "Time allows wounds to heal, and complainants who may come to court for their first appearance on crutches, or who may have been altogether unable to come to court because they were in the hospital, may recover fully by the time the case comes up again. Delay not only provides an opportunity for defendants to make themselves look better, it also puts distance between the incident and the defendant which diminishes the seriousness of the event in the eyes of the complainant and the court" (Feeley 1979:174). Thus Lawyer Time is partly a function of the convenience of the lawyer and other members of the court, but it is also sometimes a deliberate strategy of an abuser's defense. That defense will undergo scrutiny if the case includes Probation Time.

Probation Time

Probation officers in Trinidad are appointed by the government to serve as social welfare agents. Among other things, they listen to couples whose marriages are failing, parents whose sons and daughters have turned to drugs and away from school, couples who want to adopt a child, and neighbors who are quarreling over property boundaries. In Port of Spain the probation officers have separate offices, but in other districts they are housed in a room at the courthouse. Probation officers provide free counseling on a "first come, first served" basis. Parties therefore wait an uncertain amount of time before they can be seen. Probation Time figures into a case if the parties seek counseling or if the magistrate wants a probation officer's report. Alternatively, parties are given an appointment for counseling at National Family Services. Ironically, the time couples actually spend in counseling is very brief—usually only one or two sessions—because of the great shortage of probation officers and social workers. There were fewer than thirty full-time probation officers in Trinidad in 1998 and their caseloads were remarkably long. One probation officer I interviewed in Pelau estimated that she saw forty people a day. Besides taking court referrals, she spent her time counseling, making home visits, and writing reports. Disputed child custody cases constituted a significant part of her workload, but other familial problems, including domestic violence and uncontrollable juveniles, were also commonplace. Another probation officer who worked in a more rural district consulted her records for me. In 1996 the court had referred seventy cases of domestic violence to her for investigation; that number rose to 153 in 1997. Those figures do not include clients who drop by the office on her days "on call." With such heavy caseloads, probation officers cannot possibly devote long periods of time to any individual or family. Counseling services for clients are also disrupted because of the government's policy of occasionally shifting probation officers from one district to another. This policy checks corruption, but it doesn't help those who need long-term counseling. Thus, when a magistrate asks for a probation officer's report, Probation Time includes the time it takes to schedule appointments for interviews, time for the officer to write the report, time for the typist to type it, time for the magistrate to read it, time to reschedule the case, and then more time to reach a judgment.

A similar situation exists for probation officers working for the juvenile courts in the United States:

> Once a finding of delinquency has been made, the court must decide on disposition. In this it relies heavily on the probation officer's report, which is derived from his initial interview and outlines briefly the delinquent's background, general behavior, family situation, and school record. Where a case appears sufficiently clear-cut, this information will be adequate, and the probation officer makes a recommendation for disposing of the case, almost always probation. . . . However, when confronted by some problem or difficulty, the probation officer will request that disposition be postponed until he has had an opportunity to make a more thorough investigation of the case. This may require contacting other agencies involved in the case, visiting the home and parents, calling upon relatives, and/or making a variety of arrangements upon which a desired disposition will be contingent, such as gaining the youth's admittance into a special program or a boarding school. (Emerson 1969:9–10)

The involvement of a probation officer in a case thus has paradoxical consequences: it entails formal attention to "trouble" at the same time that it most certainly postpones immediate legal action.

Evidence from Barbados suggests that the state's failure to provide immediate institutional support contributes to the ineffectiveness of domestic violence legislation there: "Welfare department staff are overworked and can hardly accommodate additional clients sent to them for counseling when magistrates in Barbados comply with the mandatory counseling aspect of the domestic violence legislation. Often the system does not track offenders so that some offenders never receive the required counseling and remain at risk of re-abusing their partners" (Spooner 2001:172–73).

In Jamaica, Counseling Time, as opposed to Probation Time, plays a significant role in the outcome of family cases at the Family Court. Couples are given the opportunity to resolve their differences without formally entering the legal process. However: "The basic tenet of most counselors is to keep the relationship together, at whatever cost" (LaFont 1996:84). In short, depending on the particularities of the case, Probation Time or Counseling Time has a decided influence on the time it takes to get that case before a judge.

Magistrate Time

Finally, there is Magistrate Time. Magistrates are aware of the urgency of domestic violence cases, but they simply can't hear all of them. Therefore, decisions have to be made to reduce the caseload. One way is to dismiss the case if the complainant does not appear in court. In some instances, this automatic dismissal occurs after a complainant has already appeared on several occasions. Magistrates also speed things up by hearing immediately those cases in which men agree to give undertakings in which they confess to their violent language or behaviors and agree not to engage in future violence. As we saw from the court records in Pelau, cases involving undertakings proceed relatively rapidly to final disposition. Occasionally magistrates protect complainants who are in fear for their lives by issuing immediately interim orders that can be made ex parte (without the defendant present). Whether or not an interim order case will proceed to trial will likely depend on the complainant's next move. In other cases, of course, Magistrate's Time includes very time-consuming cases involving charges and cross-charges, witnesses, and competing attorneys. In those situations, magistrates do their best to urge attorneys to come to some resolution without a public hearing, but they are not always successful. Moreover, some defendants demand their day in court (e.g., Blumberg 1967; Conley and O'Barr 1990; Feeley 1979; Merry 1990). On the other hand, as I witnessed on a number of occasions, a complainant, defendant, or attorney who gets on a magistrate's nerves can find his or her case adjourned on the grounds that "there's no time today." Magistrates can take over time, too, as a form of impression management for an audience that includes the general public, other legal professionals, or the litigants before the bench. As Emerson commented: "The institution is very truly 'his court'" (1969:12).

In some instances, as in Hilo, Hawaii, judges organize their time to prioritize the most violent cases: "The Family Court judge's concerns are twofold: first, to stop the violence and, second, to protect the children involved. . . . He defines his task as preventing the parties from killing each other rather than finding out what the underlying issues are. There is not enough time to handle the cases that way, and his objective is to prevent violence and threats and to protect any children in the family" (Merry 1994:47).

In sum, then, at multiple points in the process of filing an application for a protection order, litigants encounter various parties who control time in ways that thwart or obstruct their ability to win the protection that the state has made available "on the books." I turn next to three representative case histories of women who applied for protection orders, but then dropped their complaints largely because of the problem of time.

It's All in the Timing

For all of the women in my study, including the cases I describe here, Applicant Time was extensive; each woman spent months or years talking to the abuser, trying to convince him to change his ways. Most women also asked family members to intervene on their behalf. A few made an effort to get counseling. Once they had made the decision to file a complaint, all of the women experienced the effects of "being on hold." On the one hand, the women recounted disabling circumstances that involved different actors in the criminal justice system. On the other hand, their stories shared a common characteristic: more than one player at more than one point in the process combined to discourage the applicant and caused her to drop her case.

For example, for more than fifteen years "Marie" had been a victim of constant emotional and verbal abuse from her husband, "Derrick." They had met in college and married with the approval of both of their families. Derrick worked for a government ministry and Marie was a social worker. To the outside world, they were an educated, respectable, middle-class couple who had built a comfortable home on land that Derrick inherited from his father. They had three handsome and intelligent sons. But Derrick was a possessive and jealous person. He did not like it when Marie went out unless it was to go to work or to a family gathering. When he became angry or jealous, he would hit her. He reserved for himself the privileges of attending cricket matches and "liming" (hanging out) with his friends, both male and female. Marie became depressed and her self-esteem suffered whenever she encountered signs of Derrick's "indiscretions." She stopped accusing him of infidelities because he always reacted to such charges by beating her, and usually in front of the children. Marie hid from the extended family what was going on at home. Occasionally she talked with a few supportive friends and once she spoke to an attorney she had known at school. Everyone advised her to work out the problems in the marriage without recourse to the law.

A particularly abusive event finally caused Marie to file for a protection order. Immediately after he was served the summons, Derrick became enraged. He screamed and cursed at her. Marie fled to the bedroom, locked the door, and called the police. Then she ran from the house. Derrick locked her out, a symbolic gesture she found very humiliating. When the police arrived, Derrick let them into the house while she remained in the street. Marie does not know what they said to him. They left a short time later without taking any official action. Derrick let her back into the house and acted sorrowful and apologetic. Over the course of the week before the court hearing, he promised to mend his ways and persuaded her to drop the case. Marie told me she stayed in the marriage for the sake of the children. Applicant Time, Police Time, and Respondent Time caused her to withdraw her case for a protection order. Subsequently, she left Trinidad for a few weeks, traveling in Canada to visit family and friends.

When I interviewed Marie about a year later, her relationship with Derrick had improved. Marie attributed the new, more peaceful coexistence between them to three causes: (1) her application to the court; (2) the call to the police; and (3) her serious threat to divorce him. Derrick admitted to Marie that he was frightened of the police and the courts. This accords with my earlier argument that some men's fear of the police and of going to jail keeps them from engaging in more violence. In addition, Marie knew that her threat to divorce him undermined Derrick's identity as a happily married, middle-class man who was expecting to eventually educate his children abroad. Derrick is of a generation in which divorce is unacceptable; it would be a great disgrace for him if his wife left him.

A second interviewee, "Sally," cited the slowness of the police in delivering a summons to "Richard," her husband, the magistrate's continuances of her cases, Richard's pleas to her to drop her charges, and finally "divine intervention" as the reasons why she eventually withdrew from the legal process in Port of Spain. Sally had married Richard at the age of eighteen, just after graduation. They had two children almost immediately. Richard drove a cab and Sally found a clerical job in a government ministry. Sally quickly learned that Richard had very traditional expectations about men's and women's work. Consequently, he never helped out with the cooking, housework, or the children. Her resentment about housework and child care increased over the years and they quarreled frequently. Richard was verbally and emotionally abusive and Sally often raised her voice to match his. To save money, Richard turned off the electricity in their house every evening. After a particularly nasty dispute, he decided not to let Sally use "his" washing machine. In retaliation, Sally refused to allow him to use "her" phone. Sometimes Richard came home drunk and he would curse and bang at the door of the room where Sally now slept with her daughters. She never opened the door. Eventually he would go to sleep, leaving one woman and two girls fearful and sleepless.

Like so many victims of domestic violence, Sally tried to seek help from a number of individuals and institutions. She spoke first to her family priest, but he advised her that she and Richard needed family counseling and Richard refused to cooperate. She then went to a Catholic charity organization for individual counseling. Those sessions strengthened her resolve to leave Richard as soon as she could manage financially. Sally also made several calls to the local police station to advise them of her situation. She never asked them to come to their home, but she told me that it comforted her to know that the officers were aware that she and the girls often feared for their safety. A good friend offered sage advice and occasionally tried to mediate quarrels between the couple—until Richard put an end to that friendship. After that, Sally went to Legal Aid to find out what options she might have if she filed for divorce. Bumping into an old friend who had become a lawyer gave her another way to obtain some free legal advice. The years passed. Sally now had her teenage daughters' support to leave Richard, but this continued to be impossible for financial reasons.

Then a fortunate incident happened. Sally's uncle got an important job overseas. Sally had always been a favorite niece and her uncle decided to give her some furniture and his ancient car. These gifts meant she could move. It took another few months to find an affordable apartment in a location near work and a good school for the girls.

Sally and her daughters moved surreptitiously—small box by small box. Richard came home from work early one day just as a friend's truck was being loaded with the last and heaviest of their things. Richard was furious and demanded the return of some items he said were his property, including two gifts he had given Sally for Christmas years ago. Sally returned everything he wanted; she was afraid he would become physically abusive if she did not. Ironically, Richard called the police to the scene as the truck was about to depart. He wanted them to make a report stating that Sally had left the home filthy and in great disarray. He was documenting her failure as a housewife in case she filed for divorce.

Sally told me she bought phone cards for her daughters as soon as they moved. She felt it was important for them to be in touch with their father and she urged them to phone him often. She and Richard worked out an arrangement so that he could see them several times a week. He paid their school fees and purchased things for them, but he refused to give Sally any child support. From Sally's perspective, Richard desperately wanted them all to move back and therefore he would show up unexpectedly and phone repeatedly. The visits and phone calls caused her severe stress and they were becoming a problem at work. Sally emphasized to me that she decided to ask for a protection order not because Richard was a violent person, but because she wanted him to stay away from her home and office and to stop calling her.[12]

Sally first went to court in February 1998. A clerk asked her questions and then advised her to also request maintenance for the two children. She took that advice. The three cases were set for the following week.

Sally learned at the first hearing that Richard had not yet received a summons to appear in court. The morning of the second hearing, she saw Richard on the street in clothes inappropriate for court and found that he still knew nothing about the case. (His summons would finally reach him two days after the second hearing.) She advised him that he was expected in court that morning. He was stunned, but he got to court before the case was called. He told the magistrate that he had not been officially summoned and that he wanted a lawyer. The magistrate concurred and set a new court date for two weeks later. Richard arrived with an attorney for the next hearing, but the magistrate did not have time to proceed. Two weeks later, Sally and Richard were both in court, but his lawyer was not. Richard did not know why. The magistrate adjourned the cases again. She inquired if Sally wanted to get an attorney. Sally replied she would proceed alone.

Meanwhile, Richard continued to call Sally to plead with her to drop the cases. He despaired that she was publicly branding him as a violent person, a wife-beater, and an irresponsible parent. At this point, however, he was willing to pay child support. Sally considered her options. She explained to me that she wanted a tolerable relationship with Richard—one that would be of greatest benefit to their children. She wanted to be able to phone him if she needed help with child care or if some unexpected bill suddenly showed up, but she also needed relief from his daily calls and frequent visits to her home and office.

Early in May, Richard's lawyer said he was ready to proceed with the domestic violence matter. The magistrate scheduled the case to be tried in the middle of the month. Without representation, Sally took the stand to explain why she had brought a case for a protection order. Her central concern was to keep Richard away from her home and office. She answered the magistrate's questions and was then cross-examined by Richard's attorney, an experience she described as one that twisted the story she was trying to tell. For example, the attorney brought to the court's attention the fact that once when Richard was ill Sally had offered to come over to the house to cook for him. He suggested that no one who feared for her safety would make such an offer. Sally protested that she would have done that for anyone who was a friend and who was ill. The case was adjourned after her cross-examination.

Then a tragedy occurred—Richard's mother died unexpectedly. Richard begged Sally again to drop the case for the protection order. Sally felt

sympathy for Richard and his family, with whom she had always shared
an affectionate relationship. How could she prosecute him when he was
burying his mother? She described to me what had happened as "divine
intervention" of the saddest nature. Sally's decision to withdraw her
case was a consequence of Police Time, Lawyer Time, Magistrate Time,
and, especially, Respondent Time. She told me she had begun to feel
very guilty about the case and she was worried about how much time
she was taking from work. When she next appeared in court, therefore,
Sally entered the witness stand to formally withdraw her request for
a protection order. In turn, Richard agreed to monthly child support.
Months later, Sally and Richard had reached an amiable relationship. He
stopped calling and showing up unexpectedly and he paid his child support on time. He also saw his children several times a week. Thus, over
time Sally found she was no longer in need of a formal protection order,
but there is no doubt that her involvement in the legal process procured
for her freedom from harassment and regular support for her children.

To cite one last case history, "Lynn," a homemaker with two small
children who tried to obtain a court order against her abusive husband,
told me this about her first court experience:

> I brought those charges against him for the restraining order and I went
> to court and you know we were living in the same house at the time. I
> did not get any cooperation from the police because, number one, they
> took very long to serve the summons so that he could come to court.
> And I was living in the house with him. It put me in a very sticky, a very
> difficult position. And he went and make friends with the police officers
> and thing. They were like his friends. When he finally got the summons
> and he came to court, now the magistrate keep putting off the case. . . .
> The case get put off about six times and I just leave it. I just dismiss it
> and did not bother.

Lynn came from a working-class family. They moved often, and she
attended several different primary and secondary schools. She did not
graduate because she became pregnant in her senior year. She parted
with the baby's father even before the child's birth. A series of poorly
paid jobs, including babysitting, restaurant cashier, and piecework in a
garment factory, followed in quick succession. When she met Rodney
she was eighteen years old, unhappy at home, caring for a baby, and fairly
desperate financially. Rodney was a working-class artisan who owned
his own home and body shop. She moved in with him, and they married
formally when she discovered she was pregnant. Violent on occasion
early in their relationship, Rodney became increasingly emotionally and
physically abusive over time. He disliked it when she left the house to

go anywhere, although he had no qualms about bringing in other women when she was out. He refused to allow her to continue her education or to work. When she went to court for a protection order, Lynn found the police, her husband, and the magistrate controlled time to her disadvantage. Police Time, Respondent Time, and Magistrate Time caused her to drop her initial domestic violence case.

About a year after first bringing her husband to court, however, Lynn succeeded in her mission to gain a protection order against him. By this time she had moved back to her father's house, a divorce was in progress, and she had secured a job as a secretary. Despite their separation, Rodney deliberately continued to provoke her: "He would come by my house and harass me. He would want to give my landlady, the landlord, money, so they could spy on me and inform him of what is happening home by me. He would harass everybody who comes by me, male. He came and took my daughter. He came a day and took her and said he was not bringing her back. And I left him with her and eventually he took me to court for legal custody."

An extremely vindictive person, Rodney sued Lynn for custody of their daughter—which he won.[13] He then transferred the little girl to his mother's home and care. Two years later, when his mother became ill, he begged Lynn to resume responsibility for their daughter. She regained physical custody of the child, although it was unclear to me as to whether legal custody had been transferred.

Why did Lynn return to court and succeed in gaining a protection order? First, experience taught Lynn what she faced in pursuing a domestic violence case. She expected the lawsuit to take considerable time, as it did. Participation in the legal process turned out to be very different from what she had initially imagined, but experience gave her important skills in seeking the justice she desired (see also Merry 1990:170, 180). Second, Rodney's harassment was persistent and it frustrated Lynn's efforts to get on with her life. It had been impossible to pursue a new relationship because Rodney was constantly present. Third, there was another magistrate on the bench whose attitude to domestic violence cases was decidedly feminist. He immediately sent the case to the probation officer for a report. Lynn and Rodney met with the probation officer at the courthouse. During that meeting Rodney emphatically denied any abusive words or actions—denials that made the probation officer question his truthfulness. Subsequently, she advised the magistrate that Lynn should have a protection order. This support gave Lynn an advocate in the criminal justice system. At the next hearing, the magistrate ordered that Rodney stay away from Lynn's home, workplace, and person.

Frightened by the order and of the police, Rodney mostly stayed away. Occasionally he used the excuse of seeing his daughter as a reason to come to their house. When he became angry about something he would "throw words," but he did not otherwise abuse her while the order was in effect. When I interviewed Lynn, her year-long protection order had just expired. She was biding her time to see if Rodney would remain on good behavior or if it would become necessary to go back to court.

In each of these stories about filing an application for protection in the magistrate's court, survivors contended with covert forms of domination that included having their cases postponed and hearing the message that the crimes committed against them were not serious enough to warrant immediate attention. For the most part, however, litigants reconstructed these experiences as idiosyncratic personal problems for which there was no remedy, rather than as structured processes of domination. I suggest, however, that the management of time in these cases contributes to the process of structural deflection that keeps already marginalized individuals and groups—in this case mostly women—from experiencing full and thus timely protection under the Domestic Violence Act.

Conclusion

As Greenhouse notes: "Time is about many things, but it is always ironic; it always implies that there is meaning beyond lived experience that nevertheless constitutes a commentary on lived experience" (1989:1632). Thus far, domestic violence scholarship has missed the meaning, centrality, and complexity of time's influence in the processing of domestic violence cases. My research demonstrates that when victims of domestic abuse refer to the problem of time, they are referencing multiple and often intertwined processes and encounters with different actors in the criminal justice system. While on paper Trinidad's Domestic Violence Act promises speedy redress for victims of abuse, in practice, domestic violence suits face lengthy adjournments. Over time, these adjournments combine to erode the sense of entitlement to be free from violence that initially engages litigants. Thus, like French, I have found that time is "both a relationship between people and a mechanism for ordering experience" (2001:695). The conscious and unconscious manipulation of time by various players in the criminal justice system makes it possible, even probable, that, in practice, formal legal protection from violence will be obtained only in a small percentage of cases. Moreover, dependency on law and the courts clearly places a litigant in a precarious and subordinate position—precisely because the dependency entails so much time, so many players, and so many processes. As we have seen in this and earlier chapters, women drop their complaints because they tire of the numerous continuances of their cases and because they are worn down by their abusers. Over time, these encounters erode the sense of agency and entitlement that bring complainants to court in the first place. In effect, they operate to return the momentary public face of domestic abuse back into the private space of family. The policy implications are therefore clear: we must address the ways in which different combinations of actors and their respective senses and uses of time figure into the litigation process. Without such attention, structural deflection will ensure that the regendered state will remain regendered in name but not in practice. The case of Trinidad thus contributes to our understanding of the degree to which law can operate as a liberating factor in postcolonial states at the same time that it renders visible the practical limitations of law.

6 Cultures of Reconciliation

"She told the magistrate she didn't want to send him
to jail or anything, and she didn't want to break up her
family. But she wanted him to stop all the abuse."

—notes following an interview with a woman whose
husband signed an undertaking

"I tell them to behave yourself and be at peace and don't
come back here. Just live in peace. You have one life to
live. Give them a little synopsis of what is life, because
they patch up and their parents might intervene and
things like that."

—notes from a taped interview with a magistrate

I have explored the ways in which court rites and the factor
of time pervade formal legal processes and dissuade women and some
men from going to the courts for protection orders or from pressing their
claims once in court. As we have seen, cases exit the legal system when
litigants are intimidated, humiliated, or silenced. Petitions for protection
are dismissed or withdrawn when complaints are delegalized, violence is
euphemized, victims get erroneous advice or instructions, or a magistrate
presides over a trial and finds the evidence does not meet the literal terms
and requirements of the Domestic Violence Act. It is clear, too, that time
is not a simple matter of delayed court dockets or scarce resources, but
is itself a form of power wielded in different ways by various actors to
manage or manipulate a case. Time changes the relationships between
applicants and defendants, as well as between litigants and officers of
the court, and it realigns positions of domination and subordination.

Court rites and time also influence the operation of agency and structure in courts. As court rites and time unfold and intertwine with cumulative effects, they change both the agency of litigants during their encounters with legal officials and the agency of those officers of the court. In each encounter, a party's purpose and power may be accepted, mitigated, or denied, but always negotiated. Simultaneously, participants face the structures of statutory law and legal procedures, as well as the structural constraints imposed by bureaucracy, as they try to strengthen their cases to their own advantage or to accomplish "success" in ways that may, but need not, include a formal protection order.

By themselves, however, neither court rites nor time sufficiently explain the statistical records that appear in chapter 2. Pelau's court records show almost 57 percent of all applications for protection orders are dismissed, about 21 percent are withdrawn, 19 percent are resolved through undertakings, and fewer than 3 percent are resolved by interim or final orders. To more comprehensively account for those numbers, this chapter explores extralegal ideas and practices that profoundly influence the meaning and consequences of taking a domestic violence case to court. In Trinidad, widely held beliefs about "family," "gender," and how people "make their living"[1] differentiate for most citizens "private" from "public" business. They guide as well what persons and forums are deemed appropriate to contact when there is "trouble."

In analyzing the ways in which these concepts are articulated and practiced, I do not claim to speak as an authoritative voice on Trinidadian families. I have instead a more modest goal—to understand why domestic violence disputes take the turns they do. Relying on my interviewees, my ethnographic experiences, and literature and research by Caribbean scholars, I posit the presence in Trinidad of a powerful "culture of reconciliation."[2] In coining the more general phrase *cultures of reconciliation,* I intend to point to ideas about family, gender, and work that intersect to keep men and women from court in Trinidad and in other places heir to the British common-law tradition. This allows for a cross-cultural comparative anthropology, denied in the postmodernist turn in the discipline (Kuper 1999:223), while retaining an appreciation for historically informed local knowledge and practice. In Trinidad, the culture of reconciliation has a long historical tradition, rooted in British colonialism, in which churches, schools, and law promoted a "Christian" perspective with respect to the duties and obligations of husbands and wives. In that tradition, the state intervenes in family life in limited circumstances. That history continues to influence not only the thinking and practice of today's laymen but, importantly, also that of the contemporary court staff, lawyers, and magistrates. As we saw in chapter 1, Trinidadian lawmakers who drafted and debated the nation's first Domestic Violence Act felt the weight of a culture of reconciliation, particularly in the decision to give an alleged abuser a second chance "to behave" (properly) in the form of an undertaking.[3]

A culture of reconciliation places enormous pressure on parties to a familial dispute to settle their differences *without* legal redress. It therefore acts as a filtering process and works against the probability that a domestic violence case will remain within the legal system. Like court rites and the effects of time, a culture of reconciliation encourages structural deflection, the situation in which formal legal rights such as protection from violence mask informal hegemonic practices that promulgate and buttress existing structures of hierarchy and obstruct peoples' opportunities to acquire the legal rights that lawmakers intended (Pierce 1996).

In the first section of this chapter, I explore what my interviewees and participant observation taught me about family, gender, and making a living in Trinidad. As I demonstrate, each construct has implications for understanding family trouble as a private matter, thus rendering public courts as mostly inappropriate sites for resolving kinship disputes.[4] The unchallenged assumption that women are primarily responsible for taking care of the emotional and physical needs of children also plays an important role in determining what women feel they can do about the violence in their lives. So, too, do the assumptions that children need their fathers and that family stability is ideal. Another important presupposition is that parents have the right to instruct and discipline their children, and sometimes even after they marry. My findings resonate with those of Trinidadian and other scholars working in nearby Caribbean states that share Trinidad's history of extended British colonialism and associated legal forms and forums.

In the second part of the chapter, I suggest that just as court rites and timing can be identified in a diverse array of common-law lower courts, so may cultures of reconciliation exercise considerable influence on the outcomes of claims to rights in other times and places. I am hardly the first to point out that efforts to keep family matters private are widespread. Research in U.S., Indian, and Israeli courts, for example, points both to the operation of powerful pressures exerted by a multitude of actors to reconcile familial conflicts outside of legal arenas, as well as to the chilling effects of such coercive measures on women's abilities to garner legal rights and protection from violence. Cross-culturally, cultures of reconciliation share some broad, common themes; they differ, of course, in their details, combinations of ideas and practices, players, and power to persuade actors from using the courts. These common themes interest me the most because my purpose is to better understand the uses and consequences of domestic violence laws and the experiences of litigants in courts. I suggest that along with court rites and the factor of time, cultures of reconciliation account for why domestic violence laws, and laws in general, so often bring such little relief to the parties they are designed to assist and protect. I begin with the case of Trinidad.

Being Family, Doing Gender, and Making a Living in the Caribbean

The kinship patterns of Trinidad's two largest ethnic groups, Afro-Trinidadians and Indo-Trinidadians, varied historically with respect to the ages when people married; whether they adopted visiting, common-law, or legal unions; the size of their family; concerns about the legitimacy of children; and patterns of residency.[5] In 1970, for example, Bell described the kinship patterns of lower-class Afro-Trinidadians as "female-centered with late marriages (when marriage occurs), low value placed on the interpersonal nature of marriage, and with minimal concern about the legitimacy of offspring" (cited in Barrow 1996:356). Afro-Trinidadians commonly resided in households spanning three generations of women whose partners might not reside within that household. More recently, Chevannes confirms the pattern: "For the African Caribbean peoples, the fact that conjugal bonds are established without formal rituals is not to say that they are not culturally sanctioned. Statistical data from the censuses for all the African Caribbean islands confirm what our ethnography and group discussions reveal, namely that the majority of first children are born to parents in a visiting union, despite its non-recognition by the state and the church" (2001:215–16).

In sharp contrast, Indo-Trinidadians were once described as "patriarchal, with great importance attached to early, arranged marriages and the legitimization of offspring" (Bell cited in Barrow 1996:356). Indo-Trinidadian families arranged the early marriages of their children and encouraged sons to remain in or near the family home. Young women married into the households of their husbands and worked under the critical eyes of their mothers-in-law. Families were organized along fairly strict patriarchal lines (e.g., Angrosino 1996:383–96; Chevannes 2001: chapter 4; Mohammed 2002a:chapter 7).

More recent studies, however, suggest that all Trinidadians are marrying later in life, their families are smaller, fewer children are illegitimate, nuclear family households are considered ideal, and more women are employed (Barrow 1996; Chevannes 2001; Yelvington 1996). While

parents of Indo-Trinidadians continue to play an important role in se-
lecting marriage partners for their children, few marriages are arranged
without the consent of the young couple as they once were in the past.
Indo-Trinidadian couples establish their first residency in the homes
of the man's parents less frequently or they do so for shorter periods of
time. Education, urbanization, and modernization are changing family
life in both ethnic communities (e.g., Barrow 1996, 1998; Chevannes
2001; Miller 1994; Momsen 1993; Munasinghe 2001; Vertovec 1992).
Not surprisingly, attitudes toward interracial marriages are liberal (St. ,
Bernard 1999).

Trinidadians are thus accustomed to a diversity of marital, kinship,
and household forms. As Munasinghe summarizes it, the "fundamental
point" is that "Caribbean peoples' behaviors continuously resist any neat
analytic compartmentalization that cannot entertain a notion of duality
or multiplicity" (2001:159).[6] Throughout the nation, people are attuned to
the changes that have come about as the economy expanded in the 1970s,
public education became readily available, women moved into the labor
market, reproductive health care improved, and changes in technology
gave people access to local and global events. These economic, political,
and social processes have influenced deeply how people conceptualize
and practice family life, how they experience gender, and where and what
they work at to make a living. These processes have also had important,
and sometimes contradictory, effects on peoples' uses of law.

Beliefs about family, gender, and work in Trinidad contribute to a
shared culture of reconciliation—one that crosses class, racial, ethnic,
and religious lines, even if some differences in family forms, gender relations, and work patterns exist between these groups. The operation
and consequences of Trinidad's culture of reconciliation are captured
repeatedly in the work of local writers and intellectuals. A recent short
story by Kanhai about "Dolly" entitled "Rum Sweet Rum" resonates
well with descriptions given to me in interviews with Indo-Trinidadians.
Kanhai writes, "The first time he beat her it was because she did not
respond quickly enough when he asked her to heat up some water for
him to bathe. She was shocked and left and went home to her mother
and father. They listened to her, sympathized, gave her a meal and sent
her back with a few dollars. They told her, 'Go back and make a living.
Is your husband, is your luck'" (1999:8).

The instructions to "Go back and make a living. Is your husband,
is your luck" encode multiple meanings. Dolly made her living working terribly hard at manual and domestic labor, in her own home and in
others, with little thanks and for little pay. She also lived her life in an

East Indian community in which "family" was constituted in particular ways, in ways that put the collective needs of the group before those of any individual, and that put the needs of men before those of women (see also Parsad 1999). Once people marry, their families are expected to remain intact. Divorce remains an uncommon option in Trinidad. A 1998 national survey of family life, for example, found just 7.6 percent of male respondents and 6.6 percent of female respondents had experienced divorce (St. Bernard 1998:56).[7] In other words, if your husband is your "luck," then the die have been cast—maybe by the time you are sixteen or eighteen years old.[8]

In another insightful account, Hodge explains how Caribbean people differently conceptualize "family." "Husbands" may be more peripheral among Afro-Trinidadians (see Barrow 1996), but other adults often play significant roles:

> Discussions of family tend to focus mainly on its role of socializing children, reflecting the tradition of the Western nuclear family as an organization designed primarily to cater for the needs of children and of husbands. A Caribbean family, on the other hand, is as much an organization for the support of adults as for the rearing of children . . . older people, adolescents and unemployed or unattached adults traditionally were not cut loose to fend for themselves, and today Caribbean people, by and large still feel a deep sense of responsibility for such family members. (Hodge 2002:480)

A Caribbean scholar who conducted research on the processing of domestic violence cases by the police and the courts in Barbados and St. Kitts–Nevis reiterates the elasticity and inclusive character of West Indian families:

> While the Unites States' legislation reflects a society that is based on individual rights and privileges, the English-speaking Caribbean remains a society based on cultural beliefs that promote close kinship between extended family members. The nuclear family is the point of reference by United States courts in which family members are increasingly identifiable and separation of household members is therefore more easily achieved in the United States than it is in the English-speaking Caribbean. Kinship groups in the English-speaking Caribbean (many of whom need not be related by blood or marriage), provide important support networks in the absence of much needed support services by the state. (Spooner 2001:78)

In these families, making a living is often a collective enterprise in which there is rarely a single breadwinner. At the same time, one's responsibility to "family" may include a large number of persons, some of whom may reside in one's household while others reside elsewhere.

We are left with the interesting thought that for many Caribbean people, the combination of the meanings and experiences of "family," "gender," and "making a living" places them within a network of persons to whom they owe major responsibilities. I suggest that these responsibilities are essential to our understanding of why domestic violence cases so often exit the court system. I have argued that the right to go to court to claim that domestic violence is unacceptable is an empowering right—and one that is used every day by Trinidadian women across the country (see also Lazarus-Black 2001). By continuing a case, however, a woman exposes the people she loves to the consequences of legal intervention and the anger of the accused. She may stand to lose critical financial aid for herself, her children, or other members of the family in which she is ensconced. Moreover, a host of agents are likely to press her to keep out of court. There is family and community pressure throughout the Caribbean to resolve family violence informally (Clarke 1998:6) and general reluctance to interfere in family matters: ". . . families are encouraged to resolve the problem themselves. Problems such as intimate partner violence often become public only if families do not have enough resources to deal with it or if the violence becomes so uncontrollable that there is serious physical wounding. Families and their support groups such as churches therefore assume great significance in the lives of abused Caribbean women" (Spooner 2001:40).[9]

Writing about women of East Indian descent in Guyana, Parsad explains: "The majority of East Indian women who experience violence do not hit back or report to agencies of social control; they prefer to rely on the help of friends, relatives and religious officials to seek conciliatory measures to deal with the problem; they find it acceptable for a man to hit his wife under certain conditions; and they place a considerable measure of blame on themselves or the effects of alcohol on their husbands' behavior" (1999:46).

To cite one last example, Cameron-Padmore, director of the Population Programme Unit, reminded readers in the *Trinidad Express*, a Trinidadian local newspaper:

Despite the fact that 57% of our households are headed by single females, the two-parent family unit continues to be the ideal. Consequently, many feel that the family should stay together at all costs. A higher value is placed on the preservation of the unit rather than on the physical and emotional well-being of family members. There is also the belief that children need their father at home regardless of the quality of the relationship within those walls. The female victim of violence knows that she must stay for the children's sake especially as their father is not violent all the time. (*Trinidad Express*, November 26, 1992)

Who are the players involved in Trinidad's culture of reconciliation? As Cameron-Padmore suggests, many women feel a family should always stay together and they remain with abusive partners for the sake of the children. The point is supported by Colón and Reddock, who find that women's responsibility for the family and children have remained "practically unchallenged," despite contemporary changes in gender relations and new economic and political circumstances (2004:500). Men also talk their wives and girlfriends into dropping their applications for protection orders with promises to change their bad behavior or by agreeing to seek counseling. Sometimes they threaten or intimidate them, or vow to cut off financial support. Children, siblings, parents, grandparents, and other relatives also try to convince couples to keep their relationships intact—even if this occasionally means assisting the woman in her decision to obtain an undertaking from the court.

One woman I interviewed several times in 1997 and 1998, for example, had married her husband at a very young age, and their relationship had always been a stormy one. Over the course of their marriage, both "Shana" and "Ramesh" had had affairs. They remained married for the sake of their children, but over time Ramesh became increasingly abusive, particularly when he was drinking. When he was intoxicated, Ramesh found fault with everything Shana did; he cursed and threatened her and sometimes he punched and kicked her. If the quarrel was a particularly bad one, Shana would take temporary refuge with her brother and his wife, both of whom influenced powerfully for many years Shana's decisions about how to remedy the violence in her life.

Shana knew about the Domestic Violence Act from the newspapers and television. She told me that she went to court having no intention of breaking up her marriage—she just wanted Ramesh to sign a paper that he would not abuse her. Shana's brother helped her find an attorney and paid his fee. In court with his own lawyer, Ramesh agreed to sign an undertaking. Shana told me Ramesh sulked for a while when they got home from court, but there was peace in the house for a long time after their hearing. She was certain that the real reason for that was Ramesh's fear of what the police might do if he breached the undertaking. In any event, the undertaking inhibited Ramesh from further violence and (temporarily) preserved the marriage.[10]

Religion and religious authorities also promote a culture of reconciliation, as Hadeed discovered in her interviews with sixteen Afro-Trinidadian women (2003:130). Catholicism is widely practiced in Trinidad and priests routinely counsel married couples to resolve their differences. They cannot advocate divorce even when there is violence in the relationship. One attorney reported to me, however, that in his experience, fundamentalist Christians were most reluctant to use the courts: "Mainly the Pentecostals. . . . I suppose also because they feel the court is not a place of truth. And with the swearing on the bible and all that sort of thing. They don't like to come to court."[11] Members of the Hindu and Muslim communities may take their troubles to respected leaders—men and women who have earned reputations as sage advisors—instead of going to court. One such Hindu leader explained to me:

> My wife and I deal with a number of family disputes—newly married couples and so on. Deal with it right here [in the family home]. They believe that my wife and I can help. They come in here sometimes to see us. One will come and then [pause]. We also do some of the family discussion thing on the [Community Service Board]. When we have family problems, we sometimes call in the two people, take them one at a time. And then we take them together. . . . And I have dealt here—my wife and I—we have dealt with a number of cases. Especially young couples. We have, recently, I am dealing with a matter right now where the husband is constantly beating the wife. Blows on her. To her face and so. A couple of nights I had to wake—I had to get up, I had to hustle out of bed, about twelve in the night and try to reach so many people.

The couple this community leader and his wife counseled never went to court. On the other hand, a female attorney in private practice in Port of Spain advised me that judging by the number of divorce cases she has handled for "young people—people 50 and under" who identified as Hindus, that community had "no problem" using the courts. Among Hindus, peoples' use of the court to resolve family conflicts are in flux: "I don't deal with old Hindu people. I can't say I have because you find that they would try to solve their problems with a pundit rather than a lawyer. . . . A lot of Hindu women above that age of 40 are not going to be willing to consider divorce. That's changing. People are more exposed and I find the children of these old Hindu women are the ones who will tell their parents 'Get out. You don't have to take this.' You wouldn't imagine that out of a Hindu family that you could produce children that would tell their mother to leave." Thus, times are changing and people are less willing to suffer abuse than they were in the past. Moreover, children will today counsel their mothers to leave violent relationships.

Advocates of the culture of reconciliation also include people who work inside the courthouse and this weighs significantly on the critical question of why so many domestic violence cases exit the legal system. They include probation officers, lawyers, and magistrates. Magistrates direct cases to probation officers when they want a report that probes more deeply into the circumstances of any case. Sometimes that involves calling the parties together in the probation office; at other times, field trips to the litigants' homes are necessary. Probation officers also have "walk-in" days when members of the public can visit them to address various problems, including domestic violence, child abuse and neglect, disputed paternity, visitation and custody rights, unruly juveniles, and alcohol and drug addiction. Each of the seven probation officers I interviewed told me they had counseled women who had suffered abuse but who preferred not to take their problems to court. One female probation officer explained: "They have been traumatized in their homes already. They don't want to be traumatized in the court. In the public and everything."

A second and more senior probation officer emphasized his role in securing therapeutic rather than legal services for families who can afford them. He told me about a case involving a perpetrator who worked in a senior position in the public service and who had been married to a teacher for over twenty years. They had four children living at home. The husband/father had been verbally and sometimes physically abusive to his wife for years. The wife finally went to see the justice of the peace about seeking a protection order. Papers were filed and the police served the summons. When the police arrived, the man became threatening and violent. One of the officers called this probation officer for advice because the couple resided in his district. He advised the police to escort the woman to a shelter where she would be safe for the night.

At the first hearing of this case, the magistrate referred the matter back to the probation officer for a report. He interviewed the family members and learned that the wife had unsuccessfully attempted suicide on two occasions and that the children suffered great stress as a result of the abusive situation in the home. The family agreed to psychological counseling. Once those arrangements had been made, the probation officer explained:

> PO: I asked the court for some time—three months to work with the family. I got a letter from the psychologist that they were responding to treatment. The four children are also attending counseling. Two professional counselors are involved. I intervened, set up the counseling and rehabilitation. Have to report to the court next

week my final findings. Once I am sure the matter can be dismissed.

M L-B: So there were never orders made against him?

PO: No. Because I did not want it to affect the firsthand counseling
process I had in place. Once they admit and talk, I don't see the
need.

M L-B: Will the case be withdrawn?

PO: Not withdrawn really. On the next occasion, based on the information from the counselors, she could withdraw it or it could be
dismissed.

He then explained that if the husband later became abusive, his wife could
reapply for a protection order. From his tone and demeanor, I could tell
this probation officer was proud about the way he had handled the case.
The parties were reconciled.

A third probation officer gave me an account of what was a more
typical scenario. He described a case involving a couple who had had a
long-term, common-law relationship. The woman applied for a protection order, but the magistrate adjourned the case, referring it to the probation officer. The probation officer spent many hours counseling these
parties, but eventually they parted without any mandates from the court.
Although he could not reconcile the relationship, protection orders were
avoided and the probation officer helped the couple work out an informal
agreement with respect to the matrimonial home, a large debt, and child
visitation rights.

Just as some probation officers prefer counseling to court orders so,
too, do some of the attorneys. As we saw in chapter 3, when we explored
the meaning of "success" with respect to domestic violence law, lawyers
are often responsible for keeping domestic violence cases out of court.
They advise their clients to try to settle without formal orders, especially
when children are involved and maintenance and visitation rights must
be negotiated. On occasion, too, lawyers convert their clients' domestic
violence cases into other kinds of matters. For example, a senior attorney
who practiced in Pelau recounted that one of his clients, an elderly man,
came to the office complaining about the behavior of his adult son who
lived at home with him. The father claimed his son was very abusive
toward him, that he was fed up, and that he wanted to press charges of
domestic violence against him. The attorney told me he realized that if
he could get the son to move out of the house, "then everything would
sort itself out." Instead of filing a case for protection, therefore, he got an
ejectment order against the son, forcing him to vacate the premises and
giving the old man the peace he desired. As we discussed other family

cases, he told me: "I think it is a last resort to come to court. They may consult, have their own family gathering and the parents may negotiate. They may do that. They may go to their parish priest. When they come to me, I try to settle it." Thus lawyers play a powerful part in sustaining a culture of reconciliation.

Finally, the conscious and unconscious conviction that reconciliation is the preferable solution to addressing domestic violence explains why, if a case must be resolved in court, it likely will be resolved by an undertaking, a promise given by a respondent to refrain from future abuse. Undertakings allow parties to reach an agreement of their own accord, rather than forcing magistrates to "order" parties to act appropriately. (Recall that undertakings constituted 19 percent of the final case dispositions in Pelau in 1997–98.) Lawyers for alleged abusers also prefer undertakings to orders because the former do not require the magistrate to hear evidence. A male attorney explained: "If the matter was to be aired, they may have to take into consideration that there is *x* years of marriage. And maybe under serious and rigorous cross-examination, many other things may come out. And this way [with an undertaking], they may have a chance for reconciliation. And I thought that personally, after *x* years of marriage, one should do everything that is possible to save the marriage."

Undertakings make it possible for magistrates to recognize and proclaim violent language and behavior as unacceptable, but with due consideration for the privacy and reputations of the parties and their respective families.[12] Undertakings give a family "one more chance" while giving the victim the right to return to court if the respondent breaches his promise. Interestingly, the 1999 Domestic Violence Act provides for another form of reconciliation of domestic violence cases—by the use of peace bonds. After hearing the evidence, a magistrate may order a respondent to be on good behavior for six months if the magistrate concludes: "(a) the incident was an isolated one; (b) there are circumstances which make it desirable to preserve the family unit; and (c) the conduct complained of is not sufficiently grave to warrant the imposition of either the Order or the penalty, as the case may be" (Laws of Trinidad and Tobago 1999:310). The law itself, in this case, specifically encourages the preservation of the family unit.

In short, when a woman in Trinidad goes to court to protest the violence in her life, she will inevitably encounter myriad players, both inside and outside the courts, who will work to convince her not to continue the case. Her kin, neighbors and friends, religious leaders, and various judicial officials with whom she may come in contact—probation officers, lawyers, and magistrates—seek to reconcile the family without formal legal redress. Judging by the statistical records from the courts, and my fieldwork and interviews, the culture of reconciliation is remarkably pervasive. Judging by historical and ethnographic research in other British-inspired legal traditions, to which I turn next, Trinidad does not stand alone in the presence and power of a culture of reconciliation that causes claims about domestic violence to vanish from the courts.

Cultures of Reconciliation, East and West

In this section, I return to historical and ethnographic studies from the United States, Israel, and India that earlier provided evidence that court rites and the factor of time critically influence the processing of domestic violence cases across an array of British-inspired courts. What is fascinating and in need of further study is that these same accounts also describe the presence of several extralegal, normative precepts akin to those I identified as characteristic of Trinidad's culture of reconciliation and that dissuade actors from claiming legal rights. First, the trope "husband-wife business is private business" is pervasive, even if its precise meaning and influence on peoples' decisions and practices take on different nuances in different times and places. Second, the notion that women are principally responsible for the daily needs of children, and the ensuing dramatic consequences of that premise for women's lives, appears everywhere in the historical, anthropological, and sociological literature on kinship and family cases. Third, the ideas that families are supposed to be stable and that stability demands a relationship between a father and his children are (mostly) unchallenged and widespread assumptions that carry powerful implications for battered women.[13] Another recurring theme is the belief that parents have the right to socialize, support, and discipline their children as they see fit—within limits that vary cross-culturally. Together, these principles coalesce into identifiable cultures of reconciliation that keep family troubles away from the courts.

Evidence of the operation of a culture of reconciliation in the United States can be found in Pleck's history of social and legal reforms against family violence. She argues that such reforms have been most difficult to enact whenever opponents successfully invoked the "Family Ideal":

> The single most consistent barrier to reform against domestic violence has been the Family Ideal—that is, unrelated but nonetheless three distinct ideas: (1) family privacy, (2) conjugal and parental rights, and (3) family stability (marriage to be a life-long relationship).

... reform against family violence is an implicit critique of each element of the Family Ideal. It inevitably asserts that family violence is a public matter, not a private issue. Public policy against domestic violence offers state intervention in the family as a major remedy for abuse, challenges the view that marriage and family should be preserved at all costs, and asserts that children and women are individuals whose liberties must be protected. (1987:7, 9)

In the American case, the demand for privacy within the domestic sphere, beliefs in unfettered conjugal and parental rights, and disdain for "broken" families combined to discourage domestic violence legislation.[14] I suggest that Pleck's "Family Ideal" operates as an American version of a culture of reconciliation—one that continues to keep abused victims out of court.[15] As Schneider points out, American women continue to be socialized to keep the family together: "Asking 'Why doesn't she leave?' hypocritically denies cultural socialization that trains young girls and women to think of marriage and family as the measure of success, to 'stand by her man' and keep the marriage together no matter what, and blames the woman if the marriage fails" (2000:78).

As we have seen in the case of Trinidad, peoples' spiritual and religious ideals may influence greatly how they respond to violence between family members. To cite an American example, Merry investigated three approaches to gender violence in contemporary Hawaii, two of which specifically describe the influence of cultures of reconciliation. The first approach, Ho'oponopono, derives from Native Hawaiian beliefs and practice and emphasizes repentance, reconciliation, and mutual respect between husbands and wives. Ho'oponopono holds the community responsible for contending with conflict, including family violence. A second approach, held by conservative Christians, emphasizes scriptural counseling and an ideal family in which the wife/mother and children are under the authority of the husband/father. Fundamentalist Christian discourse discourages divorce and instructs church members to pray for a resolution to family violence. Both worldviews dissuade the use of secular courts to resolve family conflict. The third approach, that of the secular courts, promotes women's separation from violent partners and emphasizes their safety. The courts advocate gender equality and criminalize violence (Merry 2001b:40–41).[16] Whether some of the players at the court also encourage reconciliation of the parties is unclear from this ethnographic account, but earlier historical records show that judges often reunited couples who had separated because of violence (see Merry 2000).

Other researchers have documented that American women frequently encounter reluctant prosecutors when they seek restraining orders in court: "... like the police, public prosecutors have not traditionally been overly zealous about pursuing cases against domestic violence offenders. The same type of issues that promoted a reluctance in police officers to arrest spouse abusers have made prosecutors disinclined to prosecute. These issues have included the belief that domestic violence is essentially a family matter and that, unless there is serious injury (generally resulting in a felony charge) the criminal courts should not be involved" (Hirschel and Hutchison 2001:47).

Moreover, in her survey of the literature on legal responses to domestic violence, Wan concluded: "Domestic abuse is commonly considered an inappropriate issue for family courts to deal with because these courts are primarily aimed at reconciling families, often doing so with favoritism toward the male heads of households" (2000:607). Wan's finding echoes the situation documented by Martin (1976:103–4, 110, 146–48) thirty years ago.

An American version of the culture of reconciliation also operates outside legal arenas via the influences of women's families. Wittner recounts an example from her research in Chicago: "Helen Callas, a middle-aged woman who came to Chicago from Greece in the 1950s, worked in a bakery. Her husband, Peter, was an independent contractor, in recent years only sporadically employed. After Peter threatened and shoved her in front of their children, Helen came to court. ... Helen's children were so unanimous in their opposition to their mother's action that they lied to the judge about their father's conduct on the night in question" (1998:91). However, Helen persisted in her case and against the hegemonic culture of reconciliation held by her family members. Her husband was subsequently acquitted and she became estranged from three of her four children (1998:91).

Of the forty women Ptacek interviewed in his study of applicants for restraining orders in two courts in Massachusetts, 73 percent spoke with friends and family about the violence in their lives and were supported in their decisions to seek court action. Another 20 percent, however, never talked to friends or family, indicative of "social damage inflicted by batterers" (1999:141). Three women reported that relatives discouraged them from going to court, one of them told by her mother to be a "good wife" (1999:141). Being a good wife, of course, subsumes one in a culture of reconciliation.

Pratt's study of judicial decision making in violence against women policies in Barbados and New York tested the influences of "feminism," as defined by concern for victims' rights and protections; "anomie," marked by judicial uncertainty or ambiguity; and "familism," "a social pattern in which the family assumes a position of ascendance over individual interests" (2000:26). In Barbados, measures of anomie were low, but the two other perspectives were clearly defined: "On one side, there is familism, deferring to religious and cultural traditional ideals of family and concern with male status and role, which influences judicial thinking on violence against women; at the other end of the spectrum strong views on victim protection, safety, arrest, and no tolerance for violence are expressed as feminism" (Pratt 2000:17). Interestingly, Pratt found New York judges scored even higher on the theme of familism than did the magistrates she interviewed in Barbados (2000:16).

In the religious courts that govern family law in Israel, pressures to ensure the stability of marital unions and to discourage divorce, pressures typical of cultures of reconciliation, are ubiquitous:

> The majority of the religious court judges see reconciliation as being in their community's best interest. . . . The religious court's goal is the maintenance of the family, the preservation of masculine rule, and the reproduction of the religion, culture and nation. . . . Men know that by requesting reconciliation they will harness the power of the religious court, gain legitimacy for their behavior and, very likely, regain control over their wives. Men employing this technique are also affirmed by the local community, which generally concurs that maintenance of family overrides individual complaints of violence. . . . Finally, because religious courts do not charge a fee for their services (or charge minimally), reconciliation is a relatively cheap method for staying married. In this way, the cycle of reconciliation mirrors the cycle of violence in which a batterer escalates certain controlling behaviors, apologizes to regain his partner, and returns to abusing her. Particular to this locale, the process of forced reconciliation is encouraged and institutionalized. (Adelman 2000:1242, 1243, 1244)

To cite a third example from another region, Indian families on the continent, like East Indian families in Trinidad, discourage women from returning to their families of origin after they have married, even if a woman is facing violence in her relationship: ". . . it is unusual for Indian parents—whatever their religion and no matter how fond of their daughter they may be—to actively take her side when she is having marital problems. They tend to be reluctant to take such a daughter back into their home once they have given her in marriage, often at very great expense. Thus they pressure her, or even compel her, to remain with her husband" (Vatuk 2001:239). Sitaraman explains that both economic security and concern about family honor "dictate that a wife will remain with her husband for life and maintain a harmonious relationship, not only with her husband, but also his relatives" (2002:4). Sitaraman conducted ethnographic research in India's all-women police stations. She found: "Both police and counselors believed that disputes should be ideally resolved to result in reunification of the couples" (2002:7).

In India, Family Courts were established as a result of women's activism and desire to make family law less contentious (Vatuk 2001:229; see also Singh 1994). At the same time, the Family Courts Act (FCA) was designed to protect and preserve the institution of marriage—an effort that, as legal scholars and activists point out, is a goal that is often incompatible with ensuring women's safety (Vatuk 2001:230). Moreover, those who dispense justice in the courts in India "harbor assumptions about what women are like and what roles they ought to perform—or are even capable of performing—within their families and in society at large. These assumptions predispose them to take a paternalistic approach toward the needs of the women who come before them, whether as plaintiffs or respondents, in matrimonial and other related kinds of legal suits. . . . In order to 'save' women by 'saving' their marriages, lawyers, court-appointed social workers, and judges alike make ample use of delays, attempts at mediation, and pressures to reach a compromise" (Vatuk 2001:228).

These Family Courts require couples to attend "counseling" that is "routinely referred to in case files as 'reconciliation'" prior to their court hearing (Vatuk 2001:231). In their attempts to save troubled marriages, counselors can request that couples return for repeated sessions. Compromise settlements are reached only when the counselors despair of saving the union, and then, as Vatuk points out, because "power asymmetries between husband and wife are marked and where the burden of adjustment within most marriages fall primarily on the wife, 'compromise' is a gender-linked concept" (2001:231).[17] "Compromise" involves pressure on the wife to meet her husband's needs, to adjust to a culture of reconciliation.

The spread of domestic violence legislation, and the plethora of approaches to resolving family violence, have been broadly influenced by a "transnational movement" that "imports" ideas about gender and violence and then "translates" those ideas for the "local context" (Merry 2001b:41). In this chapter I suggested that the "translation" of domestic violence laws and their implementation in the courts will be influenced profoundly by the presence and power of cultures of reconciliation—cultures that hold that women's familial responsibilities should take precedence over individual rights, that gender hierarchy is natural, that marital and family stability are preferable, and that how any one particular family makes a living is a complicated interaction of political, social, economic, and gendered ideas and practices negotiated between men and women (Mohammed 2002a) within and across different households and over generations.[18]

Conclusions

I have argued that domestic violence cases in Trinidad drop out of the legal system in such high numbers in part because men and women who become involved in the legal process are subject to different combinations of court rites and the use and abuse of time by a range of actors. To more comprehensively account for why domestic violence disputes take the turns they do, however, we must also pay attention to the simple truism that law always functions in a particular historical and cultural context. In Trinidad, that context is shaped by a powerful culture of reconciliation reflecting how Trinidadians perceive family and gender relationships and why they make certain choices to earn a living. The culture of reconciliation places enormous pressure on parties to a familial dispute to settle their differences without laws and outside of courts. It influences the attrition of domestic violence cases in the following ways. As a case for protection unfolds, it is subject to the hegemonic ideas that "husband-wife business" is "private business," that public attention to family quarrels is unsavory, that families should remain stable, that women should turn the other cheek for the sake of their children, that making a living is a matter of intersecting rights and responsibilities, and that every effort should be made to resolve family disputes by reconciliation rather than by formal legal redress. These views may be held by the complainant herself, but even if they are not, she is likely to encounter them from her partner, family and friends, religious authorities, a probation officer, and perhaps from her own lawyer. Thus, in its own determinative way, Trinidad's culture of reconciliation influences both peoples' agency as legal actors and the structural constraints of cases and legal procedures.

The historical and ethnographic evidence suggests clearly that Trinidad's culture of reconciliation is not entirely unusual and shares common themes found in other societies, east and west. In Guyana (Danns and Parsad 1989; Parsad 1999), Barbados (Pratt 2000), St. Kitts–Nevis (Spooner 2001), England (Connell 1997), Israel (Adelman 1997, 2000), India (Sitaraman 2002; Vatuk 2000, 2001, 2003), and, in the United States in Illinois (Wittner 1998), Massachusetts (Ptacek 1999), Hawaii (Merry 2001b), and Kentucky (Websdale 1998), persons seeking protection orders are regularly dissuaded from the courts by their partners, parents, friends, and legal professionals. Complainants experience pressure to reconcile families for the children, for stability, for honor, for privacy, and for the good of the family economy. Therefore, to comprehend the histories and consequences of domestic violence disputes and their legal redress, we must attend not only to the events and processes of law, to its rites and timing, but also to the extralegal ideas and practices that color law's efficacy as a form of protest and protection.

Book
focuses too
much on
explaining

experiences — I'm say
simply as success all odiments near
deeply troubling...

Conclusion: How Law Works

This book captures what law can and cannot accomplish in the matter of violence against women. It not only illustrates Trinidad's fascinating recent social and legal history and its role as a leader in implementing domestic violence law in the English-speaking Caribbean, but it also suggests answers to broader, core questions in the anthropology and sociology of law, law and society research, and gender studies. Those questions guide these concluding thoughts.

First, why and when do lawmakers write laws to protect subordinated peoples? More specifically, what conditions permit the regendering of the state, the process of bringing to public and legal attention categories and activities that were formerly (and formally) without name, but that constituted harm to women, denied them rights, silenced them, or limited their capacity to act in ways available to men?[1]

Second, why is it that in spite of laws to protect people from harm, so very little results from that legislation? What happens in and around courts that makes it so difficult for people to secure their rights? What are the signs of a state of affairs in which law grants rights and protections in name, but masks and even contributes in practice to continuing structural inequities rooted in economy, class, politics, and gender organization? What makes structural deflection possible? Even probable?

Third, what can the law mean for women's empowerment, gender equity, and protection? How do the cultural norms and practices of their communities intercept the law? What clues about how law works has the vanishing complainant left behind?

Finally, how can we apply what we have learned in this study of the implementation of domestic violence law to other courts and other cases? How does law become implicated in the everyday harm that people experience?

Making Law for Equitable Practice

Laws name behavior as a new crime when specific political, social, and economic conditions coalesce in ways that enable changes in earlier relations and structures of power. Cross-cultural research reveals, for example, that the case of Trinidad's Domestic Violence Act is not unusual; its appearance at this particular juncture in history mirrors in several ways the experiences of other states of the North and the South.[2] Internationally, a country's sense of identity as a modern nation among the community of nations, economic prosperity enabling progressive social legislation, the expansion of education, and the development of a women's movement that crosses gender, class, religious, and ethnic divides portend success in the legal struggle against domestic violence.[3] Like Boyle and Preves (2000), I found that international pressures for human rights wield considerable influence on national lawmaking; that over time less powerful states tend to comply with international standards; that national lawmaking is often a "top-down" process designed to change local attitudes; and that independent activists not dependent on government can exercise considerable influence.

My research also shows, however, why and how the language of a global discourse in lawmaking is always tempered by a provincial dialogue. Local ideologies and politics play a decisive role in jurisprudence and scholars must pay attention to these lest they miss the crucial ways in which cultural beliefs and practices constitute law, even as law constitutes cultural praxis. Trinidad's statute prohibiting domestic violence, for example, was designed to reflect the special forms and practices of Trinidadian families. As the bill was being debated, articles, editorials, and letters to the newspapers proclaimed the differences between Trinidadians and "others," particularly their widespread acceptance of common-law relationships and emphases on the importance of family networks, privacy, and kinship solidarity (Shepherd 1991). The Domestic Violence Act indexed how lawmakers conceived of their nation, their families, and their gender organization.

The implications of this history for the sociology of law are clear: to comprehensively understand the process of lawmaking, scholars must investigate the forms and forces of both the global and the local.[4] These matters are complex: there is no singular "global" just as there is no one "local." Governmental and nongovernmental agencies (NGOs) that cross international borders struggle to define the discourse on rights (e.g., Hirsch 2003), just as lawmakers and laypersons can be deeply divided about who laws should protect, from whom, against what deeds, and with what consequences. Moreover, this study suggests that the regendering process will likely be most successful when it engages a language and politics of rights shaped by community leaders; achieves widespread public support from men and women across different class, racial, and ethnic groups; and also garners support from an international constituency. Local organizing to regender the state clearly gains critical strength and support from broader, global social and legal movements to make women's rights human rights (Lazarus-Black and Merry 2003; Thomas and Beasley 1993). Regendering the state undoubtedly transforms women's agency in law, empowering them, for example, to protest violence and to seek protection orders. That effort should also change structures of domination that formerly disempowered women—at least in theory.

Law and Structural Deflection: Court Rites, Time, and Cultures of Reconciliation

Once new legislation appears, it must be publicized so that people become aware of their rights, legal professionals must be educated about the contents of the law, and agents of the state must learn how to implement and enforce the statute. These efforts require coordination and consensus, both from those who work within the legal bureaucracy and between agency representatives and ordinary citizens who turn to the courts seeking justice. In her discussion of structural deflection, Pierce (1996) alludes to the blatant manipulation of legal and policy changes by elites to ensure that reforms conform to their own agendas. My research of the microtechniques and processes that contribute to structural deflection suggest that all actors, not just elites, can and do contribute to structural deflection, and that their actions may be purposeful or unintentional.

How do we know if structural deflection is operating? In the case of domestic violence, a comparison between applications filed for protection orders and final case dispositions provides an important signal. As we have seen, in Trinidad, thousands of complainants filed for protection orders as soon as the Domestic Violence Act became available and those numbers increase every year (Trinidad and Tobago Coalition Against Domestic Violence 2005:30–31). Yet quantitative analyses of court records reveal that more than three-quarters of those applications are dismissed or withdrawn. Only a few cases alleging domestic violence actually win a court's attention, and even fewer result in an extended order for protection. Trinidad's numbers are not unusual: data from U.S. courts, for example, also show high rates of case attrition (e.g., Belknap et al. 2001; Harrell, Smith, and Newmark 1993; Hirschel and Hutchison 2001). The numbers provoke two immediate questions. What makes a case likely to result in a protection order? Why do so many cases exit the legal system?

The extended case histories of litigants interviewed for this project, and corroborated by evidence of domestic violence litigation from Great Britain, the United States, and other locales sharing the British common-law tradition, teach us that complainants are likely to win protection orders if they can satisfy two legal and sociological conditions. First, law is literal. To successfully pursue a legal claim, therefore, one must satisfy all the tenets of the statute. In the case of domestic violence law in Trinidad, that includes defining one's relationship with the abuser as constituting a relationship covered by the act; specific evidence of abuse that can be dated, timed, and located in a particular place or places; and ongoing fear of potential future abuse. In other words, the facts must be framed in such a way as to make the story of abuse into a report that is chronological and consistent or, in Trinch's language, "institutional-ized" (2003:121). Second, law is unforgiving. In accord with what scholars have learned about rape victims, a complainant who alleges domestic violence must be both believable and deserving.[5] We saw this clearly in the extended case studies. Like Rosalyn, she may be a good mother, one who has tried repeatedly to help her drug-addicted son, but who has reached the limits of her ability to endure violence and theft on her own. Alternatively, she may be a single woman like Karrene, an upstanding, hard-working member of the community who dines on Sundays with her family and who needs relief from a dangerous, obsessed former partner. Rosalyn, Karrene, and each of the other women I interviewed or observed in court who received protection orders met both the literal demands of the Domestic Violence Act and its extralegal requirement that the applicant be a worthy victim. In these cases, "success" in law means vindication of rights in the sign and form of a protection order issued by the magistrate.[6]

With regard to the second question, why so many cases exit the legal system without legal redress, we need first to acknowledge the agency of individuals in violent relationships to make choices within the contexts of the structural constraints they face beyond the courthouse and outside the law, including the powerful and power-laden organizations of gender, race, and class that generate multiple forms of oppression.[7] Extensive research shows that most women who experience domestic violence never file for protection orders and, even if they do, many subsequently decide not to pursue their cases for reasons having little to do with law. Their decisions may be rooted in emotional needs, financial dependency, language skills, love, immigration status, need for housing, fear of the abuser, desire for counseling or just to talk, religion, a child's illness, or satisfaction with having made the point that they are serious about no longer tolerating abuse by calling the police or filing at the court. And, of course, their definition of "success" in resisting domestic violence need not include a legal remedy.

This study demonstrates, however, that when domestic violence survivors choose to pursue rights and protections offered by domestic violence law, they face significant obstacles intrinsic to law and the legal process itself. Law is literal and it is unforgiving. It also draws its participants into court rites, the use and abuse of time, and the hegemonic effect of cultures of reconciliation. My ethnographic research documents that these three phenomena influence profoundly the history and outcome of every domestic violence case. Both alone and in combination, they constitute mostly unnoticed micropolitics of the everyday that contribute to structural deflection and explain why so many applicants for protection orders exit the legal system. Alena's story is telling.

Alena, it will be recalled, was a young woman who went to live with John, her boyfriend, before she had finished school. John became abusive, isolated her from family and friends, and prohibited her from working, even after he lost his own job. Evicted from several apartments, the couple went to live with John's mother. After their son was born, John's violence escalated. Alena was fortunate in that her family eventually found her, brought her and her son back home with them, and supported her efforts to obtain a protection order. She was less fortunate in court. Once she became engaged in the legal process, Alena experienced court rites and long adjournments of her case, and she used language befitting a middle-class woman and mother. These contributed to the eventual dismissal of her case and to the broader process we have identified as structural deflection. They are ubiquitous to the implementation of law more generally.

Court rites refer to the events and processes that occur in and around legal arenas and that mostly operate to dissuade people from using the courts or interfere with their ability to exercise rights. In the process of trying to make a case for justice, litigants encounter personnel who tell them their problems are not worthy of legal redress, distortions of their stories, and silencing. At court, complainants get inadequate or incorrect information. They hear comments that reinforce their fears that no one will take them seriously. The police are slow to serve summons, sometimes because they are given too little or incorrect information, but also because the respondent is a relative, friend, or someone who employs their daughter. Lawyers, magistrates, and judges work hard to process cases, but occasionally they talk to litigants and witnesses in ways that intimidate, humiliate, or objectify them. Sometimes magistrates use euphemisms that plaintiffs do not understand and sometimes they write orders for which they have no legal authority. Without anyone noticing, members of privileged groups win concessions from the courts, get second chances when they break the law, and suffer few consequences because there is no one to enforce the laws they have broken. As I surveyed the ethnographic record on courts in the United States, Great Britain, India, Israel, and Jamaica, I found that other researchers described court rites, but without synthesizing them into a model, as I have done, that explains both how these rites buttress class and gender hierarchies and make it so difficult for complainants to obtain their legal rights.[8] Thus, the protection of legal rights depends a great deal on our ability to identify and challenge court rites.

Knowing how time works in the legal process is as essential to understanding the process of structural deflection as is identifying the pervasive and critical role of court rites. Time makes and breaks cases, but in more intricate ways than has previously been imagined. In this study, I isolated different categories of time to illuminate the meaning, complexity, and consequences of the common complaint that it takes too much time to make one's case in court. As we have seen, clerks at the courthouse may list a case for the next day or the next week, the police may be more or less diligent at locating or charging respondents, magistrates may decide that there is no time to hear a new case, and attorneys can choose to delay cases as a matter of strategy or convenience. These interactions dilute the urgency of any case and discourage complainants from remaining in the legal process; they contribute to structural deflection.

Court time is complicated and unpredictable, but playing with time in law is widespread. In their study of assault cases between intimates and nonintimates in Arizona, for example, Ferraro and Boychuk found: "Victim cooperation in cases of domestic violence is viewed as such a typical problem that prosecutors have established a 'cooling off' period for such cases. Rather than file the case immediately, prosecutors hold the case until they are sure victims will follow through with testimony. This procedure was completely lacking in nondomestic violence cases. . . ." (1992:213). In criminal matters in the United States, defendants "do time" until the judge is ready to hear their cases and sometimes they are left in jail until they come up with the funds to pay their attorneys (Blumberg 1967). Moreover, as Emerson points out:

> Many control agents, notably many social workers and probation and parole officers, organize their work around *caseloads*. In this respect, the focus of much of their routine decision-making is not so much the individual case as it is this larger set of cases for which they are organizationally and administratively responsible. One commonly observed consequence is that such agents must allocate time, energy, and other organizational resources on the basis of how they assess the demands and "needs" of any given case relative to the competing demands of other cases within the caseload. (1995:162; italics in original)

Hence, the conscious and unconscious manipulation of time by various players in the criminal justice system has consequences for the history and outcome of any case. Time can function as an instrument of hegemonic power or as a tactic to challenge regnant forms of domination. In the case of domestic violence, time consistently works against women who file for protection orders and contributes to structural deflection.

Finally, any case grows yet more complicated when we place the exercise of rights and the contested character of legal processes into the context of the communities in which they are embedded. Within those communities, cultures of reconciliation include precepts and practices about peoples' appropriate behavior, including norms about who is included in family, what rights and duties those roles entail, and how gender is organized. Cultures of reconciliation posit, for example, what it means to inhabit such roles as "husband," "common-law spouse," "mother," "sibling," or "son." Although no one's identity is subsumed by a single kinship position, these statuses inform the choices we make, the paths we imagine, and how our lives unfold and are made meaningful. I identified several norms that appeared repeatedly in my interviews in Trinidad that constitute essential features of its culture of reconciliation and that are critical in influencing what women feel they can and cannot do about the violence in their lives. While Americans commonly idealize the nuclear family as the "natural" family unit (Schneider 1980 [1968]), Trinidadian families comprise more extended networks. For my interviewees, "family" committed one to a wide array of persons to whom one owes loyalty and responsibility—including the responsibility not to draw public attention to private kinship matters. People also assume that women are primarily responsible for taking care of the emotional and physical needs of children. Any disruption of those responsibilities is unacceptable. People also hold that children need their fathers, even if fathers behave inappropriately. Family "stability" is the ideal. Finally, earning one's livelihood in Trinidad is almost never about "one's" livelihood. Trinidad has a very large working class and at any given time, many people are out of work. Making a living involves multiple relationships often spread across numerous households. It includes work for wages and work for love. Members of families are regularly called upon to render assistance that may be financial or take such forms as caring for children, lending one's car, sewing school uniforms, or paying school fees. These ties should be and are celebrated, but dependency also limits possibilities and options.

In short, requesting a protection order against a family member embodies the antithesis of the precepts that govern family. Local norms about kinship, gender, and the economies of households operate against law's claim that each individual is separately entitled to protection without consideration of an alleged victim's obligations or responsibilities to family. A culture of reconciliation acts as a filtering process, exercising a powerful influence on a woman's decision to seek redress at court and then on her ability to negotiate her case to trial.

Turning to the ethnographic record, I found variations of cultures of reconciliation are everywhere and ever-present, even as they vary locally. I documented their influence in domestic violence cases in the United States, Israel, and India in chapter 6, but they also complicate matters such as divorce and child support. In India, for example, women who want to divorce have to attend counseling sessions in which the primary goal is to reconcile the family (Vatuk 2001; see Cobb 1997 and Fineman 1995 on divorce and child custody in the United States). Baumgartner also points to the effects of cultures of reconciliation in other places and times in her work on the "myth of discretion" in law:

> One of the most powerful and best documented of the social factors that constrain legal decision-making is "relational distance," or the extent to which the adversaries in a case were personally tied to each other before their disagreement. . . . In general, the greater their intimacy, the more indifferent and lenient legal officials will be. Police officers, for example, are less likely to recognize disputes between intimates as crimes, and less likely to arrest offenders in such matters; prosecutors are less likely to press charges; grand juries are less likely to indict; judges and trial juries are less likely to convict; and judges are less likely to sentence harshly. (1992:131–32)
>
> Furthermore, the effects of relational distance are not restricted to contemporary settings. In sixteenth-century Spain, for example, a governing body in Castile asked the king to order that "all lawsuits between relatives within the fourth degree be settled and determined through

compromise arbitration" and thus removed from the courts altogether.
(Baumgartner 1992:135)

Thus, cultures of reconciliation not only keep potential litigants out of court, but they also keep officials charged with implementing the law from taking seriously certain offenses.[9] Police, probation officers, lawyers, and magistrates, like litigants, are influenced by the force of cultures of reconciliation and so sometimes the very people charged with prosecuting domestic violence advise women to compromise for the sake of the family, urge them to seek counseling with the abusive fathers of their children, and press them to accept husbands' promises to refrain from future violence by signing undertakings. As a result, courts grant extended formal orders fairly rarely and only as a last resort.[10]

There are parallels between what I have described as cultures of reconciliation and what Nader identifies as "harmony ideology": "a specific cluster of beliefs . . . that operate as control by limiting the playing field to a recurrent dialectic between legality and its alternatives" (2002:120). As she explains: "The basic components of harmony as ideology are the same wherever it appears as cultural control: the emphasis on avoidance and conciliation, the belief that conflict resolution is inherently good and that its opposite, continued conflict or controversy, is bad or dysfunctional, the belief that peaceful, orderly behavior is more civilized than confrontative behavior, the belief that consensus is of greater survival value than controversy" (2002:32).

Nader first described harmony ideology as descriptive of legal consciousness and practice among village Zapotec in Mexico (1990), but it also characterizes the Alternative Dispute Resolution (ADR) movement that became pervasive in the United States in the 1970s. As she points out, ADR won support soon after the 1960s civil rights movement and to some extent it functioned to keep subordinated groups out of the formal legal system, directing them instead to semilegal arenas such as community-based forums and mediation (Nader 2002:141). ADR entailed delegalization on a grand scale (Nader 2002:14). It urged mediation and compromise, often at the expense of allowing subordinated people to experience empowering rights at court. Like ADR, cultures of reconciliation discourage the expression of conflict, undermine rights, and avoid naming and confronting the structural, material, and ideological causes of discord that sometimes erupt in violence. Such cultures intercede between the symbol and promise of law and the implementation of rights—and help us to explain why the best intentions of lawmakers to assist marginalized peoples are so often thwarted in practice.

I offer next a final ethnographic example from my fieldwork to show how court rites, the use and abuse of time, and a culture of reconciliation factor into the practices and possibilities of law, not just in domestic violence cases, but also in a variety of other kinds of legal claims. Charges and countercharges brought to court by "Lorna" and "Philip" exemplify how law works, whether we are talking about a case for a protection order, paternity affiliation, access to a child, or child maintenance.

Lorna's Cases: Domestic Violence, Paternity Affiliation, Access, and Child Maintenance

Lorna, a tall, slim woman in her early thirties, lived with her two children in her parents' home, a comfortable middle-class dwelling. She had married Philip, ten years her senior, when she was sixteen. They had a son. The couple separated and reunited on many occasions, but eventually Lorna applied for a divorce. Years later, they entered into a stormy visiting relationship, a result of which, Lorna claimed, she had a daughter. When I first interviewed Lorna on the veranda of the family home, she described herself as a "homemaker." She was financially dependent on her father, on child support ordered by the court for her son when she divorced Philip, and on occasional gifts to the boy from Philip's parents.[11]

In November 1997, Lorna appeared in court without an attorney. She had applied for a protection order, charging that Philip hit her during a quarrel about their son's schooling and that he also harassed her with excessive telephone calls. Simultaneously on that date, Lorna brought cases against Philip for paternity affiliation and child support for her daughter. Philip denied that he had committed domestic violence. He also denied that Lorna's daughter was his child. He asked for a blood test. Lorna saw this as a stalling technique, but she agreed to the test. The magistrate informed them there were expenses that they would have to assume, instructed them to obtain a letter of referral from the clerk, and reset the cases for six weeks to await the test results.[12] Once those matters were scheduled, Lorna suddenly told the magistrate that she was withdrawing her charge of domestic violence against Philip because "I want him in my daughter's life." She later explained to me that Philip had urged her to withdraw that case. She told me that she knew that the blood test would prove Philip was the father.[13] Following local kinship norms and the culture of reconciliation, she wanted Philip to play a role in their daughter's life.

The paternity and maintenance cases were scheduled for the end of

January 1998. At that time, Lorna also filed a new case against Philip •
for domestic violence. He countersued, contending she had engaged in
violence against him. He also filed applications for access to his son
and a request to decrease the amount of maintenance he was paying.
The magistrate announced that she wanted a probation report regarding
the couple's circumstances. That decision, of course, shifted the matter of agency to the probation office, brought into play new structural
constraints, and changed the timing of the cases. Because the blood test
results had not yet reached the court, the cases for paternity affiliation
and maintenance were adjourned for another month. The magistrate
agreed, however, to hear the cross-charges of domestic violence. Lorna
took the stand first. She told the magistrate she wanted "peace and my
freedom!" She complained that Philip visited her home too often, using
the pretext of seeing his son. He also annoyed her family with his constant
phone calls. When it was his turn to testify, Philip appeared extremely
nervous. He clutched some papers and asked the magistrate if he could
please read her something. She agreed. Philip read dates when he alleged
that Lorna told him he could see his child but then denied him that right.
He claimed she had once threatened to shoot him and that he was afraid
of her. He also alleged that Lorna had cursed his mother and that he had
reported her behavior to the police.

Lorna claimed Philip was lying. She denied that she had used bad
language to him or his mother, and she said she wanted him to keep away
from her premises. But then how, the magistrate asked, could he see his
son? Lorna suggested that Philip pick up their son outside the house or
that her father could deliver the boy to Philip's home at a designated
hour. In accord with the culture of reconciliation, the magistrate asked
if the parties would sign undertakings to keep away from each other.
They agreed but then launched into further accusations of bad conduct.
Eventually the magistrate decided she had heard enough. She announced
she wanted to wait for the probation officer's report. All of the cases were
rescheduled.

I was in court on the next date but neither Lorna nor Philip appeared.
Consequently, the cross-charges of domestic violence, Philip's applications for access to a child and decrease in child support, and Lorna's
suits for paternity affiliation and maintenance were dismissed. The court
record was marked "NAC" (No Appearance of Complainant). The mag- •
istrate used her agency to dismiss the cases.

Three weeks later, however, Lorna and Philip were back in court,
each having resurrected their respective charges and complaints against •
the other. Lorna accused Philip of having used abusive language against

her on three occasions and claimed they had gotten into a fight during which he had choked her. The magistrate asked for the probation officer. The officer told the magistrate that she had made appointments with both parties, but neither of them had appeared. Lorna explained she missed her appointment because to keep it she would have had to leave her children home alone. Philip said he was confused about the date. The magistrate ordered them to make new appointments. Then, finding there was still no report from the hospital regarding the blood test, she adjourned all the cases for another two weeks. Philip asked if he could say something. The magistrate told him no, that they would both have a chance to bring their witnesses and evidence, that she didn't have time to hear him today, and that she wanted a report from the probation officer. Philip experienced the court's silencing.

At the next court hearing, Philip appeared with an attorney who informed the magistrate that he hoped to resolve the domestic violence charges with mutual undertakings and that he was looking into the issue of paternity and support for the little girl. The cases were adjourned for one month to give the attorney time to prepare. As each week passed, of course, Lorna's daughter went without child support. In this way, Philip was given "second chances" to avoid paying the child maintenance he would eventually have to pay. No one feared, however, that the child would go hungry—her family would adjust. Given the inclusive definition of kin and caretaking, and the culture of reconciliation, Lorna's parents would "pick up."

Lorna hired an attorney in the period between that court adjournment and the next hearing. She told me she wanted someone "strong" to counter Philip's lawyer. On the next court date, however, the magistrate still had no report from the hospital. Therefore, she gave instructions to the lawyers to look into the matter and assigned a new court date two weeks later.

I was not in court at the next hearing. The court records show that Lorna had appeared with her attorney, that Philip was absent, but that his lawyer was in court. The cases were adjourned for six weeks. It became clear to me that Lorna and Philip could proceed with their cases in part because neither one of them was working full time. It is hard to imagine an employer willing to grant his employees as much time off work as these cases required.

At the end of June 1998, after the various allegations had been in the legal process for nearly seven months, three of the five cases were resolved. Their respective attorneys urged Lorna and Philip to withdraw their cases of domestic violence against each other, and they complied.

(Note that Philip's attorney's original plan to obtain the parties' mutual undertakings never transpired.) In effect, the domestic violence cases had been delegalized; the attorneys converted them into complaints unworthy of legal redress.

The same day those cases were withdrawn, the court heard Philip's cases for access to his son and to decrease child support. Philip's attorney argued that Philip was in poor health and working only intermittently. Therefore, he could no longer afford to pay support in the amount that the court had previously ordered. Lorna's attorney protested that their son was getting older and was more expensive to raise—not less so. The magistrate ordered Philip to the stand. Three years ago, when the child support order was issued, he explained, he had been self-employed and was earning a good salary. Now he worked irregularly as a laborer. The magistrate tried to determine exactly how much Philip was presently earning, but he was vague. He testified that he did odd jobs when they became available. He asked the magistrate to reduce the payments in half "until something presents itself." The magistrate quickly gave Philip "instructions," a common court rite. She informed him: "Things don't present themselves in life! You have to make them happen!" Did he have job applications pending? Philip said he did, but he could not recall the dates he had posted them in the mail.

Lorna's attorney led a fiery cross-examination of Philip. She demanded to know why he was working as a casual laborer when he could "do accounts." Exercising the rites of "humiliation" and "objectification," she berated him for asking to reduce the maintenance he was paying when he knew that amount could not support his son. Like the magistrate, she instructed Philip to "go out and make it happen!" Philip's attorney registered an objection to the attorney badgering the witness. The magistrate sustained the objection. She then tried again to determine exactly how much Philip earned. He offered a few pay stubs into evidence. One stub showed he had earned less than $75 TT (about U.S. $13) for a day's work. Philip testified that he lived at home and that his parents provided him with food and clothing. He was eventually permitted to step down, having been "instructed," "humiliated," and "objectified."

Lorna took the stand. She testified that it was too difficult for her father to maintain her and the children—Philip needed to do more—not less. She told the court about the clothing expenses and school and book fees she needed for their son. During cross-examination, Philip's attorney charged Lorna with being unreasonable when she knew Philip was going through a bad period. The magistrate commented that the original order for child support had been made three years before and that she "didn't recall anyone saying that prices had gone down since then." His lawyer countered: "No ma'am, but earnings did." The magistrate advised the parties that although Philip's meager pay stubs suggested he could no longer afford the child support he had previously paid, she was taking into account his "familial circumstances and the needs of the child." As we saw in chapter 4, she assumed, as magistrates do, that men find ways to make extra cash.

The magistrate finalized the paperwork for the access order because Lorna had not contested Philip's right to see his child. Meanwhile, Philip and his attorney conferred. A few minutes later, the lawyer requested leave to withdraw Philip's application for a decrease in child support. The magistrate concurred and then ordered that Philip be allowed weekly access to his son. She then adjourned for six weeks the cases for paternity affiliation and maintenance for the little girl. Although the attorneys had previously been instructed to look into the matter of the hospital report, it was clear that neither of them had done so. Thus, shifting agency to one's attorney does not necessarily speed up the processing of one's case.

I returned to the United States temporarily during that adjournment and was not present at the final hearing. The court records show that the cases were adjourned two more times before paternity affiliation and child support for Lorna's daughter were finally decided.

Lorna and Philip appeared in court for the last time almost a year after having initially filed their respective cases. By this time, they had both given up retaining attorneys.[14] In our interview, Lorna told me triumphantly that Philip accepted paternity of their daughter after the blood test report showed that he shared her blood type. She accepted his offer of a minimum of weekly support because she knew he was not working steadily. Soon after the court hearing, Philip's mother sent word that she would like to meet the little girl. Lorna told me she did not consent to that until Philip started paying child support. The court record shows that in addition to child support, Lorna requested and won legal custody of her daughter at that last appearance.

A little over a year later, I encountered Lorna in a shopping market and she invited me to visit with her family the following Sunday. She continued to reside in her parents' home and remained a full-time home-maker. The household had gained new members, however, expanding as Trinidadian households do when family members have new needs. Lorna's brother had returned home from overseas. He had a full-time job working in construction. One of his two children was visiting him for a few weeks. I also met Lorna's elderly aunt who was convalescing in the household. There was one other new resident—a niece who would be attending one of the better secondary schools in the neighborhood had moved in for the academic year. Lorna told me she hardly ever saw Philip and that he no longer harassed her in any way. In accord with family norms and practices, their children are primarily cared for by Lorna, who is in turn assisted by her parents and the other members of the household. Philip's status and role as their father is acknowledged, and his right to be involved in their lives is unquestioned. Philip's parents participate as family by providing for Philip's children financially when he is not working, by spending time with them, and by bringing them gifts when they travel overseas. In keeping with the culture of reconciliation, Philip's family embraced the child Philip had once denied.

In Pursuit of the Vanishing Complainant

Lorna and Philip went to court in dispute over paternity affiliation and support for one child, weekly maintenance and access for another, and domestic violence. In the course of the legal process, they experienced court rites that included, among others, instructions, silencing, delegalizing, and humiliation. The cases took months to resolve. According to Lorna, Philip blatantly manipulated the court's time by asking for a blood test, but neither party could control when the probation officer had time to see them or when the lab technician scheduled the blood test or sent the report to the magistrate. As their cases progressed, the litigants, their parents, and their lawyers each acted according to their own sensibilities about how family members should behave, whatever the technicalities of the law. The court established the legal paternity of the disputed child and what it perceived to be fair and reasonable child support. As applicants for protection orders, however, Lorna and Philip vanished from the legal records.

I contend that the micropolitics of court rites, the use and abuse of time, and the hegemonic influence of cultures of reconciliation operate generally in British common-law traditions. I've identified their presence, for example, in juvenile (Emerson 1969) and criminal (Feeley 1979) cases in the United States, in divorce cases in India (Vatuk 2003) and Israel (Adelman 2000), and in requests for child support in Jamaica (LaFont 1996). Although my research has been limited mostly to family matters and other cases processed in lower courts, it would be fascinating to investigate as well how these micropolitics influence cases of homicide, rape, or white-collar crime. Coutin (2000) has identified the operation of court rites in deportation hearings in the United States.

These findings about how law works are counterintuitive in two senses. First, members of the public commonly assume that an individual goes to court as an independent agent, free to apply for rights or other legal remedies and able to accomplish goals based on the strength of personal volition, the truth of the evidence, and the justice of that particular cause. This is never the case. A complainant's agency in law resides not in any single individual who presses a claim, but rather in the continuous interactions that frame a litigant's encounters with courthouse staff, police, justices of the peace, probation officers, attorneys, witnesses, and magistrates. Agency in law is always inherently unstable and constantly negotiated between litigants and legal professionals, each of whom leaves in some way their mark on the history of a case. Agency in law is thus a dialectical and dialogical process, captured only in the exchanges of relevant players at different sites along a shared legal process. The complexity of this agency, however, is mostly unnoticed and unremarked by scholars, legal professionals, activists, and the public.

Also counterintuitive to commonsense understanding (Schutz 1962) is the finding that the rules, procedures, and precedents that govern judicial proceedings are never static. We think of structural constraints at the courthouse as including, among other things, the precise words and actions that constitute illegal behavior, contingent forms and fees, the hours the court is open, the number of benches available for people to sit on as they wait for their hearings, the number of police officers available to serve summons, or statutes of limitation that apply to different offenses. These seem to us "objective" in form and content.

In the micropolitics of everyday legal practice, however, what counts as a structural constraint to one clerk, attorney, or judge does not always count as such to another; legal officials interpret and use discretion as they read and respond to codes and procedures, not to mention the definition of a decent lunch break. Hence so-called structural constraints at times become roadblocks to further action in a case, but at other times those constraints are ignored or dismissed. Importantly, other structures, powerful in their influences but less determinative than the scholarly literature usually allows, also weigh upon litigants. In the case of domestic violence, these include the structures of kinship, gender, economy, and politics. These structures shape whether an abused woman has someone to watch her children when she wants to file her case, whether she can afford to live on her own if her husband locks her out, whether she too can pay an attorney after she goes to court and learns that the respondent is represented by counsel and has filed countercharges, and whether politicians have located the court in an accessible place. These structures constrain and contain—like rules at the courts—but they can be and are resisted. Structures are blueprints. Like agency, they are subject to the sway of court rites, time, and cultures of reconciliation.

In May 2004, Trinidad and Tobago took new steps to alter the structure of the courts that process family law. A Family Court was opened as a pilot project in the boundaries of the St. George West Magisterial District and the Port of Spain High Court. In June 2006, I visited this innovative program to talk with a member of the court's planning and monitoring committees, a judge, and courthouse staff, and to read the first evaluative study of its operation.

The Family Court combines in one building a magistrate court and a High Court, as well as probation, counseling, and mediation services. It thus brings together in one place law and other options for resolving familial conflicts. In its first year of operation, parties brought 6,885 matters to the Family Court, of which 1,858 were filed at the High Court and 4,348 were filed at the magistrate's court (Hann, Boucaud, and Murrell 2005:5). Some 87 percent of the High Court cases entailed divorce, and 57 percent of the magistrate cases concerned maintenance (Hann, Boucaud, and Murrell 2005:29, 30). The Family Court is not yet charged with adjudicating domestic violence cases unless those matters are brought in conjunction with other family suits. Moreover, hearings for breaches of domestic violence cases must be held in another magistrate's court.[15] Even so, 11 percent of cases filed in the magistrate's court were domestic violence complaints (Hann, Boucaud, and Murrell 2005:30). Thus, as we saw in the ethnographic study of Lorna's and Philip's encounters in the magistrate's court in Pelau, the data from the Family Court lend further support to the pervasiveness of violence, to its manifestations in other types of family troubles, and to peoples' desire to seek the law's intervention and protection.

Officials anticipate that the Family Court will eventually process all applications for protection orders and that the project will be rolled over into other jurisdictions. The new institution represents an impressive effort to reform legal structures and the matter of client agency.[16] Whether this new, innovative, and empowering organization can overcome the process and the consequences of structural deflection will also depend, I suggest, on participants' understanding of how court rites, time, and cultures of reconciliation intertwine with law.

Understanding how law works teaches us about law's power to speak to the identity of a people, to proclaim a nation's values, to promote gender equity, and to empower formerly marginalized people. As we have seen, given the opportunity to speak the truth about violence, survivors of domestic abuse will speak out; they will exercise newly acquired rights. Domestic violence laws allow states to gaze into bedrooms and backyards, as well as workplaces. These laws regender the state. They empower women, give them new leverage in their familial relationships, and, more generally, shift power in gender organization. While appreciative of this power of law to make a nation modern and to give voice to formerly subordinated people, knowing how law works also makes us less sanguine about what law can accomplish for any one person who has suffered harm. Legal reform can be and often is undermined in the legal process. The micropolitics that I have identified in the enactment of court rites, the crucial influence of actors' engagement with time, and the subtle but powerful push and pull of cultures of reconciliation mostly contribute to social orders that favor "how things are" rather than "how things might be," and weigh against the possibility that law can be a harbinger of radical change. The protection of women who protest violence, then, requires the efforts of legal officials who are aware of their own agency in law and who are cognizant of and flexible in their interpretation of structures inside and outside the legal process. Discerning the complexities of how law works reveals the real work that is necessary to address everyday harm, to implement domestic violence law, and to make a future free of violence against women. We know better, now, how law works, and why it is such uneven and uncertain terrain.

NOTES

Introduction

1. My use of this case, which happens to involve Indo-Trinidadians, in no way implies that domestic violence and wife murder do not occur among other social groups in the country. As has been found by all researchers investigating domestic violence in multiracial and multiethnic societies, no one group is free of domestic violence (see, for example, Danns and Parsad 1989; Gopaul and Cain 1996; Parsad 1999; Razack 1998; Sokoloff 2005). The details of this particular crime, and information about the perpetrator, Richard Daniel, and the victim, Ramdaye Daniel, were compiled from reputable newspapers. One account of the conclusion of the trial reads: "Before passing sentence [the judge] told [the defendant]: 'You and your wife were married for 20 years. It appears you had a good marriage until your wife began to commit adultery. She at first lied to you about it, but afterwards brazenly admitted her guilt and determination to continue in adultery. To your credit, you tried to effect a reconciliation but your wife was by this time a confirmed adulteress and addicted to the lust of adultery. You killed her against that background and then tried to commit suicide'" (*Trinidad Express,* December 16, 1994). The Caribbean Association for Feminist Research and Action (CAFRA) registered a protest against the judge's description of a woman who was killed by her husband after she committed adultery as "addicted to the lust of adultery" (*Trinidad Express,* December 23, 1994).

2. In 1997–98, the period of my initial fieldwork, there were two main daily newspapers, the *Trinidad Guardian* and the *Trinidad Express.* Each paper published a Sunday edition. In addition, there were several popular tabloids available two or three times a week.

3. My analysis is based on newspaper accounts of "domestic violence" (1991 through mid-1995) collected by staff members at the Hugh Wooding Law School, the University of the West Indies, and the CAFRA resource center. I found ten incidents in which men seriously wounded or killed their girlfriends, common-law wives, or spouses without harm to themselves, and twenty-two accounts of men who caused serious harm to their partners or former partners and then (usually successfully) attempted to take their own lives. Commonly, they drank what the newspapers referred to as "weedicide," which made them froth at the mouth. Agricultural workers in Trinidad, in particular, have ready access to potent pesticides. Pesticides are also used by young persons to commit suicide when they suffer from unrequited love or their families force them to wed against their will (see also Miller 1994:62; Yelvington 1995:180–81). For discussions of the problem

of wife murder in nineteenth-century Trinidad, see Brereton 1981; Reddock 1994; Trotman 1986; and Wood 1968. Miller (1994:175) also noticed the regularity of cases of "horning" that led to suicide or murder and suicide.

4. The newspaper collections described in the previous note also included eleven cases in which an initial charge of wife murder was later reduced to manslaughter. I found only one case in which a man murdered his wife and got the death penalty. A second case in which the murder charge held involved a man who killed his five children because his common-law wife had left him for another man. In 2000, Minister of Culture and Gender Affairs Daphne Philips reported: "In Trinidad and Tobago between 1990 and 1995, a total of 80 women, 2 men and 23 children were murdered as a result of domestic violence—yielding an average of 14 women and 4 children per year. In 1996, there were 16 murders—4 were children, 3 men and 9 women. In 1997, there were 12 such murders, 3 were children, 1 man and 8 women. The 1998 figures indicate that 23 persons were killed through domestic violence—13 women, 6 children and 4 men" (Philips 2000:181).

5. Technically, the Bahamas passed into law the 1991 Sexual Offences and Domestic Violence Act two weeks before Trinidad's statute became law (*Acts of the Commonwealth of the Bahamas* 1991:47–54). The Bahamas act was limited in scope, protecting from domestic violence only parties in legal unions and children of the family. Thompson-Ahye assessed the act as "woefully deficient" both in the restricted categories of applicants to whom the law applies and in its definition of the limited conduct that constitutes domestic violence (2004:73). In contrast, Trinidad's 1991 Domestic Violence Act was a separate and far more comprehensive piece of legislation. Readers should note that what many people understand as "domestic violence" was of course already outlawed in Trinidad's criminal statutes under categories such as "assault" or "aggravated assault." There is a common misperception about Caribbean domestic violence laws, even within the region: "A common misperception is that these statutes *criminalise* behaviour that hitherto was ignored by law. In reality, much of the behaviour we describe as domestic violence already fitted the definition of an existing crime. At most the legislation creates quasi-criminal relief. When the applicant proves in court that violence has occurred no criminal sanction follows, only the possibility of court orders designed to protect the applicant from further abuse. Criminal sanction is withheld until violence occurs again, in breach of the court order. What therefore is criminalised is not domestic violence *per se*, but breach of protection orders" (Robinson forthcoming; italics in original).

In contrast to the United States where one can apply for civil or criminal remedies for domestic violence, domestic violence law in Trinidad is a civil matter that enables quasi-criminal relief. In a civil case, a magistrate or judge can render a decision quickly based on the preponderance of the evidence presented.

6. Trinidad and Tobago's 1991 Domestic Violence Act precluded: "(a) the persistent intimidation of a person by the use of abusive and threatening language; (b) the damaging of the property of a person; (c) the persistent following of a person from place to place; (d) depriving a person of the use of his personal property; (e) the watching or besetting of the house or other place where a person resides, works, carries on business or happens to be; and (f) the wilful or reckless neglect of a child or dependent person" (*Laws of Trinidad and Tobago* 1991:91). The offense for contravening a protection order was a fine of not more than $5,000

TT (about $835 U.S.) or six months' imprisonment or both. I am using a simple conversion rate of U.S. $1 to $6 TT; the exact rate varies.

7. Following Comaroff and Roberts, a norm "is a statement of rule that is indigenously regarded as relevant to the regulation of social conduct" (1981:28). Social groups and communities develop norms regarding domestic violence that vary over time and place.

8. I am using "discourse" in the Foucauldian sense, described by Conley and O'Barr as "the broad range of discussion that takes place within a society about an issue or a set of issues. . . . Discourse in Foucault's sense is not simply talk itself, but also the way that something gets talked about. Logically, the way that people talk about an issue is intimately related to the way that they think about it and ultimately act with respect to it. Discourse is thus a locus of power. Different discourses compete for ascendancy in the social world; one is dominant for a time and then may be challenged and perhaps replaced by another. The dominance of a particular discourse reflects the power structure of society. At the same time, however, the repeated playing out of the dominant discourse reinforces that structure" (1998:7). My emphasis is on law in practice, recognizing the multiple and sometimes opposing influences of law's power and consequences.

9. The term "hegemony" is widely used today: "Hegemony refers to power that 'naturalizes' a social order, an institution, or even an everyday practice so that 'how things are' seems inevitable and not the consequence of particular historical actors, classes, and events" (Hirsch and Lazarus-Black 1994:7). Hegemony denotes a condition of consent that operates in everyday institutions such as schools and churches, but that is deeply rooted in each society's economically dominant form of production.

10. As a general mode of inquiry, however, violence between intimates has thus far received little attention from anthropologists (Levinson 1989, 1996). This project contributes to a growing and theoretically exciting literature that investigates domestic violence and its legal redress using anthropological perspectives and methods (e.g., Adelman 1997, 2000; Adelman, Erez, and Shalhoub-Kevorkian 2003; Alonso 1995; Counts, Brown, and Campbell 1992; Lazarus-Black 2001; Lazarus-Black and Merry 2003; London 1997; Merry 1994, 1995a, 1995b, 2000, 2001a, 2001b, 2003; Vatuk 2001, 2003).

11. Assessing the state of research and policy and legal responses to violence against women in the Caribbean five years after the Beijing Conference, Pargass and Clarke conclude: "Notwithstanding the enactment of domestic violence legislation in the majority of countries in the region, there is still no adequate statistical database to assess the impact of the legislation in any of the countries where such legislation has been enacted" (2003:52). Their comprehensive review of current practices in the region investigates not only domestic violence, but also state and nongovernmental responses to sexual offenses, marital rape, and sexual harassment.

12. By 2000, two-thirds of all Caribbean territories had passed domestic violence legislation: Antigua and Barbuda (1999); Bahamas (1991); Barbados (1992); Belize (1997); British Virgin Islands (1992); Cayman Islands (1992); Guyana (1995); Jamaica (1995); St. Lucia (1995); St. Vincent and the Grenadines (1995); and Trinidad and Tobago (1991, 1999) (Robinson 2000:102). Caribbean nations have adopted widely international accords and agreements protecting women's rights. As Par-

gass and Clarke write: "At the formal level therefore, Caribbean governments may be said to have accepted that violence against women constitutes a violation of fundamental human rights requiring state action" (2003:41).

13. In an earlier publication, I spoke of "rites of domination" at court (Lazarus-Black 1997). I have revised my thinking to allow court rites to exemplify both domination and moments of resistance to more general patterns of oppression and hierarchy. I explain the paradoxical and sometimes ironic functions and consequences of court rites in chapter 4.

14. I build on the work of anthropologists and sociologists who have analyzed how the form, language, and staging of legal proceedings in courts function, often oppressively, as mechanisms of social control (e.g., Atkinson and Drew 1979; Baumgartner 1988; Blumberg 1967; Carlen 1974, 1975, 1976a, 1976b; Cicourel 1968; Comaroff and Roberts 1981; Conley and O'Barr 1990, 1998; Coutin 1993, 2000; Eaton 1986; Emerson 1969; Feeley 1979; Fineman 1995; Garfinkel 1956; Hirsch 1994, 1998; Hirsch and Lazarus-Black 1994; Holstein 1993; LaFont 1996; Matoesian 1993, 1995, 2001; Merry 1990, 1994, 2000; Mileski 1971; Moore 1992; O'Barr 1982; Sudnow 1965; White 1991; Yngvesson 1993, 1994).

15. As many scholars attest, race and ethnicity are often contentious issues in Trinidadian politics (e.g., Munasinghe 2002; Ryan 1996, 1999), but these were not salient in any obvious or patterned way in the implementation of Trinidad's domestic violence law in the courts that I observed. That is not to discount, of course, that parties to domestic violence cases may encounter prejudiced officials who negatively influence in myriad ways peoples' abilities to secure justice. Moreover, groups practicing different customs or religious practices may make use of alternative forms of dispute resolution in lieu of courts. Two examples are East Indians' use of *panchayat,* a traditional forum for conflict resolution led by respected village elders, and fundamentalist Christians' decisions to avoid the courts (Lazarus-Black and McCall 2006). Note that Danns and Parsad (1989) report negligible ethnic differences in domestic violence rates in Guyana. Similarly, Rawlins's analysis of a sample of 100 men and 100 women of diverse ethnic backgrounds from two communities in Trinidad confirmed that "differences in terms of first hand experience of domestic violence in adulthood by ethnicity were not statistically significant" (2000:165). In Trinidad, members of each of the two largest ethnic groups regularly told me that the problem of domestic violence was mainly a problem found among persons of the other ethnic group (see also Cain 1996:iii.) The topic of race/ethnicity, gender violence, and the criminal justice response needs further attention from Caribbean scholars. In the case of the United States, domestic violence research documents both the intersectionality of race, class, culture, and gender in the matter of violence against women, and the persistent racism encountered by victims in the criminal justice system (see, especially, the recent edited collection by Sokoloff 2005.)

16. This insight is a consequence of feminist scholarship and methodology across several disciplines. Minow succinctly summarizes important points:

> First, feminist work explores and expresses the relationship between the knower and the known: how does the material historical perspective of the investigator influence or shape what is seen or understood? Second, feminist methods look for wholes and relationships rather than simply separate parts and they emphasize experience and intuition, not just analysis of distinct and

separate units. Third, feminist work specifically reflects upon relationships between people rather than treating people as autonomous, with identities existing prior to their social relationships. Feminists criticize the assumption of autonomous individualism behind American economic and political theory and legal and bureaucratic practice, for this assumption rests on a picture of public and independent man rather than private and often dependent, or interconnected, woman. And fourth, feminist work expresses a suspicion of general rules abstracted from context and instead considers the significance of contexts and particularities. (1990:194)

17. My understanding of agency resonates with William H. Sewell's compelling conceptualization: "To be an agent means to be capable of exerting some degree of control over the social relations in which one is enmeshed, which in turn implies the ability to transform those social relations to some degree. As I see it, agents are empowered to act with and against others by structures: they have knowledge of the schemas that inform social life and have access to some measure of human and nonhuman resources. . . . Structures . . . empower agents differentially, which also implies that they embody the desires, intentions, and knowledge of agents differentially as well. . . . Agency entails an ability to coordinate one's actions with others and against others, to form collective projects, to persuade, to coerce, and to monitor the simultaneous effects of one's own and others' activities" (1992:20, 21).

To this definition I would add Greenhouse's important insights that "agency" itself is a cultural concept, and that terms like "hegemony" and "resistance," and "structure" and "agency," name the practices of recognition by which some forms of agency and some agents are acknowledged, while others are denied (1996:4, 234). Coutin (2000:12, 173) reminds us that "agency" is not the same thing as "resistance" or "autonomy"; see also Butler (1992:13) and Razack (1998:26). Other recent discussions of the agency of survivors of domestic violence include Abraham (1995, 2000, 2005), Richie (1996), Sokoloff (2005), and Sokoloff and Dupont (2005a, 2005b).

18. Trinch (2001, 2003) demonstrates how Latina women's stories of sexual abuse and violence are heard and recorded by court workers who are charged with creating formal, institutional reports to be used later in their hearings. In an argument similar to the one I am making here regarding litigants' interactions at the court, she finds that victims' sworn statements are not singular products but rather the outcome of the encounter between the victim and the court worker who interviews her. In some cases, a third party, a translator, also plays a role in the construction of the affidavit. The discrepancies between spoken, unofficial accounts and written, official reports are vast, leaving victims vulnerable to tests of their credibility.

19. Like Sewell, I conceptualize "structure" as "process" rather than as a steady state: "Structure is dynamic, not static; it is the continually evolving outcome and matrix of a process of social interaction. Even the more or less perfect reproduction of structures is a profoundly temporal process that requires resourceful and innovative human conduct" (1992:27).

20. Structural and cultural analyses of domestic violence in the United States have proliferated in recent years so that we now have quite sophisticated studies of how the intersections of race, class, and gender combine in ways that subject

women to multiple forms of domination that often include physical, psychological, and sexual violence. I direct the reader's attention, for example, to recent collections by Fineman and Thomadsen (1991), Fineman and Mykitiuk (1994), Schneider (2000), and Sokoloff (2005).

21. The category of "other" or "not stated" may include indigenous peoples and those who identify as "European," "Middle Eastern," "Portuguese," and "Spanish." Insightful works on the history, ethnicity, and "mixing" of diverse peoples in Trinidad are found in Khan 1993; Munasinghe 2001, 2002; Reddock 1999; and Segal 1993.

22. The 2001 elections in Trinidad were unprecedented in that the two major political parties, the People's National Movement (PNM) and the United National Congress (UNC), each won eighteen seats in Parliament. Patrick Manning has served as prime minister since December 24, 2001. George Maxwell Richards became head of state in March 2003. Of the nineteen members of the PNM cabinet, five are women. They hold the positions of attorney general, education minister, minister of legal affairs, minister of culture and tourism, and minister of social development.

23. The oil production and refining segment of the economy is supported by asphalt and natural gas resources, methanol, and fertilizers. Trinidad and Tobago is one of the world's largest exporters of liquefied natural gas. Sugar, cocoa, rice, citrus, coffee, vegetables, poultry, and fishing diversify the country's economy, as do tourism, food processing, beverages, and cotton textiles. The United States is currently Trinidad's leading import and export partner.

24. Trinidad and Tobago's judiciary includes the Supreme Court of Judicature and the Magistracy. The head of the judiciary is the chief justice responsible for the administration of justice in the nation. The Supreme Court consists of the Court of Appeal and the High Court and was established by the constitution of the republic. The Magistracy, presided over by a chief magistrate who reports to the chief justice, is governed by the Summary Courts Act, Chapter 4:20, and the Petty Civil Courts Act, Chapter 4:21. The Magistracy theoretically includes one chief magistrate, one deputy chief magistrate, thirteen senior magistrates, and twenty-nine magistrates (in 2001, seven positions were unfilled.) The country is divided into thirteen magisterial districts. To qualify for the office of magistrate, an attorney must have practiced a minimum of five years (Judiciary of the Republic of Trinidad and Tobago). Note that a case involving domestic violence might include additional criminal charges and so become transformed into a case that might find its way to the Privy Council (Robinson forthcoming).

25. It is possible to apply at the High Court for an injunction against domestic violence; however, an injunction is expensive, requires the services of an attorney, and must be brought with another matter, such as a divorce application. My analysis is limited to the much more prevalent applications for protection brought to the lower courts.

26. For example, investigating violence among East Indian women in Guyana, Parsad finds: "Based on a cultural acceptance of male dominance and female subservience, routine violence is legitimized by socially shared definitions as normative, necessary and expressive of social control. In Guyana, much of the physical violence directed against wives finds acceptance among spouses and tolerance from the authorities of social control. Physical abuse of wives is both accepted

and tolerated in the Guyanese context by the adage that 'teeth and tongue must bite.' Not only by this do we openly sanction violence and abuse in man-woman relationships but we also hold firm to a position that whatever occurs between a man and his wife is their business" (1988:2). Historical research from Guyana confirms this pattern among Afro-Guyanese, Chinese-Guyanese, and Indo-Guyanese peoples (Moore 1995:105). Curiously, Moore does not mention domestic abuse in relation to Guyana's white community. Acceptance of domestic violence by Caribbean peoples under certain circumstances, but not others, is discussed by Chevannas (2001).

27. For the sake of brevity in this book, I often use the colloquium "Trinidad" to refer to the nation-state of Trinidad and Tobago. I want to be clear, however, that my experiences were limited to the locations described in this and later chapters.

28. In court I observed women at every stage of their lives—married and unmarried, with and without children, and homemakers and working women—applying for protection orders. Of the twelve applicants whom I interviewed in depth, two were in their twenties. One was single, unemployed, and raising a child in her parents' home. The other was unmarried, employed, childless, and living with her parents. Four of my interviewees were in their thirties. One reconciled with a former abuser. She remained married to him and they were raising their children together. A second ended her relationship with the abuser and married someone else with whom she was raising her children. A third woman in her thirties was working full time raising her children alone, and the fourth was divorced from the abuser and raising her two children in her parents' home. One of two interviewees in their forties lived alone once she managed to get her abusive common-law partner out of her home. She supported herself in a low-paying job. The other worked full time at a better salary. She was separated from her abusive husband and raising the children with some financial assistance from their father. Finally, three women interviewed were in their fifties. One was single and still supporting children. The other two were married, employed, and their children were young adults either already living in their own households or soon to depart. By local standards, six of these interviewees were middle class and six working class.

29. My research focused on the creation and implementation of a *new* law, rather than the consequences of reforming an old statute. See Horney and Spohn (1991) for a classic study that found that in the United States, reform of previously existing rape laws intended to better define the offense, protect victims, and increase offender conviction rates—all intentions shared by those who helped reform the 1991 Domestic Violence Act in Trinidad—had limited consequences on final case dispositions in most of the jurisdictions surveyed. My project confirms Horney and Spohn's conclusions that those who implement the law wield considerable power over the fate of legal cases, and also that law provides important symbolic messages regarding women (see chapter 3). A more complete analysis of the 1999 Domestic Violence Act and its consequences for litigants must await future research.

30. Later I would learn that these explanations replicated those told to Websdale in his interviews with battered women in the United States (1998:xxii, xxv). Of course, some people whom I approached to ask if they would participate in the study turned me down. (I did not keep a count of these.) Most were men convicted

of the offense of domestic violence. I was not surprised when they declined to be interviewed as there is stigma attached to being convicted of domestic violence. Two women turned down my request for an interview when I explained that there was no financial compensation for participation in the study. A few attorneys and one magistrate also declined to be interviewed. For the most part, however, people generously shared their experiences.

31. The 1991 Domestic Violence Act and the more recent statute of 1999 do not require a complainant to obtain an attorney to seek a protection order. Most complainants and defendants that I observed in the magistrates' courts were not represented. Attorneys handling domestic violence cases are not influenced by whether the prosecution of any particular case is also good for their career (see, for example, Frohmann 1991 and Hirschel and Hutchison 2001). Indeed, the stakes are low for the attorneys involved in domestic violence cases in Trinidad. These cases are not considered very important; they are mainly prosecuted in the lower courts, and fees are minimal.

Chapter 1: Imagining and Implementing Domestic Violence Law

1. A word of caution about the process of regendering the state: it is not necessarily a process that makes women the "equal" of men, either legally or in everyday practice. As Alonso demonstrates in her analysis of nineteenth-century domestic violence law in Mexico, "the regulation by men as agents of the state of the abusive behavior of men in households had as one of its effects a construction of domestic violence as a practice of deviant men, deflecting potential criticism of the inequities of marriage as a whole, and of the ways in which women's subjectivities and subjection were constituted through legal means" (1995:43). Nevertheless, for both Namiquipan and Trinidadian women, domestic violence law is empowering "within the terms of their overall subordination" (Alonso 1995:43). Regendering is an ongoing process that names some actions and words as crimes; time and politics will produce others.

2. Alexander's important work on law and the politics of sexuality in Trinidad and Tobago and the Bahamas uncovers "racialized legislative gestures that have naturalized heterosexuality by criminalizing lesbian and other forms of nonprocreative sex" as part of the "process of decolonization and reconstruction of the self, a project which has been seriously disrupted in most 'postcolonial' nation-states" (1994:5, 6). As she suggests, criminalization is a technique of power; a mode for forging a nation whose citizens are specifically heterosexual. At the same time, however, feminist mobilization has made possible certain concessions from the state, including the tale I tell here about the Domestic Violence Act: "it becomes clear that some areas of patriarchy have been challenged while others have been resolidified" (Alexander 1994:7).

3. Historians will find interesting the fact that in the nineteenth century the state had once enacted a statute to protect indentured immigrant women from abusive behavior from their husbands or common-law partners, although that act did not protect the public more generally. The end of the nineteenth century was a tense period in Trinidad. The sex ratio among East Indian immigrants was highly skewed, with few women, and the years 1870–1900 were difficult times for the sugar industry because of the sugar duties imposed by Great Britain, the

development of the sugar beet, and the closure of many estates in Trinidad (Reddock 1994:33). Violence was high in the immigrant community and legislators were moved to act. Ordinance No. 6, 1881, later incorporated into the Indian Immigration Ordinances of 1881 and 1899, made it illegal to "entice away," cohabit with, or harbor an immigrant's wife on penalty of twenty pounds, six months in prison, or both. Immigrants were also prohibited from threatening violence to the women they cohabited with, a crime punishable by one month in prison. Moreover, if a stipendiary justice of the peace found evidence of domestic violence, he could transfer the defendant to another estate, allow the victim to move from the household, and/or order alimony and child support—unless there was evidence of the woman's adultery (Reddock 1994:34–35).

4. Garland cites Gay's notion of "overdetermination" as "the sensible recognition that a variety of causes—a variety, not infinity—enters into the making of all historical events, and that each ingredient in historical experience can be counted on to have a variety—not infinity—of functions" (1990:280). My task here is to uncover the most important of the causes surrounding the passage of the Domestic Violence Act. I view the act as part of the process of decolonization and nation building that began formally in Trinidad with independence from Great Britain in 1962, continued with the formation of the republic in 1976, and characterizes contemporary political, social, and economic programs. Sources on Trinidad's recent history include Brereton 1981, 2004; Deosaran 1993; Kiely 1996; Munasinghe 2001; Reddock 1994, 1995; Ryan 1991, 1996, 1999; Segal 1987; and Vertovec 1992. Reddock (1986) and Colón and Reddock (2004) point out that regional organizing for social change and justice for women has also been important in the Caribbean. The Caribbean Association for Feminist Research and Action (CAFRA), organized in 1985, is one example (see also Cain 2000). Based on interviews with thirteen women involved with the prevention of violence against women and children, Cain found evidence of "interactive globalization, rather than hegemony or acceptance by the women of an occidentalist denial of difference" (2000:253). She also points to the importance of women's roles in the professions, government, and public service in efforts to abolish gender inequality (2000:255–56).

5. In contrast to Antigua and Barbuda, where women have organized politically to enact legislation that protects their own and the rights of their children in "private ways" rather than in public forums (Lazarus-Black 1994:chapter 9), Trinidadian women have a long history of participation in political organizing, although they have not often won positions of leadership (Colón and Reddock 2004; Reddock 1994, 1998b).

6. That Caribbean lawmakers are influenced both by local ideologies and practices and by the new global order is summarized succinctly by Robinson:

> Caribbean family law in the post-independence era reflects the evolving attitudes of those governing and being governed about the status, rights and responsibilities of women, men and children in families. The reform initiatives of the last twenty-five years have endeavored to create more culturally relevant laws. Attempts have been made to respond to Caribbean realities such as the dominance of family structures which do not have marriage at the center, a high percentage of Caribbean children born to parents who are not married to each other, and a significant number of households headed by

women who need economic support in raising their children. The changes in Caribbean family law also mirror global trends, particularly the emphasis on the welfare of the child and the move towards gender equality. (2000:101)

The rapid timing and similar contents of domestic violence legislation in the English-speaking Caribbean also suggest international influence as predicted by Boyle and Preves (2000). Clarke (1997, 1998), Babb (1997), and Bissessar (2000) also note the importance of international attention to gender-specific violence in the Caribbean. Bissessar and I reached independently the conclusions that the global women's movement had a significant impact on local activists in Trinidad and that the passage of the first domestic violence law could not have been possible without the local women's movement. She also describes some of the problems associated with implementing domestic violence law, such as insufficient attention to local causes of violence, lack of economic security and shelters for victims, bureaucratic incompetency, and varying interpretations of policy (Bissessar 2000:57–59).

7. As Reddock (1998b) points out, the PNM was successful very soon after its emergence in large part because it swiftly incorporated many organizations and mobilized women members. These included the Teachers' Education and Cultural Association (TECA), the People's Education Movement (PEM), the People's Education Group (PEG), and the Federation of Women's Institutes (UWI). Women organized many grassroots events, although they were rarely chosen for leadership positions in the PNM. The PNM gained power in 1956 and was undefeated until 1986 when it lost to the National Alliance for Reconstruction (NAR), under whose leadership the Domestic Violence Act became law.

8. Miller reports: "I had found people quite capable of creative normativity around recently developed or adopted rituals that blithely ignore all those transnational factors that should have counted against this. At Christmas, for example, virtually the entire population may be found eating the same things, highlighting certain values that center very clearly on a common notion of being Trinidadian" (1997:33). Living, teaching, and interviewing in Trinidad, one finds that people identify things and events that comprise "Trini" culture. In addition to Carnival, Christmas, music, literature, dance, and food, my interviewees took pride in Trinidad's relative wealth, literacy, health care, and general modernity and development.

9. During colonialism, education was in the hands of religious authorities and the schools catered to the children of the elite. Primary education expanded after World War II. Boys were encouraged to go to school for at least a few years, but many Indian families deliberately kept their daughters away from schools, particularly after the age of ten or when they reached puberty (Barriteau 1998:202; Kassim 1997:6; Mohammed 1998:17). Canadian Presbyterians provided formal education to East Indians in Trinidad, but they did so at the price of conversion. "Ironically, the first Hindu-Muslim school was founded in 1930 as a reaction to the Canadian mission's dictum that all Indians had to convert to get jobs" (Mohammed 1998:19). Mohammed argues that "education was one of the avenues which Indian women used to negotiate terms for a deferment of marriage age, the extension of the period of childhood and age of sexual maturity, and by this means as well to have the option of choice in a marriage partner" (Mohammed 1998:21). See Campbell (1997) for the history of education in Trinidad and To-

bago, 1939–86. In his article on education in the region from 1930–90, Campbell concludes: "A virtual revolution in female participation and success in the school systems has occurred in the twentieth century" (2004:624). Bailey (2003) cautions us, however, that women's access to education and high levels of achievement need not necessarily translate into conditions of empowerment in politics or the labor market.

10. To understand the complexity of gender relations and how they do (and do not) change over time, Barriteau urges scholars to investigate both the "ideological dimension of gender" and the "material dimension of gender" (1998:190; 2001:29–30). The state intercedes along these two dimensions in important ways that change a gender system over time. For example, the state may end wage discrimination or renounce certain social practices as "appropriate" for men but not women (Barriteau 1998:190, 191).

11. By the mid-1980s, however, the government had an unmanageable external debt. As a consequence, the IMF/World Bank implemented structural-adjustment policies that cut welfare and food subsidies, devalued the currency, and privatized some state enterprises (Miller 1997).

12. By 1995–96, women constituted 68 percent of undergraduates in the faculty of law, 50 percent in medical sciences, 56 percent in natural sciences, 67 percent in social sciences, 61 percent in agriculture, 78 percent in arts and general studies, and 20 percent in engineering (Reddock 1998a:14). In 1998–99, women comprised 65.5 percent of all students at the three campuses of the University of the West Indies (Bailey 2003:115). This should not mask the truism that "while developments in education and training systems brought a number of changes and improvements in women's status, and some women have successfully entered previously all-male fields, there still remains a complex of mechanisms, both structural and ideological, hindering women's attainment of equality with men" (Seebaran-Suite 1991:241; see also Bailey 2003 and Lindsay 2002).

13. The original sexual offenses bill was designed to criminalize marital rape and to decriminalize homosexuality. After extensive public debate, however, both proposals were dropped. Among other things, the 1986 Sexual Offences Act criminalized some sexual activity previously ignored, made homosexual and lesbian sex punishable as "serious indecency," prohibited employers from taking sexual advantage of minor employees at the workplace, made sex with a girl up to age 14 a statutory offense, and criminalized marital rape in specific situations, such as when there was a decree nisi of divorce or a judicial separation (Alexander 1991). Nevertheless, as Mohammed explains, the controversy over the law had important ramifications: "First the issue of sexual violence had to be taken seriously; second, women had united across class, ethnic and political barriers to demand their rights and had proved themselves a force to be reckoned with; and third, they had found support among many men as well. Most importantly, by having the clause reintroduced, admittedly in a watered-down form, another battle had been won in the rights of all women—the act of marriage should not and could not in any way interfere with the right of women to control over their bodies and their lives" (1991:45).

14. Services to victims of violence increased steadily through the 1990s, although there is certainly need for additional programs and shelters. A domestic violence unit was established at the Ministry of Culture and Gender Affairs,

which operates the Domestic Violence Hotline. In 1998, the hotline received 2,611 calls, 84 percent from women and 16 percent from men. There are approximately fifteen shelters in the country, including one in Tobago, and sixteen counseling centers for victims of domestic violence. Of these, the Family Services Division of the Ministry of Social and Community Development is the official agency. The Probation Department of the Ministry of Social and Community Development is also an official counseling agency. In addition, the government collaborates with a variety of nongovernmental organizations such as the Rape Crisis Society, the Coalition Against Domestic Violence, Men Against Violence Against Women, Families in Action, Working Women for Social Progress, and Caribbean Association for Feminist Research and Action. Finally, the police are receiving special training and have begun to collect statistical data on domestic violence cases. Gender-sensitivity training for public officials, key individuals in the private sector, social workers, magistrates, and the police were all initiated during the late 1990s (Ministry of the Attorney General and Legal Affairs 2000:35, 36, 45, 53). By 2003, 670 persons had received special training for police officers on domestic violence (Economic Commission for Latin America and the Caribbean 2003:23). James-Sebro (2001) offers a study of two very different local organizations devoted to working on behalf of abused women.

15. The 1960s and 1970s in the United States, for example, had seen the rebirth of feminism that Pleck finds "was necessary for the rediscovery of wife beating. The women's movement put pressure on the police, social agencies, and the state and federal government to respond adequately to the problem. It forced policy makers to consider remedies that had been unthinkable only a few years before" (1987:183). The National Organization for Women formed in the United States in 1966, but it did not turn its attention to the problem of domestic abuse until 1977, the date of the International Women's Year Convention (Pleck 1987:183).

16. These include: (1) the International Covenant on Economic, Social and Cultural Rights; (2) the International Covenant on Civil and Political Rights; (3) the Optional Protocol to the International Covenant on Civil and Political Rights; (4) the Convention on the Political Rights of Women; (5) the Convention on the Nationality of Married Women; (6) the Convention on Consent to Marriage, Minimum Age for Marriage and Registration of Marriages; and (7) the Convention on the Elimination of All Forms of Discrimination Against Women (CEDAW). In May 1991, Trinidad and Tobago adopted the American Convention on Human Rights and recognized the Inter-American Court of Human Rights (Human Rights Internet 1993:9–10).

17. Women continue to gain representation in party politics in Trinidad, although they remain underrepresented at the decision-making levels. Of thirty-six elected members of Parliament in 2000, four were women. Of thirty-one nominated members in the Senate, nine were women; one was also a minister. In the public sector in 1996, women comprised approximately 42 percent of legislative senior officials and managers, 40 percent of professionals, 53 percent of technicians and associate professors, and 48 percent of service workers. With respect to the judiciary, women were overrepresented in the lower courts and underrepresented in the High Courts. Approximately 33 percent of the Court of Appeals judges, 14 percent of the High Court judges, 67 percent of Masters of the High Court, 47 percent of senior magistrates, and 77 percent of magistrates were women as

the century closed (Ministry of the Attorney General and Legal Affairs 2000:66, 67).

18. This account of the controversy is based on interviews with participants, politicians, attorneys, scholars, staff, and graduate students at the University of the West Indies; a few published and unpublished papers by Trinidadian scholars and attorneys; and newspaper accounts (see especially *Trinidad Express*, February 20, 21, 28, 1991; March 6, 7, 8, 1991; April 18, 1991; *Sunday Guardian* March 10, 1991; and *Trinidad Guardian* March 11, 1991). In this chapter, I speak of "advocates" and "opponents" of the Domestic Violence Act. This simplifies reality, for some "opponents" and "advocates" supported one or more tenets of the original bill and rejected others. The law had widespread support from feminist organizations, particularly a number of nongovernmental organizations. Some feminists wanted an even stronger act, such as Puerto Rico's, which protects girlfriends and ex-girlfriends from abuse (e.g., *Trinidad Express*, February 1, 1991). In contrast, opposition to the law came mainly from individuals who argued against changing the constitution, state intervention in family life, extending police powers, removing men from their homes, and the bill's failure to provide supportive services for victims. In short, there was opposition from both conservatives and liberals.

19. The full titles of these acts are the Matrimonial Proceedings and Property Act, 1988, and the Attachment of Earnings (Maintenance) Act, 1988 (Daly 1992:75, 96). The first is primarily a divorce bill; the latter is a statute to collect child support from delinquent fathers.

20. "De facto spouse" refers to a person living with the respondent as his wife or her husband although not legally married. The term also includes a person who has a child with the respondent, whether or not they reside together at the time of the incident. Parent may be a parent by blood, marriage, or adoption. Children include children of the respondent or spouse under the age of eighteen who normally reside with one of the parties or of whom the respondent or spouse is a parent or guardian. Dependents are persons over the age of eighteen who reside with the parties and who rely on them because of some disability (Daly 1992:36). As noted earlier, there is no protection for victims of violence in gay or lesbian partnerships.

21. The magistrate considers: (1) the need to protect a person from violence; (2) the welfare of children or the spouse or respondent; (3) the domestic needs of the parties; (4) hardships resulting from the orders; (5) financial needs and responsibilities of the parties; and (6) other matters the court deems relevant (Daly 1992:39).

22. A magistrate is required by law to consider "any hardship that may be caused to the respondent or to any other person as a result of the making of the order" (Laws of Trinidad and Tobago 1991:94). Interestingly, the concern that disturbed so many of the legislators—namely, the thought that men would be deprived of the right to remain in their homes—hardly ever came up during my court observations. When an order included the provision that the respondent keep away from the complainant's premises, it was almost always the case that the couple had already separated or planned to separate. I return to this point in later chapters.

23. The relationship between the "authentic" state and "ethnic" groups in

Trinidad is a complex matter. Yelvington describes the relationship between ethnicity and nationalism in Trinidad as characterized by two related but opposing processes: "On the one hand, there is the conflation of nation/state/ethnicity to construct a 'non-ethnicity,' in which there are 'Trinidadians' and 'others,' that is, 'ethnics.' On the other hand, there is the construction of ethnic and cultural differences to prove and justify contribution, authenticity, and citizenship" (1995:59). Smith (1996), however, warns scholars of the theoretical limitations of recasting status struggles as ethnic conflicts. For a recent critical account of the relationship between ethnicity and nationalism, I refer the reader to Munasinghe (2001).

24. For example, Lynette Seebaran-Suite, an attorney, and Cathy Shepherd, CAFRA's documentalist, discussed the domestic violence bill at a public forum at the city hall on March 15, 1991. The program was organized by Working Women in collaboration with CAFRA (*Trinidad Express*, March 17, 1991). See also interviews with R. Saith and Senator D. Mahabir-Wyatt in the *Trinidad Guardian*, March 10, 1991.

25. The petitions voiced opposition to amendments limiting the scope of the protection order and protested against attempts to limit the definition of spouse: "We have a wide range of family forms in Trinidad and Tobago. Victims need protection against violence, irrespective of which domestic arrangement they choose. . . . The argument that a woman should be in a relationship for two weeks, five months, or one year before being eligible to obtain legal protection from abuse is downright ridiculous. We say no time frame for taking licks." The petitioners also denounced the proposal to permit an abuser to give an undertaking—a promise to the court that he would not abuse again—on the grounds that "it essentially gives him the opportunity to abuse at least one more time before the victim can benefit from full legal protection" (*Trinidad Express*, March 14, 1991).

26. Commenting on my chapter, Robinson pointed out that the law recognizes women's rights but makes it clear that sex does not include sexual orientation.

27. The power of the police to investigate domestic violence disputes was expanded in the 1999 Domestic Violence Act. In the new law, police must respond to every report of domestic violence and complete a report on the incident. An officer may request a warrant to enter a premise to prevent the commission of an offense, or may enter a premise without a warrant if he has reasonable cause to suspect an act of violence is being committed or is about to be committed (Laws of Trinidad and Tobago 1999).

28. I thank attorney and author Roberta Clarke and law professor Tracy Robinson for clarifying for me the origins and importance of the undertaking in the Trinidadian statute. Clarke, who was active in Trinidad in support of the first domestic violence law, explained that the provision in the Trinidadian statute for undertakings evolved in response to the concerns of several senators that the domestic violence law could too readily force a man from his home. They believed the undertaking gave an offender one more opportunity to apologize and to make amends, that it was less harsh on the respondent psychologically, and that the consequence might therefore be more conducive to preserving the family. In contrast to Trinidad, Robinson's research finds that most of the Caribbean countries that have passed domestic violence legislation modeled their statutes on the CARICOM model legislation. The model legislation does not include a provision for undertakings. However, Connors's "generalized account" of "cur-

rent strategies employed by governments to confront violence against women" reports: "In many countries there is a procedure for lodging a complaint of threatened or actual violence before a magistrate or justice, who then can request the violent party to enter into an undertaking, with or without a pledge of money, to keep the peace or be of good behavior" (1994:182, 185). I have not been able to determine the specific source for the Trinidadian undertaking.

29. Perhaps its cultural emphasis on modernity, individualism, progress, social status, and materialism also helps explain why Trinidad's "route" to domestic violence legislation and its lawmakers' proposed solutions may more closely parallel those of the United States than of Great Britain:

> In Britain, there was almost universal acceptance of activists' pragmatic solution for refuge and housing provision, and legislation was quickly passed, but feminist conceptions of the social and cultural causes of the violence were generally ignored or rejected in favor of ideas focusing on individual inadequacy and poor family background. The solution was adopted while the nature of the problem was denied or transformed. In the United States, the focus of the initial hearings was on civil rights and obtaining equal rights to legal protection from violence. . . . In the United States, like no other country, extreme individualism coupled with a perpetual concern about one's status and position combined with unrestrained ideals of striving and success are powerful forces shaping individual rather than collective solutions. (Dobash and Dobash 1992:112, 216)

I posit this as a hypothesis for future research.

Chapter 2: A Look at the Numbers

Patricia L. McCall is a professor in the Department of Sociology and Anthropology, North Carolina State University.

1. As Urla also notes: "Who or what gets counted, by whom, and for what purposes are questions of immediate consequence to the distribution of economic and political power and to the experience of everyday life in modern civil society" (1993:819; see also Bograd 2005:29). Given the legal reforms and resources committed to handling domestic violence cases throughout the region, the social, political, and economic stakes are high.

2. I am indebted to Patty L. McCall for the innovative approaches she took in creating a quantitative record from data that was collected by an anthropologist unaccustomed to thinking about statistics and for her endless patience as she introduced me to the properties and perils of quantitative research. Along the way, we had help from Margaret (Peg) Brant, Mike Maltz, and Joe Peterson and we want to acknowledge the generous time and efforts of these colleagues.

3. The court data from Pelau was gathered between September 11, 1997, and August 20, 1998. I observed the court on a weekly basis for about ten months. Because quantitative analysis through a statistical program was not planned at the time that field notes were collected, court information was entered into the software, retaining as much detail as possible. Unique identifiers were devised by McCall to follow the cases while protecting the anonymity and identity of

the litigants. This procedure also provided avenues for determining the duration of case processing and for data checks.

4. This assertion is based on participant observation in the magistrates' courts and interviews with legal professionals. In addition, one of the extended cases I followed involved a mother whose adult son was a drug addict. Her story is recounted in chapter 3. Readers should be aware that Trinidadians can be creative in their naming practices and usages.

5. Defendants are protected by res judicata; that is, placing a person in double jeopardy. However, a complainant can bring a defendant back to court on other grounds and citing other incidents. The same rules apply to withdrawn cases; if no evidence has been laid before the court, the case can be brought back. Once evidence is given in court, that case is never reheard.

6. There has been considerable research on the question of why applications for protection orders are dismissed or withdrawn (e.g., Connell 1997; Eigenberg 2001; Ford 1991; Harrell, Smith, and Newmark 1993; Hirsch 1998; Martin 1976; Merry 1990, 2000; Ptacek 1999; Trinch 2003; and Wittner 1998). Belknap and colleagues identified the following barriers that sixty-five women in the United States encountered in going to court: "By far the most commonly reported barrier, cited by almost half of the participants, was *fear of the batterer.* Three other barriers to going to court reported by approximately one-quarter of the respondents were problems with getting time off work, wanting to work things out with the abuser, and pressure from the abuser's family/friends" (2001:323). Other reasons included prior negative experiences with the courts, lack of child care, pressure from the victim's friends or family, finding transportation, and the victim's fear of possible arrest (Belknap et al. 2001:323–24). Bennett et al. (1999) add the courts' failure to provide information to complainants about case processing and lack of follow-up of cases by court personnel as other reasons applications are dropped. Given these typical barriers to going to court, we were not surprised to find that the great majority of complainants in Pelau (87 percent) made just one application for protection during 1997–98. Eleven percent, however, applied for two orders and less than 2 percent brought three applications.

7. About 37 percent of the complainants were present for all of the hearings in their cases; almost 29 percent were present for at least half. Thirty-two percent were never present. Respondents are not required to be present at hearings until they receive an official summons. Almost 38 percent were present at all of the hearings; 19 percent were there for at least half of their hearings. If there is evidence that a defendant has been served but has not appeared in court, a warrant for his arrest can be sworn. That happened infrequently—in only three cases in this sample. Lack of summons service to the respondent was also a factor in dissuading American women from returning to domestic violence court for a final protection order (Harrell, Smith, and Newmark 1993:32). Feeley wrote about the practice of nonappearance of defendants in an American criminal court: "My observations of the court lead me to believe that nonappearance is more likely to be accounted for in terms of how well defendants understand the operations of the court (for example, are they in the correct courtroom?), how much respect they have for the court, how seriously they take the proceedings, how aware they are of their scheduled court appearances, and what they believe the consequences will be if they fail to appear. In other words, the *interaction between the court organiza-*

tion and the accused is likely to provide the best explanation for appearance or nonappearance" (1979:232). Similar considerations likely influenced respondents with respect to court appearances in domestic violence cases in Trinidad.

8. Some examples illustrating this point include Adelman 1997; Comaroff and Roberts 1981; Conley and O'Barr 1990; Connell 1997; Coutin 2000; Fischer and Rose 1995; Ford 1991; Frohmann and Mertz 1995; Gordon 1988; Greenhouse 1986; Greenhouse, Yngvesson, and Engel 1994; Hirsch 1998; Hirsch and Lazarus-Black 1994; Lazarus-Black 1994, 1997; Lazarus-Black and Hirsch 1994; Mahoney 1991, 1994; Mather and Yngvesson 1980/81; Maurer 1997; Merry 1990, 2000; Razack 1998; Websdale 1998; Wittner 1998; and Yngvesson 1993.

9. Tabulations also were made focusing on case dispositions involving parties who had the same surname. Identical surnames can indicate several possible relationships: (1) marriage; (2) parent/child; (3) other familial relationships such as siblings or grandparent/grandchild; or (4) the assumption by a woman of her partner's name when they have been in a long-term, common-law relationship. In terms of case dispositions, there was very little difference between cases involving parties with the same surnames and those of the general sample. Of cases that involved litigants with the same surnames, 57 percent were dismissed, 20 percent were withdrawn, 19 percent were resolved through undertakings, 2 percent won formal protection orders, and 1 percent closed with an interim order. Cases involving parties with the same last name were less likely to be dismissed as a result of the failure of the complainant to attend the hearing: 25 percent in contrast to 50 percent in the general sample.

10. This was changed to twenty-one days in the 1999 Domestic Violence Act.

11. The 1999 Domestic Violence Act provides for complaints about additional forms of abuse, such as emotional and financial abuse. It will be interesting to see if future research finds changes in the contents of magistrates' court orders. Like Ptacek (1999:155–56), I found magistrates varied in which remedies for domestic violence they offered to victims.

12. One officer told me that breach cases are rare because the police have difficulty establishing the evidence to bring such cases to court. For example, a woman with a protection order might meet the respondent on the street and he might use abusive and insulting language. Alarmed, she would go to the police to report the incident. If the police followed through and spoke with the man, he would almost certainly deny that he was abusive. At that point, and unless there were witnesses willing to go to court, it would be her word against his. The police are more likely to respond to a case in which there is physical evidence of abuse. Several magistrates also advised me that the police might bring breaches of protection orders to court as other criminal matters, such as "assault" or "intention to wound," instead of filing them as breach cases.

13. Reluctance to send men to prison for domestic violence matters has also been identified by research on this topic in the United States: "A 1995 study of 140 domestic violence arrests in 11 jurisdictions found that only 44 made it to conviction, plea, or acquittal, and of these, only 16 served any time" (Hanna 1998:1523). See also Ventura and Davis (2005) and Crocker (2005).

14. I conducted participant observation in Cocoa in February and March 1998, interviewed Cocoa's magistrate and several attorneys who practiced there, and collected a sample of one month of court cases. I attended the magistrate's court

in Port of Spain between February and August 1998, and followed a selected sample of cases as they progressed through the system. When I could not attend court, my research assistant observed the final hearings and case dispositions of those cases. I observed two magistrates adjudicate in Town, one of whom was interviewed for this study, and most of the attorneys I spoke to had at least some experience practicing in Port of Spain. The sample of 2,711 domestic violence cases from Town covers the same two-year period as those from Pelau. We used the same methods to analyze the cases in both courts. A more comprehensive comparison of the court records of domestic violence cases from Pelau and Port of Spain appears in Lazarus-Black and McCall (2006).

15. This description of the parties involved in domestic violence cases draws heavily from Lazarus-Black and McCall (2006:144).

16. As noted earlier, different areas and neighborhoods in Trinidad are populated with different proportions of people of varying ethnic, racial, religious, and socioeconomic backgrounds. For example, Afro-Trinidadians' flight from the plantations after slavery left them heavily concentrated in towns and cities where they entered various professions and trades (Munasinghe 2001:77). Rural Tobago's population is comprised almost entirely of persons of Afro-Trinidadian heritage. Rural southern Trinidad, in contrast, is populated by a high percentage of persons with Indo-Trinidadian ancestry. As a result, different groups are more or less represented at different courts.

17. It was necessary to combine undertakings and final orders because I found this particular clerk in Cocoa did not always differentiate between them in the court records. On February 2, 1998, for example, there were two undertakings but neither is specifically marked that way. On the other hand, other undertakings are listed later in the month.

18. The charges of possession of a weapon and intention to wound were resolved by putting the defendant on a peace bond to keep the peace for three years. The fine for breaking the peace bond was $500 TT.

19. I discuss claims about the misuse of the Domestic Violence Act in chapter 3.

20. The report does not stipulate whether the category "protection orders issued" included interim orders, final orders, and undertakings, but we presume the category is inclusive.

21. We suspect the figures for Port of Spain and Court E are erroneous and actually represent cases that were dismissed or withdrawn rather than cases that were granted orders. Supporting this hypothesis, Bissessar reports that "statistics from the Magistrates Court in Port-of-Spain . . . revealed that during the period 1991–1994, although a large number of cases were brought before the Court, less than one quarter (22.5%) of the applications led to the granting of Protection Orders and seventy-five per cent were dismissed" (2000:70).

22. Again, we presume these statistics collapse our categories of "dismissed" and "withdrawn" cases, as well as cases ending in either "protection orders" or "undertakings." The coalition's report found that "available statistics are not comprehensive enough to properly understand the reasons why so many domestic violence matters are dismissed" (Trinidad and Tobago Coalition Against Domestic Violence 2005:32). Why domestic violence petitioners vanish from the courts becomes clearer over the course of later chapters in this book.

23. A recent survey by the Economic Commission for Latin America and the

Caribbean that evaluated the implementation of domestic violence law in Antigua and Barbuda, St. Kitts–Nevis, St. Lucia, and St. Vincent and the Grenadines provides limited data on case dispositions for applications for protection orders in these states. The study found thirty-six of forty cases for protection orders drawn from case files in Antigua and Barbuda were granted to applicants. This was highly unusual; protection orders were granted more sparingly in the other regions, although in percentages that were higher than those in Trinidad. For example, 55 percent of applicants for protection orders in St. Lucia in 1997–2000 received protection orders and 39 percent of applicants achieved the protection orders they sought in St. Vincent and the Grenadines in 1996 through April 2001 (Economic Commission for Latin America and the Caribbean 2001a:45–46). One possibility for Antigua's different rate might be its use of affidavits in support of applications for protection in the magistrates' courts (Economic Commission for Latin America and the Caribbean 2001a:viii). These courts also serve smaller populations and court personnel may be familiar with the parties and their troubles. Therefore, if a case overcomes other impediments and appears before a magistrate, it may result in a protection order.

24. A 1998 study of 200 randomly selected women in Trinidad by CAFRA determined that 19 percent of the sample were presently experiencing abuse at home and that 49 percent admitted to having been in situations of abuse in the past (CAFRA 1998:50). In most cases, the respondents reacted to domestic violence by getting upset, crying, or simply accepting the abuse (CAFRA 1998:61). One-third of the victims fought back or left the abuser (CAFRA 1998:62). Fifty-one percent of this sample were aware of the Domestic Violence Act (CAFRA 1998:84).

Chapter 3: The Meaning of Success

1. There is a vast literature on the topic of "entitled" and "inappropriate" or "undeserving" victims of domestic violence. For the case of Israel, see Adelman (1997, 2000); for Mexico, see Alonso (1995); for England, see Connell (1997); for the European continent, see Corrin (1996); and for the United States, see Bograd (2005), Crocker (2005), Gordon (1988), Klein (1982), Loseke (1992), Mahoney (1991, 1994), Maurer and Merry (1997), Merry (1994, 2000), and Sokoloff (2005). Razack (1998, 1999) discusses who counts as an entitled victim in Canada, while Sitaraman (2002) and Vatuk (2001) address the issue in different locales in India.

2. During 1997, the court convened with a regular list of Thursday cases on forty-seven occasions. Three public holidays fell on Thursdays: Labor Day, Divali (a Hindu celebration), and Christmas Day. On two occasions, the court sat just briefly, the magistrate hearing thirty-five matters on one date and two on another. These five dates have been eliminated from the 1997 sample. In 1998, the court met on fifty Thursdays. Excluded from my 1998 sample are two public holidays, New Year's Day and Corpus Christi Day (June 11, 1998), as well as Christmas Eve, which had an unusually short list of cases. The difference in the average number of cases heard each week between 1997 and 1998 can be partially explained by the fact that toward the end of 1998, a second magistrate was appointed in Pelau. The domestic violence cases were heard by one of these two magistrates.

3. Magistrates differed in how they interpreted the meaning of hearing domestic

violence cases "privately." Some magistrates cleared the courtroom before they turned to the domestic violence cases on their dockets. Others moved to their private chambers to hear them. A third approach involved calling the parties to the bench and adjudicating in a low voice so that the general public in the courtroom could not hear how events unfolded.

4. In formal and informal conversations during my research, many recommendations for improving case processing came to light. For example, cases could be handled much more expeditiously if resources were spent to ensure that summonses to persons accused of domestic violence were served immediately. One magistrate recommended that when people go to court to file cases of domestic violence or to receive summonses to answer charges, they should be given a one-page sheet outlining the court's procedures, a summary of the offenses covered by the act, and what constitutes evidence in a legal case. A third suggestion made to me by several persons was that additional probation officers and family counselors be made available to families seeking counseling. For recommendations to Caribbean governments to improve current legislation and its enforcement, see Joseph, Henriques, and Ekeh 1998 and Trinidad and Tobago Coalition Against Domestic Violence 2005.

5. In that case, the magistrate had sentenced him to a fine of $160 TT (about U.S. $27) or three months in prison. Everett went to prison because he did not have the money to pay the fine. By the time the case for a protection order was filed, therefore, Everett was a known petty criminal and the magistrate was well aware of his drug problem. When the magistrate spoke to Everett during the in camera hearing, she called him by his first name. It was clear that she and the defendant knew each other from his previous court cases.

6. When I analyzed the court records for Pelau for 1997 and 1998, I discovered that Rosalyn had first filed for a protection order against Everett in November 1997. She appeared as the complaining witness on the first hearing date, but Everett had not been served. The case was adjourned for one week. That record reads "Magistrate Out," without further commentary and the case was adjourned to the first week of December. On that date, Rosalyn did not appear and the magistrate dismissed the case.

7. This was verified in court when, at the end of the hearing for the protection order, Everett asked the magistrate, "What about the other cases?" The magistrate instructed the clerk to find out when those cases were scheduled. They had been adjourned for a later date.

8. Rosalyn's neighbor, the police constable, warned her not to encourage Everett to visit the apartment. If she did, he could claim that she entrapped him to breach the protection order.

9. I am summarizing lengthy testimony and omitting some of the incidences of alleged abuse to protect the anonymity of the parties and in the interests of brevity.

10. A "lime" refers to a spontaneous or sometimes prearranged social event that generally involves a small group of people. A lime may begin at one location and move on to another. It may include parties of both sexes or only one sex. For example, people lime on weekends and before and after Carnival events, but men are also said to lime when they muster friends for a fishing trip and all-day cookout during which the cooks are fortified with lots of alcohol.

11. "Community policing," so popular in the United States, has also found its way to Trinidad. Certain officers are specially trained to deal with family and neighborhood problems in their local communities and to work with youth in the schools.

12. As an anonymous reader of an earlier version of this chapter pointed out, I am discussing the kinds of cases that appear before the court and that are most likely to win protection orders. That discussion is separate from the question of what causes domestic violence more generally. Based on a survey of 407 men and women in Barbados in 1990, Handwerker (1997) concludes that violence inheres in the nature of the social relationship between intimates. A startling one out of four of his sample experienced physical and emotional abuse as children, with girls and boys equally subjected to parental abuse from male and female caretakers. Moreover, more than half of the sample reported their mothers experienced significant abuse. Powerful women (as defined by education, employment, supportive family and friends, and home ownership) were able to protect themselves and their children from abusive partners. Powerless women, in contrast, suffered more partner abuse and also abused their children.

13. In 1989, two years before there was a domestic violence act in Trinidad, Mohammed wrote: ". . . sexual violence, the ultimate and most fundamental form of control over women, is the mechanism which is used to keep women from 'getting outta hand' in Trinidad" (1989:38). Yelvington (1996) investigates flirting behavior in Trinidad as manifesting "symbolic violence," replete with tensions of domination and submission between the sexes. As he and others have pointed out: "Gender relations and the public display of sexuality pervade all aspects of life in the Caribbean" (1996:315). In part, these tensions are consequences of the different standards of behavior deemed appropriate for each sex and of the West Indian "dual-marriage system," in which men marry women who are their status equals but form nonlegal liaisons with women of lower status (Smith 1987; see also Douglass 1992). As Yelvington notes, in Trinidad: "Notwithstanding portrayals of the East Indian patriarchal, patrilocal extended family and the Black female-headed one, differences between Black and East Indian family forms and mating practices seem to be eroding" (1996:320).

14. Loseke (1992) uses a reflexive analysis to demonstrate how the categories of "battered woman," "wife abuse," and "shelters for the battered woman" have emerged as collective representations in American society and how, in turn, those representations structure the possibility of a woman's admission to, and residence in, a battered woman's shelter. Similarly, Razack found: "Asylum seekers who cannot present themselves as the victims of unusually patriarchal and culturally dysfunctional cultures are not granted asylum in Canada" (1998:20).

15. For example, Ford's sample of American women who brought charges of domestic violence against their partners dropped their cases for a variety of reasons. In some instances, threat of prosecution resulted in his staying away or he agreed to a divorce or another settlement. Some abusers agreed to get counseling. A number of women did not want to contend with the legal process or did not want to see the defendant go to jail or lose his job. Some defense attorneys convinced applicants to drop charges (1991:326). Wittner's study revealed other reasons women withdraw cases: (1) they calculate the costs of continuing the case and decide it is not worth the financial drain; (2) they consider the costs to their

families if they pursue the charges; and (3) they resolve the problem themselves by other alternatives, such as moving (1998:90–92). As she notes, even if they did not complete their cases, these women "demanded that the system of criminal justice make space for them in the official proceedings and respond to their self-defined needs" (Wittner 1998:103). Spooner found women in St. Kitts–Nevis and Barbados remain in abusive relationships because of shame, fear, commitment to marriage, religion, and economic dependency (2001:178–81).

16. There was room for judicial discretion here. I observed cases in which the parties never lived together and had no children, but which earned the applicant a protection order. Some magistrates, however, chose not to hear applications for domestic violence unless the parties had resided together, had children in common, or were economically dependent on one another. For discussions of judicial discretion in handling domestic violence cases, see Crocker (2005), Crowell and Burgess (1996), and Ptacek (1999). Ptacek (1999:7), Belknap et al. (2001:319), and Eigenberg (2001:269, 281) point out that the majority of research on domestic violence and the criminal justice response has focused on the police and has ignored the role that the courts and judges play in the processing of domestic violence cases. Based on observations and interviews in two courts in Massachusetts, Ptacek (1999) documents that there are significant differences in the ways judges respond to applicants for protection orders. That is also the case in Trinidad.

17. As one anonymous reviewer commented, the use of domestic violence law to evict a partner or spouse is an example of the use of the law for purposes other than those intended by lawmakers. According to my sources, magistrates used exclusion orders regularly when the Domestic Violence Act first became law. Informal discussions in the legal community about possible abuse of the act, however, led to more conservative use of exclusion orders. The accuracy of these accounts could be tested by investigating whether, and in what ways, the contents of protection orders changed over time. In the sample drawn from Pelau's court records of specific mandates ordered by magistrates (chapter 2, table 2.8), some 20 percent of interim orders and undertakings, and 47 percent of final orders, included directives for the respondent to keep away from the complainant's premises. However, that mandate was almost always a component of a broader array of prohibitions to limit offensive language, assault, and abuse at the complainant's workplace, suggesting the magistrate had heard evidence that convinced him that violence had occurred. In my experiences in court, applicants for protection orders sometimes quarreled with alleged abusers over who had the right to live where, but none seemed to have trumped up charges of domestic violence when none existed. One justice of the peace I spoke with also believed that the persons he interviewed at the court had genuinely experienced violence. On the other hand, one respondent I interviewed thought ejectment was a motive held by his common-law wife for bringing him to court, and a few attorneys believed domestic violence charges were sometimes falsely laid, particularly in cases of contentious divorce brought to the High Court. A study of the implementation of domestic violence legislation in the Eastern Caribbean also considered whether that legislation "would be used as a sword by unscrupulous applicants to acquire de facto property rights (exclusive possession)" and found that "in Antigua and Barbuda where a significant percentage of applications for occupation orders have been granted, no case could be cited as an example of

such cynical use of the legislation" (Economic Commission for Latin America and the Caribbean 2001a:43).

18. Loseke found that, in the United States, "the label 'wife abuse' is not really a label for an event, per se, since it is defined explicitly as a *pattern* of physical abuse, or as a continuing *series* of abusive and degrading acts. Thus, as constructed, wife abuse is a label for a series of events and hence a 'battered woman' is explicitly defined as a woman who has been 'systematically and severely beaten by her husband for many years.' As explicitly constructed, then, wife abuse is not a label for an 'occasional slap'" (1992:18). Moreover, as in Trinidad, the cultural construction of "wife abuse" in the United States includes the condition that the victim be terrified of the abuser (Loseke 1992:20).

19. A Women and Development Program located in England found the tendency to try to keep families together is commonplace throughout the Commonwealth, although no statistics are provided for readers (1992:33). Clarke (1998:6) also notes there is family and community pressure in the Caribbean to "work out" family violence issues. I pursue this point in chapter 6.

20. As I documented in chapter 2, of twenty-five closed breach cases filed in Pelau in 1997–98, only two men were fined for complaints filed as breaches of protection orders and both in amounts substantially below what the law allowed.

21. In a study comparing the court's response to assaults between intimates and nonintimates in the United States, Ferraro and Boychuk (1992) found the courts treated people prosecuted for crimes of violence leniently—whether or not their crimes were committed against intimates or nonintimates. Prison sentences were rare. They conclude: "Tolerance for wife beating in this context may simply be an extension of the more general lack of concern within the criminal justice system for violence that involved those of the same racial and economic group. The purpose of this system is to maintain the social order. Crime that does not threaten this order will be treated leniently if at all" (1992:224). It may also be the case that when Trinidadian men are tried for violence, or for breaching orders, they do not suffer much in the way of penalties.

22. I found his comment accurate. Here is a sample of the titles of newspaper articles gathered the last week in November and the first week in December, 1997: "Viewpoint: Rape and Domestic Violence" (*Sunday Guardian,* November 23, 1997); "Women against Violence Hold Candlelight Procession Tomorrow" (*Newsday,* November 24, 1997); "Prime Minister Says Expose Family Violence" (*Newsday,* November 26, 1997); "Bissessar: Turning Point on Domestic Violence, Minister Praises Media for Coverage of Crimes against Women" (*The Independent,* November 26, 1997); "Rush to Meet AG's Deadline: Legal Architects Framing Stiffer Sentences for Rape" (*Trinidad Express,* December 3, 1997); "Our Opinion: Making It Safe for Our Women" (*Trinidad Express,* December 13, 1997). See also Shepherd (1991).

23. The 1997 public forums were sponsored by the Ministry of Legal Affairs, with the assistance of the Ministry of Social Development and the Ministry of Culture, Community Development, and Women's Affairs. A forum of approximately two hours in duration was held in Port of Spain on November 25, in Chaguanas on November 26, in Tobago on December 1, and in San Fernando on December 3.

24. Keep in mind, too, that not all women who go to court for protection orders

actually want their applications to result in formal court orders; see, for example, research by Fischer and Rose 1995; Ford 1991, 1993, 2003; Haniff 1998; Harrell, Smith, and Newmark 1993; Ptacek 1999; Websdale 1998; and Wittner 1998.

Chapter 4: Court Rites

1. As Rheinstein explains, the central problems of Weber's sociology of law are that of the nature of legal thought in general, and, secondly, the relationship between the type of legal thought that developed in the West and modern capitalism (1954:xxxix, xliii). Feeley points out that it is discretion rather than bureaucratic organization that allows American lower courts to function: "The essence of bureaucracy, as Weber noted, is that decision making is dictated according to a 'calculable set of rules,' that is, that bureaucracy is characterized by routine application of clearly enunciated rules. The antithesis of bureaucracy is discretion, the ability to base decisions on individual judgments rather than on rules. And it is the *discretionary* capabilities of the prosecutor and judge and the many options of the defense which facilitate rapid processing of vast numbers of cases" (Feeley 1979:16).

2. There is a large literature on men's and women's different uses and experiences of courts and of their differential access to symbolic and material resources (e.g., Conley and O'Barr 1990, 1998; Coombe 1991; Eaton 1986; Fineman 1995; Fineman and Mykitiuk 1994; Fineman and Thomadsen 1991; Frohmann 1991; Grossberg 1994; Hirsch 1994, 1998; Holstein 1993; Jackson 1982; LaFont 1996; Lazarus-Black 1994; Merry 1990, 1994, 2000; Moore 1994; Philips 1994; Seng 1994; Starr 1989, 1992; White 1991; and Yngvesson 1993).

3. I am using the traditional anthropological method of choosing one case to illustrate patterns I observed watching dozens of domestic violence cases in four courts in Trinidad and that also emerge in ethnographic work on lower courts in other English common-law jurisdictions.

4. I have often been asked if I believe that the rites are intentionally practiced or if they occur without the conscious realization of members of the criminal justice system. I believe that the answer is both. Legal professionals and litigants sometimes practice these rites intentionally, as a deliberate strategy to strengthen their side of the case. But research in the courts and my reading of other ethnographic accounts convince me that sometimes legal professionals don't realize the full impact of the choices they make in processing cases.

5. I learned later that while her case was pending in Pelau, Alena returned to John's mother's apartment to collect her clothing and some of the baby's things. She let herself in with the key she still held, thinking the apartment was empty. But John was home, sleeping off a late-night bout of drinking. He woke up and immediately became abusive, hitting her in her face, calling her a bitch and a whore, and tearing her blouse. Alena started screaming and headed for the door. John dragged her back into the apartment and continued to beat her. She slipped into unconsciousness. When she woke up several hours later, she was in terrible pain. She called for help from the door of the apartment. Someone called the police. When they arrived, they took her statement and escorted her to the hospital for a medical report. Alena later filed criminal charges of assault and attempted rape. Those cases were still pending when I left Trinidad. These were the cases

the magistrate had alluded to that were "outside her jurisdiction." Alena told me months later by telephone that something went wrong every time she went to court. Sometimes her attorney couldn't make it; on one occasion, the two cases were listed separately and one was wrongly dismissed. Her lawyer requested that both matters be heard together. The judge agreed and set a new date three months later. John remained without an attorney. She described his demeanor in court as "smug." John paid no child support and made no effort to see his son, but he stopped harassing Alena.

6. Conley and O'Barr uncovered this phenomenon in their work in small claims courts in the United States. Instead of blaming the system or concluding that law was not concerned with justice, laypersons instead blamed themselves or the particular judges who heard their cases: "The litigants held themselves responsible for their failure to prepare for the transformations their stories had undergone. ... Whatever its therapeutic value for litigants, this personalizing reaction to adverse experiences clearly works to the benefit of the system" (1998:96). This means, of course, that law's hegemony remains unchallenged (1998:96).

7. Alena's story is especially interesting in that her middle-class status was not an advantage in her case. She came from a family who immediately hired an attorney for her. In contrast, John was working class, frequently unemployed, and could not afford an attorney to represent him. Yet, as we have seen, he left the court without any sanction and she lost her right to a protection order. Ironically, as I demonstrate later in this chapter, Alena's socialization as a middle-class woman and mother, someone who would not ordinarily use "inappropriate" language, was partly responsible for her failure to obtain an order. As Hirsch points out for Swahili women, women's speech may index "gendered subject positions routinely devalued through patriarchal ideologies linking gender, discourse, and conflict" (1998:15).

8. Elsewhere Carlen describes how people are very carefully spaced and placed in British courts: "Within the courtrooms of the magistrates' courts tacit control of their spatial and temporal properties is the monopoly of the police and the judicial personnel. In practice both the staging and the prosecution of the criminal business becomes the responsibility of the police. This renders absurd the judicial rhetoric of an adversary justice where, so the plot goes, both prosecution and defense stand as equals before the law" (1976b:19–20). Eaton also notes the "respect and deference" expected of defendants in London's lower courts (1986:80).

9. Emerson (1969:203) makes this point with respect to American juvenile courts: "The judge and other court officials may openly express disapproval of the appearance, behavior, and comments of delinquents." Holstein finds that all of the behavior of patients in courtrooms, not just their testimony, bears upon their hearings for commitment for insanity (1993:138).

10. In Bourdieu's terms, intimidation is a form of symbolic violence: "It is already partly true to say that the cause of the timidity lies in the relation between the situation or the intimidating person (who may deny any intimidating intention) and the person intimidated, or rather, between the social conditions of production of each of them. And little by little, one has to take account thereby of the whole social structure" (1991:51).

11. Other important discussions of the phenomenon of silencing in legal arenas can be found in Atkinson and Drew 1979; Carlen 1976b; Hirsch 1998; Hirsch and

Lazarus-Black 1994; Lederman 1984; Matoesian 1993, 2001; Moore 1994; Philips 1998; Tsing 1990; and White 1991. See Gal (1991) for a fine review of the meaning of silence in research on language and gender. As Schneider points out, crimes such as rape, intimate violence, sexual harassment, and incest have become more visible, but "this visibility does not mean that women are really being listened to, or that the listener (or society at large) gets the point" (2000:103).

12. Conley and O'Barr (1990, 1998) have written extensively about two contrasting ways of speaking in court: "rule-oriented accounts" versus "relational accounts." Rules-based accounts stick to the issues of interest to the court, such as dates and contractual obligations. Relational accounts, like Alena's, rely on general ideas about entitlements to fair and decent treatment. "Because relational accounts focus on personal status and social position, they tend to be full of details about the life of the speaker, details that the law usually deems irrelevant. Issues of time and of cause and effect are often dealt with in highly idiosyncratic ways" (1998:68). More recently, Matoesian makes the case that "language is not the mere passive vehicle for the imposition or transmission of law but actually constitutes and transforms evidence, facts, and rules into relevant objects of legal knowledge" (2001:3). Alena's case certainly lends credence to Matoesian's claim.

13. My thanks to Bill Black for raising this point in discussion. Schneider (2000: chapter 9) discusses how judicial discretion can operate to women's detriment in the prosecution of battered women who are mothers. Stereotypes of "good" and "bad" mothers play out in these trials and judges have tremendous power in deciding whether or not, or to what degree, to allow evidence of domestic abuse or expert testimony. See also Roberts (1993).

Chapter 5: Time and the Legal Process

1. French's erudite argument presents "to a legal audience a chronological smorgasbord of the types of thinking that have surrounded the issue of time" and shows "some of the ways in which these ideas might be useful in both legal analysis and legal practice" (2001:671). She argues correctly that legal theory and practice needs "a richer and more subtle understanding of time's relationship to law and law's relationship to time" (2001: 672). For a more general discussion of theories of time put forward by prominent anthropologists, see Gell (1992) and Greenhouse (1996).

2. The reader can consult, for example, Baumgartner (1988), Carlen (1976a, 1976b), Clarke (1998), Conley and O'Barr (1990), Coutin (2000), Emerson (1969), Feeley (1979), Greenhouse, Yngvesson, and Engel (1994), Harriott, Brathwaite, and Wortley (2004), LaFont (1996), Martin (1976), Merry (1990), Mileski (1971), Moog (1997), Nimmer (1978), Ryan (2001), and Yngvesson (1993).

3. Investigating district-level civil courts in the northern state of Uttar Pradesh, India, Moog finds the long delays in these courts are most certainly *not* a matter of simple supply and demand or of too many cases and too few judges. Instead, he finds "the behavior of these courts can be explained to a large extent by the actions of certain principal groups of actors within them who are pursuing their own interests through the use of whatever power is at their disposal" (1997:2). Moog shows how litigants, advocates, court officers, process-servers, and judges

each have their own (often conflicting) goals and that informal rules and constraints on the parties operate around and against official procedures. For example, advocates in India are paid after each court appearance; it is therefore in their own interests to focus on litigation rather than on compromise solutions (1997:74). They also work out symbiotic relationships with other court officials that can work against their clients' best interests (1997:87). Conflicting concerns and goals also characterize the participants in domestic violence cases in Trinidad. As in India, however, competing interests are mitigated by the need for daily coexistence, concern for professional standards, and a shared interest in maintaining the organization (1997:5). See Blumberg (1967), Cohn (1965), and Emerson (1995) for insightful discussions of the working relationships that form in courts.

4. In breaking up time in this way, I am contradicting the commonsense notion of law as timeless and of legality as constant and unchanging, beliefs held by many Americans: "Ironically, legality's timeless, transcendent status as something distant and removed from everyday life is achieved not by representing it as intangible, but by associating it with material phenomena: buildings, courtrooms, benches, pews, tables, files, codes, and prison cells. By identifying legality with concrete things that occupy space, our respondents explain how legality is able to overcome fleeting time and become timeless" (Ewick and Silbey 1998:95). My findings support French's notion that variables such as age, social group, and professional status, as well as context, have great influence on how time is perceived (2001:695–96). To take a simple example, litigants generally found their cases moved slowly, but their lawyers often saw nothing unusual about how much time the case was taking.

5. Coutin makes the important point that courthouse officials control time but also space: "Just as they manage official time, court officials also govern legal space. The judge's sovereignty over a courtroom is analogous to the state's sovereignty over national territory, because judges decide who can officially exist within U.S. borders. One judge drew attention to this parallel during an in-absentia deportation, commenting, 'The respondent has seemingly chosen to remove herself from the jurisdiction of the court. She can do so physically but not legally. We will proceed in absentia'" (2000:113).

6. Interviewing litigants, legal professionals, and ordinary members of the community, I found that Trinidadians share with working-class Americans a sense that not all and every act of violence deserves the attention of the law. As Merry reports: "Plaintiffs are very reluctant to bring marital problems to court and typically do so only when the situation seems desperate. One of the most common justifications is violence. As plaintiffs talk, however, it is protection from excessive and undeserved violence—not protection from all violence—which they seek. There is an underlying assumption that violence can be deserved, that women have an obligation to tolerate some abuse, and that the issue is what the limits are" (1990:51). Similarly, Trinidadians insisted that some violence could be deserved—as in a case of adultery or public disrespect or humiliation of one's partner. What is not tolerated is "excessive" and "undeserved" violence. Danns and Parsad (1989), LaFont (1996), and Spooner (2001) reached similar conclusions in their research on domestic violence in, respectively, Guyana, Jamaica, and St. Kitts and Nevis and Barbados. See also Chevannes (2001).

7. The women in Massachusetts who did not seek any help cited shame and

concerns about family privacy as reasons for remaining silent. They were the most isolated victims (Ptacek 1999:141).

8. The justice of the peace with whom I was most familiar regarded his role as that of "facilitator." He told me that "it is always up to the magistrate to decide whether or not there is a case." He also explained, however, that he saved the magistrate time by excluding cases between parties not covered by the Domestic Violence Act and others belonging to different jurisdictions. The justice of the peace also offers alternatives to victims who come to court, but then change their minds about pressing the case. Counseling is available through the probation office or, in some districts, at the police station with a member of the specially trained "community" police.

9. This point is discussed at length by Yngvesson (1993) who describes clerks as "watchdogs" whose business is to keep "garbage cases" from the courts. See also Merry (1990) who shows that clerks transform what litigants perceive as legal disputes into issues of morality and therapy that are unworthy of the law's attention. Courthouse Time is considerable in U.S. cases in which legal officials determine the merit of immigrants' claims to legality: ". . . officials who conduct proceedings are concerned with managing time. Proceedings need to be run efficiently, witnesses are urged to get to the point, and heavy caseloads and overcrowded calendars make advocates compete for officials' times and attention. . . . The consequences of arriving late or failing to arrive at all are severe. When informing one respondent of the date and time of his next hearing, a judge warned, 'Be on time! If you are more than fifteen minutes late, I will order you deported!'" (Coutin 2000:105, 112).

10. Vatuk explains: "Even the police seem to view with skepticism the motives of those women who come for the purpose of charging their spouse with domestic abuse. Although their job is to enforce the law that is on the books, in practice they often consider it counter-productive to do so. Instead, they tend to try to take the law into their own hands, first by meting out immediate punishment, in the form of a beating, to the man involved and then by extracting a promise from him, possibly having him put it in writing, that he will behave better in the future. They reason that this approach will enable the couple to resume their life together for what they see as the long-term benefit of the wife" (2000:9).

11. The Trinidadian Bar Association publishes standard fees for different kinds of cases. Some attorneys charge these rates, but as they gain in experience and success, many lawyers charge higher fees. Rates are highest in Port of Spain; less so in the rural villages.

12. I spent many hours with Sally over the course of three long interviews, two of which ended with us sharing a meal in a local fast-food restaurant, and one of which included my being invited to her home to meet her daughters. In the course of her telling me her life history, she mentioned many incidents that left me no doubt that at least by legal standards Richard had behaved violently. (Only some of these incidents have been recorded here, both to protect the couple's anonymity and for the sake of brevity.) I concluded that Sally believed Richard was not a violent person because he did not physically beat her.

13. Lynn's explanation for why she did not fight to retain legal custody of her daughter reflects her experiences of emotional abuse, harassment, and fear: "I did not object. He have this kinda way about him that I decided to leave him if that

is what he wanted. I would leave and see what would happen. Maybe if he had the child with him he would have no reason to come by me. So I left the child in his care. He got custody of her and I left him with her."

Rodney's demand for custody of their daughter occurred after Lynn took him to court to ask for maintenance for herself and their child. She was awarded maintenance, although she claimed that Rodney never paid it. Instead, he took her to court for child custody. As she explained, she did not fight his claim because he was constantly using their child as an excuse to emotionally abuse and harass her.

Chapter 6: Cultures of Reconciliation

1. Williams distinguishes between "making a living" and "making life" in her insightful ethnographic account of the Guyanese villagers of Cockalorum: "Most often, when they refer to someone's ability to making a living, they are speaking of the person's industry, skill, and ambition, all of which result in material rewards. When they speak of someone's ability to make life, they are referring to their own assessment of the individual's interest in the socioeconomic well-being of others and his inclination to balance work against sociability—the enjoyment of life through participation in organized and casual forms of socializing, on the one hand, and conspicuous consumption, on the other" (1991:56).

2. Anthropologists have used "culture" in the most general sense to refer to collective identities and to signify "difference" and "opposition to something else" (Kuper 1999:2, 14). Theoretically, among other ideas, "culture" has been understood to imply "civilization," a collection of customs and institutions, a body of postulates and presumptions about the nature of the universe, a separate system of symbols and meanings, and a semiautonomous sphere within a more comprehensive sociology of action. Kuper ultimately concludes:

> In short, it is a poor strategy to separate out a cultural sphere, and to treat it in its own terms . . . unless we separate out the various processes that are lumped together under the heading of culture, and then look beyond the field of culture to other processes, we will not get far in understanding any part of it. For the same sort of reason, cultural identity can never provide an adequate guide for living. We all have multiple identities, and even if I accept that I have a primary cultural identity, I may not want to conform to it. . . . Finally, there is a moral objection to [an autonomous] culture theory. It tends to draw attention away from what we have in common instead of encouraging us to communicate across national, ethnic, and religious boundaries, and to venture between them. (1999:247)

3. Another example of how Trinidad and Tobago law promotes the culture of reconciliation is found in the process of divorce. When filing a petition for divorce, an attorney must include a certified copy of the marriage certificate, a statement of arrangements for any children, and a certificate of reconciliation that states whether the lawyer has discussed with the petitioner the possibility of reconciling and has provided names of parties qualified to assist in such a reconciliation (Thompson-Ahye 2002:12).

4. Illuminating common threads in the causes of domestic violence in the Ca-

ribbean, LeFranc and Rock (2001) point to "the culture of tolerance and shame" that characterizes victims' responses to abuse. My sense is that while most Trinidadians would prefer to see family matters resolved without the police or the courts, people understand and sympathize with a battered woman's decision to call the police and to file an application for protection in cases of serious physical abuse.

5. The reference in the previous subhead is to the title of a 1987 article, "Doing Gender," by Candace West and Don H. Zimmerman in *Gender & Society*, vol. 1, pp. 125–51.

6. My experiences in Trinidad lend support to the long-held theoretical contention, argued most recently by Munasinghe (2001), that West Indian kinship can be brought into a single conceptual framework, that of "creolization," which accommodates a continuum of different racial, ethnic, and religious groups. Members of these groups sometimes recognize similarities in their kinship practices with those of other groups, but at other times identify as having very different norms and traditions. As a heuristic tool, creolization enables scholars to recognize the inclusive but sometimes contradictory character of Caribbean kinship.

7. The survey revealed that unfaithfulness and incompatibility were the two main reasons Trinidadians divorced. Interestingly, 6.4 percent of divorced women reported that an abusive spouse was the main reason for their divorce (St. Bernard 1998:56).

8. Parsad found similar notions among East Indians in Guyana: "Within the East Indian community, where the family is the core unit for ethnic and social identity, notions of individual identities and rights are likely to be subsumed by more general notions of family obligations and demands. Since few East Indian women express their identities in isolation of family obligations, it is hardly likely that ideologies of individualism and women's rights will assume much relevance within the East Indian community" (1999:59). She advocates an approach to gender violence that focuses on the family: "Such an approach, taking the family as the unit of focus, is sensitive to the contextual reality of non-western traditions which lack the ethos of individualism and gender equality, characteristic of contemporary western, industrialized societies" (1999:59).

9. Spooner found that addressing domestic violence by the use of protection orders "represents a progressive change in philosophical thinking among policymakers in the English-speaking Caribbean, but not among the masses of Caribbean people. As such protection orders legislation is insufficient to address the problem of women's abuse in societies as culturally complex as the English-speaking Caribbean" (2001:10). Protection orders had limited success in deterring repeat abuse in Barbados, but were slightly more successful in St. Kitts–Nevis. In both countries, victims "remain unwilling to report abuse to the police and legal system and women remain subjected to economic and social barriers in the wider society" (Spooner 2001: v; see also Spooner 2004).

10. I contacted Shana during my fieldwork in Trinidad in 1999. She told me Ramesh's bad behavior escalated as soon as the undertaking expired—he even notified Shana on the day when "the law finish." Eventually, and again with the assistance of her brother, she took him back to court for domestic violence. Both of the couple's adult children, however, appeared as witnesses for Ramesh. Not surprisingly, Shana lost her case. (This is similar to what happened in "Helen's"

case, described later in chapter 6 on page 153.) The couple separated. Ramesh went to live in the country and Shana moved in with her brother, who then urged her to obtain a divorce. Ironically, within a few months after their divorce, Shana and Ramesh were again in a visiting relationship. Shana's brother told me that he would allow Ramesh to move back into Shana's room with her because he finally understood that the couple loved each other and would not be parted. He did warn them that he was not about to put up with any violence in his home.

11. See Greenhouse (1986) for a superb treatment of an American fundamental Christian sect and its beliefs and practices concerning law and courts.

12. In this respect, undertakings are like the contact orders issued to victims of domestic abuse who request temporary restraining orders in Hilo, Hawaii. As the name suggests, a contact order permits contact between a victim and a batterer. The couple may continue to reside together or engage in limited contact when, for example, they take custody of the children according to the visitation schedule. In contrast, a judge may issue a "no-contact" restraining order that prohibits the respondent from any contact with the victim (Merry 2001a:24–25; 2001b:ff 4, 5). Yet undertakings also highlight the boundaries of the culture of reconciliation because they are granted only if there is no previous evidence of abuse. My thanks to Lisa Frohmann for this observation.

13. For example, a Women and Development Program located in England found the tendency to try to keep families together is commonplace throughout the Commonwealth, although no statistics are provided for readers (Women and Development Program 1992:33).

14. Peterson del Mar traces the history of wife abuse in Oregon beginning in the 1840s. Like Pleck, he found "wife beating varied over time" (Peterson del Mar 1996:6) and that respect for family privacy "consistently undercut community intervention in domestic violence" (1996:171). As marital and gender roles shifted, so did the nature and pervasiveness of violence toward wives: "In the mid-nineteenth century, during the settlement era, husbands used violence largely to enforce claims to patriarchal authority. . . . Later in the nineteenth century, violence against wives became less common as an ethos of self-restraint and women's public influence spread. . . . Beginning in the 1890s, men's violence became more expressive of general male anxieties and misogyny, a trend that became more pronounced with the twentieth century's emphasis on marital intimacy and self-realization. Both husbands' violence and wives' agency increased as the twentieth-century ethos of self-gratification supplanted self-restraint" (Peterson del Mar 1996:170). Peterson del Mar's work reminds us that "a history of violence against wives must always begin with a consideration of its context, very broadly defined" (1996:171).

15. At any one time, of course, there are always many "American versions" of the family ideal. Abraham's (2000) study of marital violence among South Asian immigrants in the United States provides one example of a variation of Pleck's model. South Asian immigrants hold that marriage creates alliances between two families, not just two persons, and encourages strong extended family ties. These precepts led Abraham to include extended kin in her analysis of marital violence (Abraham 2000:3).

16. Merry found that these three approaches shared "a surprising similarity in their technologies of personal transformation. All emphasized making choices

and holding people accountable, knowing and controlling feelings, and building self-esteem for those who batter as well as for their victims. In all three settings, men and women were told they could make their own choices about how they feel, how they view situations, and how they respond to them" (2001b:42).

17. As Kelkar points out, Hindu women are also disadvantaged because Hindu laws of property and ownership "give women negligible rights as independent entities, to family income, assets, and property" (1989:5). Women also commonly waive their land rights to their brothers (1989:6). Kelkar asserts that Indian women face "subordination in the structure of material production, the organization of marriage and family and the sexual division of labor" (1989:6). Thus, in India, as in so many other places, including Trinidad, whether you can "make a living" has significant impact on how women respond to domestic violence.

18. See Mohammed (2002a) for an important discussion of the negotiation of gender relations among East Indians in Trinidad, 1917–47. As she explains: "Cultural definitions of masculinity and femininity are never arrived at permanently but are themselves continually contested in the real lives of men and women" (2002a:14). These negotiations are conducted by individuals, but also by groups and institutions, including the judicial system, and involve "varying degrees of collusion, compromise and accommodation, resistance and subversion" (2002a:15).

Conclusion

1. Over the past decade, investigations of crime and victimization have emerged as critical concerns in the Caribbean, but these studies mostly analyze more conventional crime categories such as murder, rape, and robbery (e.g., Harriott, Brathwaite, and Wortley 2004). In recounting the evolution of this social movement and its legacies in Trinidad, my study contributes to Caribbean history, criminal justice, and the ethnography of lawmaking and legal praxis in the postcolonial state at the end of the twentieth century. As I described in chapter 1, I drew on scholarship that identifies how former colonial states claim identities as modern and progressive nations, and chronicled the critical role of the contemporary women's movement in Trinidad, a subject that has received too little attention in Caribbean anthropology (Slocum and Thomas 2003:561).

2. Among the sources I consulted on this point for the United States were Abraham (1995, 2000); Breines and Gordon (1983); Dobash and Dobash (1992); Frohmann and Mertz (1995); Gordon (1988); Loseke (1992); Matthews (1994); Pleck (1987); Ptacek (1999); Rosen (2000); Schneider (1999, 2000); and Straus and Gelles (1986). See Dobash and Dobash (1979, 1992) for the United Kingdom, Smyth (1996) for the Republic of Ireland, and Walker (1990) for Canada. Sources on European women's movements include Miller and Barberet (1994) and Valiente (1996) for Spain and Szalay (1996) for Hungary. See Corrin (1996) for an overview of case studies from Europe. Adelman (1997, 2000, 2003) investigates women's efforts to combat domestic violence in Israel within the context of divorce and under conditions of militarization. Thomas and Beasley (1993) discuss women's human rights in Brazil. Research on women's social movements and domestic violence legislation in the Caribbean includes Rivera (1995) and Romany (1994) on Puerto Rico and Alexander (1991, 1994), Bissessar (2000), James-Sebro (2001),

Lazarus-Black (2001), Mohammed (1989, 1991, 2002a), Rawlins (2000), Reddock (1995), and the Trinidad and Tobago Coalition Against Domestic Violence (2005) on Trinidad and Tobago. Alexander (1994, 1997) investigates women and the law in the Bahamas, Spooner (2001) describes the contemporary situation in Barbados and St. Kitts–Nevis, and Morrow (1994) researched the U.S. Virgin Islands. Pargass and Clarke (2003) provide an overview of gender violence and state and nonstate responses in the wider Caribbean region.

3. Surveying the international struggle for women's rights, Fraser concludes: "The history of the drive for women's human rights indicates that only when women are literate, when they can articulate their view of life in publications and before audiences, when they can organize and demand equality, when girls are educated and socialized to think of themselves as citizens as well as wives and mothers, and when men take more responsibility for care of children and the home, can women be full and equal citizens able to enjoy human rights" (2001:58).

4. Having signed declarations such as the United Nation's Convention on the Elimination of All Forms of Discrimination Against Women (CEDAW), Trinidad has been pressed to demonstrate its compliance with and commitment to human rights through reports to the UN and so the nation is, at least to some degree, "policed" by the international community (Lazarus-Black and Merry 2003; Merry 2003; Ministry of the Attorney General and Legal Affairs 2000).

5. See chapter 3 for literature documenting that both rape and domestic violence victims must be believable and deserving victims. Scholars working in the field of law and language have demonstrated that a victim's believability in law is demonstrated in part by consistency in reporting (e.g., Conley and O'Barr 1998; Matoesian 2001; Trinch 2003).

6. Recall that Karrene later learned that the police had misplaced a copy of her protection order. Thankfully, Mohan did not further abuse her; he would have presumed the order was in effect.

7. The literature on this topic is vast, particularly for the United States. In addition to race, class, and gender, scholars in the United States also identify sexual orientation, immigration status, disability status, ethnicity, religion, and cultural practices as loci of multiple forms of oppression that intersect with gender violence. Some excellent recent discussions include Bograd (2005); Collins (2000); Crenshaw (1994); Dasgupta (2005); Kanuha (2005); Razack (1998); Richie (1996, 2005); Schneider (2000); Sokoloff (2005); Sokoloff and Dupont (2005a, 2005b); Volpp (2005); and West (2005).

8. Recall that court rites occasionally reverse class and gender hierarchies (see chapter 4).

9. On the other hand, as we saw in chapters 3 and 6, cultures of reconciliation also name deserving victims.

10. In some American domestic violence courts, victims can readily win a temporary restraining order by appearing before a judge and explaining a situation of abuse. These orders expire in a few weeks unless the plaintiff pursues the matter. Winning an extended order is a much more protracted process (Ptacek 1999; Wittner 1998).

11. My policy was to interview complainants after their cases concluded, but in this instance, Lorna came over to me to ask who I was and what I was doing. I

explained the research and she offered to participate in the study. I did not attempt to contact Philip because a number of persons at the courthouse advised me he would be unreliable as an interviewee for reasons I shall not disclose because I cannot verify them. Lorna and Philip were not strangers to the court staff; they had quarreled about child support and visitation rights on earlier occasions.

12. Lorna told me they went to the hospital in Port of Spain early in January. They waited several hours, until the clinic closed, and they were told to return on another date, significantly delaying the case. At their second visit, a few weeks later, the tests were administered. The results were sent directly to the magistrate. That left the principal parties unaware of the outcome of the test and so neither of them could use the test results to decide whether to pursue litigation. In this way, the litigants' agency shifted away from them.

13. The simple blood test reveals only the blood groups of the tested parties, but it is widely assumed that a match "proves" paternity affiliation.

14. I interviewed Lorna's attorney after these cases were resolved. She said that initially she was puzzled by the fact that the two parties used the courts so frequently, but that she understood Lorna's desire both to determine paternity affiliation and maintenance for her daughter and her protest of Philip's attempt to reduce child support for their son. Once she realized, however, that both of the litigants' parents seemed to accept their roles in supporting their own offspring and the children of that union, she decided to withdraw from the remaining time-consuming litigation. In contrast, Lorna told me her attorney became fed up with her ex-husband, found him "very impossible" and suggested she should "let the magistrate deal with him" (alone). Lorna also hinted, however, that there was some disagreement with her attorney about legal expenses. It seems likely that there was a mutual decision for the two to part company.

15. The planning committee arranged for the Family Court to go into operation expeditiously and with relatively few changes in extant legislation. (The Family Court is guided by the *Family Proceedings Rules, 1998*.) The decision that the Family Court would not entertain petitions for domestic violence unconnected to other family matters ensured that the caseloads of the magistrates would remain manageable. In the first year of the court's operation, the majority of domestic violence applications (over 70 percent) were determined within a three-month period (Hann, Boucaud, and Murrell 2005:52). The report does not provide information on the final outcome of determined cases.

16. The Family Court is located in the old magistrate building in Port of Spain. The interior of the building has been completely redesigned and access to the courts no longer poses a formidable experience. Instead, clients encounter trained intake workers who listen to their troubles privately and then direct them to appropriate personnel who may schedule a hearing for the magistrate's court or High Court or recommend counseling, mediation, or another social service. The evaluation team found: "People are taking advantage of the new services offered by the court. During the first year, 226 cases were referred to mediation directly from intake, and 453 cases were referred directly to counseling" (Hann, Boucaud, and Murrell 2005:220). An additional 111 cases were referred to mediation from the High Court and 80 from the magistrate's court (Hann, Boucaud, and Murrell 2005:220). Probation received referrals for 439 cases, 84 percent of which came from the magistrate's court (Hann, Boucaud, and Murrell 2005:221).

Two other important changes at the Family Court created small private court-rooms in which magistrates and judges preside and the immediate scheduling of hearing dates and times, which alleviated the lengthy waiting periods of the past. The building also contains a law library, a cafeteria, and supervised waiting rooms for young children and youth, allowing parents peace of mind while they tend to their affairs. All the records are entered into a computer system, trials are recorded and can be transcribed, and the new case-management system makes possible statistical evaluation of the number, type, and timing of the cases. The pilot project is successfully meeting its target goals of easier access for the public, responsiveness by trained staff, safety, convenience, affordable costs, more rapid case handling, and greater client and attorney satisfaction. It is facing personnel shortages, problems serving summonses and orders, increasing backlogs, and heavy workloads for judicial officers and support staff—all issues faced by the magistrates' courts prior to the pilot project. For further information about the Family Court, see Hann, Boucaud, and Murrell (2005) and Trinidad and Tobago Coalition Against Domestic Violence (2005).

BIBLIOGRAPHY

Abraham, Margaret. 1995. "Ethnicity, Gender, and Marital Violence: South Asian Women's Organizations in the United States." *Gender & Society* 9(4):450–68.

———. 2000. *Speaking the Unspeakable: Marital Violence among South Asian Immigrants in the United States.* New Brunswick, N.J.: Rutgers University.

———. 2005. "Fighting Back: Abused South Asian Women's Strategies of Resistance." In *Domestic Violence at the Margins: Readings on Race, Class, Gender, and Culture.* Natalie J. Sokoloff, ed. Pp. 253–71. New Brunswick, N.J.: Rutgers University.

Abrams, Philip. 1988. "Notes on the Difficulty of Studying the State." *Journal of Historical Sociology* 1(1):58–89.

Acts of the Commonwealth of the Bahamas. 1991. Sexual Offences and Domestic Violence Act. No. 9.

Adelman, Madelaine. 1997. "Gender, Law, and Nation: The Politics of Domestic Violence in Israel." Ph.D. dissertation, Duke University, Durham, N.C.

———. 2000. "No Way Out: Divorce-Related Domestic Violence in Israel." *Violence Against Women* 6(11):1223–54.

———. 2003. "The Military, Militarism, and the Militarization of Domestic Violence." *Violence Against Women* 9(9):1118–52.

Adelman, Madelaine, Edna Erez, and Nadera Shalhoub-Kevorkian. 2003. "Policing Violence Against Minority Women in Multicultural Societies: Community and the Politics of Exclusion." *Police & Society* 7:103–31.

Alexander, M. Jacqui. 1991. "Redrafting Morality: The Postcolonial State and the Sexual Offences Bill of Trinidad and Tobago." In *Third World Women and the Politics of Feminism.* Chandra Talpade Mohanty, Ann Russo and Lourdes Torres, eds. Pp. 133–52. Bloomington: Indiana University.

———. 1994. "Not Just (Any) Body Can Be a Citizen: The Politics of Law, Sexuality and Post-Coloniality in Trinidad and Tobago and the Bahamas." *Feminist Review* 48:5–23.

———. 1997. "Erotic Autonomy as a Politics of Decolonization: An Anatomy of Feminist and State Practice in the Bahamas Tourist Economy." In *Feminist Genealogies, Colonial Legacies, Democratic Futures.* Jacqui M. Alexander and Chandra Talpade Mohanty, eds. Pp. 63–100. New York: Routledge.

Alonso, Ana Maria. 1995. "Rationalizing Patriarchy: Gender, Domestic Violence, and Law in Mexico." *Identities: Global Studies in Culture and Power* 2(1/2):29–47.

Angrosino, Michael. 1996. "Sexual Politics in the East Indian Family in Trinidad."

In *Family in the Caribbean: Themes and Perspectives.* Christine Barrow, ed. Pp. 383–96. Kingston, Jamaica: Ian Randle.

Atkinson, J. Maxwell, and Paul Drew. 1979. *Order in Court: The Organization of Verbal Interaction in Judicial Settings.* Oxford: Wolfson College, Centre for Socio-Legal Studies.

Babb, Cecilia. 1997. "Taking Action against Violence: A Case Study of Trinidad and Tobago." In *Women against Violence Breaking the Silence: Reflecting on Experience in Latin America and the Caribbean.* Ana Maria Brasileiro, ed. Pp. 100–114. New York: United Nations Development Fund for Women (UNIFEM).

Bailey, Barbara. 2003. "The Search for Gender Equity and Empowerment of Caribbean Women: The Role of Education." In *Gender Equality in the Caribbean: Reality or Illusion.* Gemma Tang Nain and Celia Babb, eds. Pp. 108–45. Kingston, Jamaica: Ian Randle.

Bailey, Wilma, Elsie LeFranc, and Clement Branche. 1998. "Partnering and Violence." *Caribbean Dialogue: A Journal of Contemporary Caribbean Policy Issues* 4(1):1–8.

Barriteau, Eudine. 1998. "Theorizing Gender Systems and the Project of Modernity in the Twentieth-Century Caribbean." *Feminist Review* 59:186–210.

———. 2001. *The Political Economy of Gender in the Twentieth-Century Caribbean.* New York: Palgrave.

Barrow, Ayanna, Allison Francis, Elizabeth Richards, and Raquel Sukhu. 1995. "Domestic Abuse and Its Relation to Childhood Exposure of Women to Abuse in the Home of Upbringing." University of the West Indies, Department of Sociology, St. Augustine, Trinidad and Tobago. Unpublished manuscript.

Barrow, Christine. 1996. *Family in the Caribbean: Themes and Perspectives.* Kingston, Jamaica: Ian Randle.

———, ed. 1998. *Caribbean Portraits: Essays on Gender Ideologies and Identities.* Kingston, Jamaica: Ian Randle.

Bartky, Sandra Lee. 1988. "Foucault, Femininity, and the Modernization of Patriarchal Power." In *Feminism and Foucault: Reflections on Resistance.* Irene Diamond and Lee Quinby, eds. Pp. 61–86. Boston: Northeastern University.

———. 2002. *Sympathy and Solidarity and Other Essays.* New York: Rowman & Littlefield.

Baumgartner, M. P. 1988. *The Moral Order of a Suburb.* Oxford: Oxford University.

———. 1992. "The Myth of Discretion." In *The Uses of Discretion.* Keith Hawkins, ed. Pp. 129–62. Oxford: Clarendon.

Belknap, Joanne, Ruth E. Fleury, Heather C. Melton, Cris M. Sullivan, and Amy Leisenring. 2001. "To Go or Not to Go? Preliminary Findings on Battered Women's Decisions Regarding Court Cases." In *Women Battering in the United States.* H. M. Eigenberg, ed. Pp. 319–26. Prospect Heights, Ill.: Waveland.

Bennett, Lauren, Lisa Goodman, and Mary Ann Dutton. 1999. "Systemic Obstacles to the Criminal Prosecution of a Battering Partner: A Victim Perspective." *Journal of Interpersonal Violence* 14(7):761–72.

Biolsi, Thomas. 1995. "Bringing the Law Back In: Legal Rights and the Regulation of Indian-White Relations on Rosebud Reservation." *Current Anthropology* 36(4):543–71.

———. 1998. *Organizing the Lakota: The Political Economy of the New Deal on the Pine Ridge and Rosebud Reservations.* Tucson: University of Arizona.

———. 2001. *Deadliest Enemies: Law and the Making of Race Relations on and off Rosebud Reservation.* Berkeley: University of California.

Birth, Kevin K. 1999. *Any Time Is Trinidad Time: Social Meanings and Temporal Consciousness.* Gainesville, Fla.: University Press of Florida.

Bishop, Joan, and Tara Rahamut. 1996. "Proposals for Collaborative Solutions to Reduce Domestic Violence in Trinidad and Tobago." *Creating the Strategies: Workshop on Domestic Violence: Seeking Collaborative Solutions through Personal, Professional, and Community Empowerment.* Tunapuna, Trinidad and Tobago: Caribbean Association for Feminist Research and Action (CAFRA).

Bissessar, Ann Marie. 2000. "Policy Transfer and Implementation Failure: A Review of the Policy of Domestic Violence in Trinidad and Tobago." *Caribbean Journal of Criminology and Social Psychology* 5(1/2):57–80.

Blankenhorn, David. 1995. *Fatherless America: Confronting Our Most Urgent Social Problem.* New York: Harper Perennial.

Blumberg, Abraham. 1967. "The Practice of Law as a Confidence Game." *Law & Society Review* 1:15–39.

Bograd, Michelle. 2005. "Strengthening Domestic Violence Theories: Intersections of Race, Class, Sexual Orientation, and Gender." In *Domestic Violence at the Margins: Readings on Race, Class, Gender, and Culture.* Natalie J. Sokoloff, ed. Pp. 25–38. New Brunswick, N.J.: Rutgers University.

Bourdieu, Pierre. 1991. *Language and Symbolic Power.* John B. Thompson, ed. Gino Raymond and Matthew Adamson, trans. Cambridge, Mass.: Harvard University.

Boxill, Eileen. 1997. "The Reform of Family Law as It Affects Women." In *Gender: A Caribbean Multi-Disciplinary Perspective.* Elsa Leo-Rhynie, Barbara Bailey, and Christine Barrow, eds. Pp. 91–105. Kingston, Jamaica: Ian Randle.

Boyle, Elizabeth Heger, and Sharon E. Preves. 2000. "National Politics as International Process: The Case of Anti-Female-Genital-Cutting Laws." *Law & Society Review* 34(3):703–37.

Bradley, Christine. 1994. "Why Male Violence against Women Is a Development Issue: Reflections from Papua New Guinea." In *Women and Violence: Realities and Responses Worldwide.* Miranda Davies, ed. Pp. 10–27. London: Zed Books.

Breines, Wini, and Linda Gordon. 1983. "The New Scholarship on Family Violence." *Signs* 8(3):490–531.

Brereton, Bridget. 1981. *A History of Modern Trinidad 1783–1962.* Kingston, Jamaica: Heinemann.

———, ed. 2004. *General History of the Caribbean. Volume 5: The Caribbean in the Twentieth Century.* Paris and London: UNESCO and MacMillan.

Bumiller, Kristin. 1991. "Fallen Angels: The Representation of Violence against Women in Legal Culture." In *At the Boundaries of Law: Feminism and Legal Theory.* Martha Albertson Fineman and Nancy Sweet Thomadsen, eds. Pp. 95–111. New York: Routledge.

Burchell, Graham, Colin Gordon, and Peter Miller, eds. 1991. *The Foucault Effect: Studies in Governmentality with Two Lectures by and an Interview with Michel Foucault.* Chicago: University of Chicago.

Butler, Judith. 1992. "Contingent Foundations: Feminism and the Question of Postmodernism." In *Feminists Theorize the Political.* Judith Butler and Joan W. Scott, eds. Pp. 3–21. New York: Routledge.

Buzawa, Eve S., and Carl B. Buzawa, eds. 1996. *Domestic Violence: The Changing Criminal Justice Response.* Westport, Conn.: Auburn House.

———, eds. 1992. *Do Arrests and Restraining Orders Work?* Thousand Oaks, Calif.: Sage.

Cain, Maureen. 1996. "Crime and Criminology in the Caribbean: An Introduction." *Caribbean Quarterly* 42(2/3):i–xviii.

———. 2000. "Orientalism, Occidentalism and the Sociology of Crime." *British Journal of Criminology* 40:239–60.

Cameron-Padmore, Jacqueline. 1992. "Age of Violence and Aggression." *Trinidad Express,* November 26, p. 9.

Campbell, Carl C. 1997. *Endless Education: Main Currents in the Education System of Modern Trinidad and Tobago, 1939–1986.* Barbados, Jamaica, Trinidad and Tobago: The Press University of the West Indies.

———. 2004. "Education in the Caribbean, 1930–90." In *General History of the Caribbean. Volume 5: The Caribbean in the Twentieth Century.* Bridget Brereton, ed. Pp. 606–626. Paris and London: UNESCO and MacMillan.

Caribbean Association for Feminist Research and Action (CAFRA). 1991. "Report on the Regional Meeting on Women, Violence and the Law." Tunapuna, Trinidad and Tobago. January 28–30.

———. 1998. "A Pilot Survey on the Incidence of Violence and Responses to Such Violence among 200 Randomly Selected Women in Trinidad." Conducted by CAFRA Regional Office, Tunapuna, Trinidad and Tobago.

Carlen, Pat. 1974. "Remedial Routines for the Maintenance of Control in Magistrates' Courts." *British Journal of Law and Society* 1(2):101–17.

———. 1975. "Magistrates' Courts: A Game Theoretic Analysis." *The Sociological Review* 23:347–79.

———. 1976a. "The Staging of Magistrates' Justice." *British Journal of Criminology* 16(1):48–55.

———. 1976b. *Magistrates' Justice.* London: Martin Robertson.

Chaudhuri, Molly, and Kathleen Daly. 1992. "Do Restraining Orders Help? Battered Women's Experience with Male Violence and Legal Process." In *Domestic Violence: The Changing Criminal Justice Response.* Eve S. Buzawa and Carl. G. Buzawa, eds. Pp. 227–52. Westport, Conn.: Auburn House.

Chevannes, Barry. 2001. *Learning to Be a Man: Culture, Socialization and Gender Identity in Five Caribbean Communities.* Barbados, Jamaica, Trinidad and Tobago: The Press University of the West Indies.

Cicourel, Aaron. 1968. *The Social Organization of Juvenile Justice.* New York: John Wiley & Sons.

Clarke, Roberta. 1991. "Domestic Violence Act—Trinidad and Tobago." *CARICOM Perspective.* P. 86. July–December.

———. 1997. "Combating Violence Against Women in the Caribbean." In *Women Against Violence Breaking the Silence: Reflecting on Experience in Latin America and the Caribbean.* Ana Maria Brasileiro, ed. Pp. 51–62. New York: United Nations Development Fund (UNIFEM).

———. 1998. *Violence against Women in the Caribbean: State and Non-State*

Responses. United Nations Development Fund for Women (UNIFEM). Inter-American Commission of Women (CIM).

Cobb, Sara. 1997. "The Domestication of Violence in Mediation." *Law & Society Review* 31(3):397–440.

Cohn, Bernard. 1965. "Anthropological Notes on Disputes and Law in India." *American Anthropologist* 67(6):82–122.

Collins, Patricia Hill. 2000. *Black Feminist Thought: Knowledge, Consciousness and the Politics of Empowerment,* 2nd ed. New York: Routledge.

Colón, Alice, and Rhoda Reddock. 2004. "The Changing Status of Women in the Contemporary Caribbean." In *General History of the Caribbean. Volume 5: The Caribbean in the Twentieth Century.* Bridget Brereton, ed. Pp. 465–505. Paris and London: UNESCO and MacMillan.

Comaroff, John L. 2001. "Colonialism, Culture and the Law: A Forward." *Law and Social Inquiry* 26(2):305–14.

Comaroff, John L., and Simon Roberts. 1981. *Rules and Processes: The Cultural Logic of Dispute in an African Context.* Chicago: University of Chicago.

Conley, John M., and William M. O'Barr. 1990. *Rules versus Relationships: The Ethnography of Legal Discourse.* Chicago: University of Chicago.

———. 1998. *Just Words: Law, Language, and Power.* Chicago: University of Chicago.

Connell, Patricia. 1997. "Understanding Victimization and Agency: Considerations of Race, Class and Gender." *PoLAR (Political and Legal Anthropology Review)* 20(2):115–43.

Connors, Jane. 1994. "Government Measures to Confront Violence against Women." In *Women and Violence: Realities and Responses Worldwide.* Miranda Davies, ed. Pp. 182–99. London: Zed Books.

Coombe, Rosemary. 1991. "Contesting the Self: Negotiating Subjectivities in Nineteenth-Century Ontario Defamation Trials." *Studies in Law, Politics, and Society* 11:3–40.

Corrin, Chris, ed. 1996. *Women in a Violent World: Feminist Analyses and Resistance across Europe.* Edinburgh: Edinburgh University.

Counts, Dorothy, Judith Brown, and Jacquelyn Campbell, eds. 1992. *Sanctions and Sanctuary: Cultural Perspectives on the Beating of Wives.* Boulder, Co.: Westview.

Coutin, Susan Bibler. 1993. *The Culture of Protest: Religious Activism and the U.S. Sanctuary Movement.* Boulder, Co.: Westview.

———. 2000. *Legalizing Moves: Salvadoran Immigrants' Struggle for U.S. Residency.* Ann Arbor: University of Michigan.

Coutin, Susan Bibler, Bill Maurer, and Barbara Yngvesson. 2002. "In the Mirror: The Legitimation Work of Globalization." *Law & Social Inquiry* 27(4):801–43.

Crenshaw, Kimberle. 1994. "Mapping the Margins: Intersectionality, Identity Politics, and Violence Against Women of Color." In *The Public Nature of Private Violence.* Martha Fineman and Roxanne Mykitiuk, eds. Pp. 93–118. New York: Routledge.

Creque, Merri. 1995. "A Study of the Incidence of Domestic Violence in Trinidad and Tobago from 1991 to 1993." Port of Spain, Trinidad and Tobago: Commissioned by the Shelter for Battered Women and Coalition Against Domestic Violence.

Crocker, Diane. 2005. "Regulating Intimacy: Judicial Discourse in Cases of Wife Assault (1970 to 2000)." *Violence Against Women* 11(2):197–226.

Crowell, Nancy A., and Ann W. Burgess, eds. 1996. *Understanding Violence Against Women.* National Research Council. Washington, D.C.: National Academy Press.

Daly, Stephanie. 1992. *Child and Family Law: Trinidad and Tobago.* Port of Spain, Trinidad and Tobago: Government Printery.

Danns, George K., and Basmat Shiw Parsad. 1989. *Domestic Violence and Marital Relationships in the Caribbean: A Guyana Case Study.* Georgetown, Guyana: University of Guyana, Women's Studies Unit.

Dasgupta, Shamita Das. 2005. "Women's Realities: Defining Violence against Women by Immigration, Race, and Class." In *Domestic Violence at the Margins: Readings on Race, Class, Gender, and Culture.* Natalie J. Sokoloff, ed. Pp. 56–70. New Brunswick, N.J.: Rutgers University.

Deosaran, Ramesh. 1993. *A Society under Siege: A Study of Political Confusion and Legal Mysticism.* St. Augustine, Trinidad and Tobago: University of the West Indies, The McAL Psychological Research Centre.

———. 1996. "Youth, Poverty and Delinquency in the Caribbean: Policy Challenges." *Contemporary Issues in Social Science: A Caribbean Perspective* 3:1–69.

Dobash, R. Emerson, and Russell P. Dobash. 1979. *Violence against Wives: A Case against the Patriarchy.* London: Zed Books.

———. 1992. *Women, Violence, and Social Change.* London: Routledge.

Dobash, R. Emerson, Russell P. Dobash, and Lesley Noaks, eds. 1995. *Gender and Crime.* Cardiff: University of Wales.

Douglass, Lisa. 1992. *The Power of Sentiment: Love, Hierarchy, and the Jamaican Family Elite.* Boulder, Co.: Westview.

Eaton, Mary. 1986. *Justice for Women? Family, Court and Social Control.* Philadelphia: Milton Keynes.

Economic Commission for Latin America and the Caribbean. 2001a. *An Evaluative Study of the Implementation of Domestic Violence Legislation: Antigua and Barbuda, St. Kitts/Nevis, Saint Lucia, and Saint Vincent and the Grenadines.* Subregional Headquarters for the Caribbean. Caribbean Development and Cooperation Committee.

———. 2001b. "Report of the Working Group Meeting on Data Collection Systems: Domestic Violence." Port of Spain, Trinidad: UNECLAC. http://www.eclac.cl/publicaciones/PortOfSpain/2/LCCARG642/G0642.html.

———. 2001c. "Report of the ECLAC/CDCC Ad Hoc Expert Group Meeting on Strategies to End Violence against Women: Data Collection Systems for Domestic Violence in the Caribbean." Port of Spain, Trinidad: UNECLAC. http://www.eclac.cl/publicaciones/PortOfSpain/4/LCCARG674/cargo674.pdf.

———. 2003. "Report of the ECLAC/CDCC/CIDA Gender Equality Programme Regional Conference on Gender-Based Violence and the Administration of Justice." Port of Spain, Trinidad: UNECLAC. http://www.eclac.cl/publicaciones/PortOfSpain/2/LCCARG744/G0744.pdf.

Economy of Trinidad and Tobago. 2005. Wikipedia Encyclopedia. http://www.en.wikipedia.org/Wiki/Economy_of_Trinidad_and_Tobago.

Eigenberg, Helen M. 2001. *Woman Battering in the United States: Till Death Do Us Part.* Prospect Heights, Ill.: Waveland.

Emerson, Robert M. 1969. *Judging Delinquents: Context and Process in Juvenile Court.* Los Angeles: University of California.

———. 1995. "Holistic Effects in Social Control Decision-Making." In *The Law and Society Reader.* Richard L. Abel, ed. Pp. 161–84. New York: New York University.

Escobar, Arturo. 1995. *Encountering Development: The Making and Unmaking of the Third World.* Princeton, N.J.: Princeton University.

Ewick, Patricia, and Susan S. Silbey. 1998. *The Common Place of Law: Stories from Everyday Life.* Chicago: University of Chicago.

Fagan, Jeffrey. 1996. *The Criminalization of Domestic Violence: Promises and Limits.* Washington, D.C.: U.S. Department of Justice, National Institute of Justice.

Feeley, Malcolm. 1979. *The Process Is the Punishment: Handling Cases in a Lower Criminal Court.* New York: Russell Sage Foundation.

Ferraro, Kathleen J., and Tascha Boychuk. 1992. "The Court's Response to Interpersonal Violence: A Comparison of Intimate and Nonintimate Assault." In *Domestic Violence: The Changing Criminal Justice Response.* Eve S. Buzawa and Carl G. Buzawa, eds. Pp. 209–25. Westport, Conn.: Auburn House.

Ffolkes, Suzanne. 1997. "Violence against Women: Some Legal Responses." In *Gender: A Caribbean Multi-Disciplinary Perspective.* Elsa Leo-Rhynie, Barbara Bailey, and Christine Barrow, eds. Pp. 118–27. Kingston, Jamaica: Ian Randle.

Fineman, Martha Albertson. 1995. *The Neutered Mother: The Sexual Family and Other Twentieth-Century Tragedies.* New York: Routledge.

Fineman, Martha Albertson, and Roxanne Mykitiuk, eds. 1994. *The Public Nature of Private Violence: The Discovery of Domestic Abuse.* New York: Routledge.

Fineman, Martha Albertson, and Nancy Sweet Thomadsen, eds. 1991. *At the Boundaries of Law: Feminism and Legal Theory.* New York: Routledge.

Fischer, Karla, and Mary Rose. 1995. "When Enough Is Enough: Battered Women's Decision Making around Court Orders of Protection." *Crime & Delinquency* 41(4):414–29.

Ford, David A. 1991. "Prosecution as a Victim Power Resource: A Note on Empowering Women in Violent Conjugal Relationships." *Law & Society Review* 25(2):313–34.

———. 1993. *The Indianapolis Domestic Violence Prosecution Experiment.* Final report submitted to the National Institute of Justice. Indianapolis: Indiana University–Purdue University Indianapolis, Department of Sociology.

———. 2003. "Coercing Victim Participation in Domestic Violence Prosecutions." *Journal of Interpersonal Violence* 18:669–84.

Ford, David A., and Mary Jean Regoli. 1992. "The Preventive Impacts of Policies for Prosecuting Wife Batterers." In *Domestic Violence: The Changing Criminal Justice Response.* Eve S. Buzawa and Carl G. Buzawa, eds. Pp. 181–207. Westport, Conn.: Auburn House.

Ford, David A., Ruth Reichard, Stephen Goldsmith, and Mary Jean Regoli. 1996. "Future Directions for Criminal Justice Policy on Domestic Violence." In *Do*

Arrests and Restraining Orders Work? Eve S. Buzawa and Carl G. Buzawa, eds. Pp. 243–65. Thousand Oaks, Calif.: Sage.

Forde, Norma Monica. 1981. *Women and the Law.* Barbados, Jamaica, Trinidad and Tobago: The Press University of the West Indies.

Foucault, Michel. 1978. *The History of Sexuality. Vol. 1. An Introduction.* Robert Hurley, trans. New York: Pantheon.

———. 1979. *Discipline and Punish: The Birth of the Prison.* Alan Sheridan, trans. New York: Vintage Books.

———. 1980. *Power/Knowledge: Selected Interviews and Other Writings, 1972–1977.* Colin Gordon, ed. Leo Marshall, John Maugham, and Kate Soper, trans. New York: Pantheon.

Fraser, Arvonne S. 2001. "Becoming Human: The Origins and Development of Women's Human Rights." In *Women, Gender, and Human Rights: A Global Perspective.* Marjorie Agosin, ed. Pp. 15–64. New Brunswick, N.J.: Rutgers University.

French, Rebecca R. 2001. "Time in the Law." *University of Colorado Law Review* 72(3):663–748.

Frohmann, Lisa. 1991. "Discrediting Victims' Allegations of Sexual Assault: Prosecutorial Accounts of Case Rejections." *Social Problems* 38(2):213–26.

Frohmann, Lisa, and Elizabeth Mertz. 1995. "Legal Reform and Social Construction: Violence, Gender, and the Law." *Law & Social Inquiry* 19(4):829–51.

Gal, Susan. 1991. "Between Speech and Silence: The Problematics of Research on Language and Gender." In *Gender at the Crossroads of Knowledge: Feminist Anthropology in the Postmodern Era.* Micaela di' Leonardo, ed. Pp. 175–203. Berkeley: University of California.

Galanter, Marc. 1974. "Why the Haves Come Out Ahead: Speculations on the Limits of Legal Change." *Law & Society Review* 9(1):95–160.

Garfinkel, Harold. 1956. "Conditions of Successful Degradation Ceremonies." *American Journal of Sociology* 61:420–24.

Garland, David. 1990. *Punishment and Modern Society: A Study in Social Theory.* Chicago: University of Chicago.

Gell, Alfred. 1992. *The Anthropology of Time: Cultural Constructions of Temporal Maps and Images.* Washington, D.C.: Berg.

Goffman, Erving. 1963. *Stigma: Notes on the Management of Spoiled Identity.* Englewood Cliffs, N.J.: Prentice Hall.

Gopaul, Roanna, and Maureen Cain. 1996. "Violence between Spouses in Trinidad and Tobago: A Research Note." *Caribbean Quarterly* 42(2/3):29–41.

Gordon, Linda. 1988. *Heroes of Their Own Lives: The Politics and History of Family Violence.* New York: Penguin.

Gramsci, Antonio. 1971. *Selections from the Prison Notebooks.* London: Lawrence and Wishart.

Greenhouse, Carol J. 1986. *Praying for Justice: Faith, Order, and Community in an American Town.* Ithaca: Cornell University.

———. 1989. "Just in Time: Temporality and the Cultural Legitimation of Law." *The Yale Law Journal* 98(8):1631–51.

———. 1996. *A Moment's Notice: Time Politics across Cultures.* Ithaca: Cornell University.

Greenhouse, Carol J., Barbara Yngvesson, and David M. Engel. 1994. *Law and Community in Three American Towns*. Ithaca: Cornell University.

Grossberg, Michael. 1994. "Battling over Motherhood in Philadelphia: A Study of Antebellum American Trial Courts as Arenas of Conflict." In *Contested States: Law, Hegemony and Resistance*. Mindie Lazarus-Black and Susan F. Hirsch, eds. Pp. 153–83. New York: Routledge.

Hadeed, Linda. 2003. "Domestic Violence in Trinidad and Tobago." Ph.D. dissertation, Columbia University, New York.

Hagley, Lystra. 1995. "Imprisonment in Trinidad and Tobago from 1935–1990: Policy and Practice." Master of Science Thesis in Sociology, University of the West Indies, St. Augustine, Trinidad and Tobago.

Hampton, Robert L., Ricardo Carrillo, and Joan Kim. 2005. "Domestic Violence in African American Communities." In *Domestic Violence at the Margins: Readings on Race, Class, Gender and Culture*. Natalie J. Sokoloff, ed. Pp. 127–41. New Brunswick, N.J.: Rutgers University Press.

Handwerker, W. Penn. 1997. "Power and Gender: Violence and Affection Experienced by Children in Barbados, West Indies." *Medical Anthropology* 17(2):101–28.

Haniff, Nesha Z. 1998. "A Study of Domestic Violence in the British Virgin Islands." Caribbean Association for Feminist Research and Action (CAFRA) Library Collection, Tunapuna, Trinidad and Tobago. Unpublished manuscript.

Hann, Robert G., Donna Boucaud, and Franklyn Murrell. 2005. *Family Court Evaluation First Year Report*. Port of Spain, Trinidad and Tobago: Family Court of Trinidad and Tobago.

Hanna, Cheryl. 1998. "The Paradox of Hope: The Crime and Punishment of Domestic Violence." *William and Mary Law Review* 39:1505–84.

Harney, Stefano. 1996. *Nationalism and Identity: Culture and the Imagination in a Caribbean Diaspora*. London: Zed Books.

Harrell, Adele, and Barbara E. Smith. 1996. "Effects of Restraining Orders on Domestic Violence Victims." In *Do Arrests and Restraining Orders Work?* Eve S. Buzawa and Carl G. Buzawa, eds. Pp. 214–42. Thousand Oaks, Calif.: Sage.

Harrell, Adele, Barbara Smith, and Lisa Newmark. 1993. *Court Processing and the Effects of Restraining Orders for Domestic Violence Victims*. Washington, D.C.: Urban Institute.

Harriott, Anthony, Farley Brathwaite, and Scot Wortley. 2004. *Crime and Criminal Justice in the Caribbean*. Kingston, Jamaica: Arawak Publications.

Hartley, Carolyn Copps. 2001. "'He Said, She Said': The Defense Attack of Credibility in Domestic Violence Felony Trials." *Violence Against Women* 7(5):510–44.

Headley, Bernard. 1994. *The Jamaican Crime Scene: A Perspective*. Washington, D.C.: Howard University.

Henderson, Thelma. 1988. "The Contemporary Women's Movement in Trinidad and Tobago." In *Gender in Caribbean Development*. Patricia Mohammed and Catherine Shepherd, eds. Pp. 363–72. Women and Development Studies Project. Barbados, Jamaica, Trinidad and Tobago: The Press University of the West Indies.

Hirsch, Susan F. 1994. "Kadhi's Courts as Complex Sites of Resistance: The State, Islam, and Gender in Post-Colonial Kenya." In *Contested States: Law, He-*

gemony and Resistance. Mindie Lazarus-Black and Susan F. Hirsch, eds. Pp. 207–30. New York: Routledge.

———. 1998. *Pronouncing and Persevering: Gender and the Discourses of Dispute in an African Islamic Court.* Chicago: University of Chicago.

———. 2003. "Problems of Cross-Cultural Comparison: Analyzing Linguistic Strategies in Tanzanian Domestic Violence Workshops." *Law & Social Inquiry* 28(4):1009–44.

Hirsch, Susan F., and Mindie Lazarus-Black. 1994. "Performance and Paradox: Exploring Law's Role in Hegemony and Resistance." In *Contested States: Law, Hegemony and Resistance.* Mindie Lazarus-Black and Susan F. Hirsch, eds. Pp. 1–31. New York: Routledge.

Hirschel, David, and Ira W. Hutchison. 2001. "The Relative Effects of Offense, Offender, and Victim Variables on the Decision to Prosecute Domestic Violence Cases." *Violence Against Women* 7(1):46–59.

Hodge, Merle. 2002. "We Kind of Family." In *Gendered Realities: Essays in Caribbean Feminist Thought.* Patricia Mohammed, ed. Pp. 474–85. Barbados, Jamaica, Trinidad and Tobago: The Press University of the West Indies and Centre for Gender and Development Studies, Jamaica.

Holstein, James A. 1993. *Court-Ordered Insanity: Interpretive Practice and Involuntary Commitment.* New York: Aldine De Gruyter.

Horney, Julie, and Cassia Spohn. 1991. "Rape Law Reform and Instrumental Change in Six Urban Jurisdictions." *Law & Society Review* 25(1):117–53.

Human Rights Internet. 1993. *Trinidad and Tobago: Women's Human Rights.* Ottawa, Ontario: University of Ottawa.

Jackson, Jean. 1982. "Stresses Affecting Women and Their Families." In *Women and the Family.* Joycelin Massiah, ed. Pp. 29–61. Women in the Caribbean Project. Barbados, Jamaica, Trinidad and Tobago: The Press University of the West Indies.

James-Sebro, Meryl. 2001. "Flagwomen: The Struggle against Domestic Violence in Trinidad and Tobago." Ph.D. dissertation, American University, Washington, D.C.

Joseph, Janice, Zelma Weston Henriques, and Kaylene Richards Ekeh. 1998. "The Legal Response to Domestic Violence in the English-Speaking Caribbean Countries." *Caribbean Journal of Criminology and Social Psychology* 3(1/2):174–87.

Judiciary of the Republic of Trinidad and Tobago. http://www.ttlawcourts.org.

Just, Peter. 2001. *Dou Donggo Justice: Conflict and Morality in an Indonesian Society.* New York: Rowman & Littlefield.

Kabeer, Naila. 1994. *Reversed Realities: Gender Hierarchies in Development Thought.* London: Verso.

Kanhai, Rosanne. 1999. "Rum Sweet Rum." In *Matikor: The Politics of Identity for Indo-Caribbean Women.* Rosanne Kanhai, ed. Pp. 3–17. St. Augustine, Trinidad and Tobago: University of the West Indies, School of Continuing Education.

Kanuha, Valli Kalei. 2005. "Compounding the Triple Jeopardy: Battering in Lesbian of Color Relationships." In *Domestic Violence at the Margins: Readings on Race, Class, Gender, and Culture.* Natalie J. Sokoloff, ed. Pp. 71–82. New Brunswick, N.J.: Rutgers University.

Kassim, Halima. 1997. "Muslim Women and the Growth of Islamic Educational Institutions in Trinidad (1917–1962)." Paper presented at the Annual Conference of the Association of Caribbean Historians, Martinique. April 7–12.

Kelkar, Govind. 1989. "Violence Against Women: An Understanding of Responsibility for Their Lives." In *Women and Violence*. Niroj Sinha, ed. Pp. 1–15. New Delhi: Vikas Publishing House.

Khan, Aisha. 1993. "What Is a Spanish?: Ambiguity and Mixed Ethnicity in Trinidad." In *Trinidad Ethnicity*. Kevin A. Yelvington, ed. Pp. 180–207. Knoxville: University of Tennessee.

Kiely, Ray. 1996. *The Politics of Labor and Development in Trinidad*. Barbados, Jamaica, Trinidad and Tobago: The Press University of the West Indies.

Klein, Dorie. 1982. "The Dark Side of Marriage: Battered Wives and the Domination of Women." In *Judge, Lawyer, Victim, Thief: Women, Gender Roles, and Criminal Justice*. Nicole Han Rafter and Elizabeth A. Stanko, eds. Pp. 83–107. Boston: Northeastern University.

Kuper, Adam. 1999. *Culture: The Anthropologists' Account*. Cambridge, Mass.: Harvard University.

LaFont, Suzanne. 1996. *The Emergence of an Afro-Caribbean Legal Tradition: Gender Relations and Family Court Use in Kingston, Jamaica*. San Francisco: Austin & Winfield.

Lamb, Sharon. 1999. "Constructing the Victim: Popular Images and Lasting Labels." In *New Versions of Victims: Feminists Struggle with the Concept*. Sharon Lamb, ed. Pp. 108–38. New York: New York University.

Laws of Trinidad and Tobago. 1991. Domestic Violence Act. No. 10. (Repealed)
———. 1999. Domestic Violence Act. No. 27.

Lazarus-Black, Mindie. 1991. "Why Women Take Men to Magistrate's Court: Caribbean Kinship Ideology and Law." *Ethnology* 30(2):119–33.

———. 1994. *Legitimate Acts and Illegal Encounters: Law and Society in Antigua and Barbuda*. Washington, D.C.: Smithsonian.

———. 1995. "My Mother Never Fathered Me: Rethinking Kinship and the Governing of Families." *Social and Economic Studies* 44(1):49–71.

———. 1997. "The Rites of Domination: Practice, Process and Structure in Lower Courts." *American Ethnologist* 24(3):628–51.

———. 2001. "Law and the Pragmatics of Inclusion: Governing Domestic Violence in Trinidad and Tobago." *American Ethnologist* 28(2):388–416.

———. 2002. "The Rites of Domination: Tales from Domestic Violence Court." Centre for Gender and Development Studies. Working Paper Series, *Working Paper No. 7*. St. Augustine, Trinidad and Tobago: University of the West Indies.

———. 2003. "The (Heterosexual) Regendering of a Modern State: Criminalizing and Implementing Domestic Violence Law in Trinidad." *Law & Social Inquiry* 28(4):979–1008.

Lazarus-Black, Mindie, and Susan F. Hirsch, eds. 1994. *Contested States: Law, Hegemony and Resistance*. New York: Routledge.

Lazarus-Black, Mindie, and Patricia L. McCall. 2006. "The Politics of Place: Practice, Process, and Kinship in Domestic Violence Courts." *Human Organization* 65(2):140–55.

Lazarus-Black, Mindie, and Sally Engle Merry. 2003. "The Politics of Gender

Violence: Law Reform in Local and Global Places." *Law & Social Inquiry* 28(4):931–39.

Lederman, Rena. 1984. "Who Speaks Here? Formality and the Politics of Gender in Mendi, Highland Papua New Guinea." In *Dangerous Words: Language and Politics in the Pacific.* Don Brenneis and Fred Myers, eds. Pp. 85–107. New York: New York University.

LeFranc, Elsie, and Letnie Rock. 2001. "The Commonality of Gender-Based Violence." *Journal of Eastern Caribbean Studies* 26(1):74–82.

Leo-Rhynie, Elsa, Barbara Bailey, and Christine Barrow, eds. 1997. *Gender: A Caribbean Multi-Disciplinary Perspective.* Kingston, Jamaica: Ian Randle.

Levinson, David. 1989. *Family Violence in Cross-cultural Perspective.* Newbury Park, Calif.: Sage.

———. 1996. "Spousal Violence." In *Encyclopedia of Cultural Anthropology. Vol. 4.* David Levinson and Melvin Ember, eds. Pp. 1252–1253. New York: Henry Holt.

Lindsay, Keisha. 2002. "Is the Caribbean Male an Endangered Species?" In *Gendered Realities: Essays in Caribbean Feminist Thought.* Patricia Mohammed, ed. Pp. 56–82. Barbados, Jamaica, and Trinidad and Tobago: The Press University of the West Indies and Centre for Gender and Development Studies, Jamaica.

London, Scott. 1997. "Conciliation and Domestic Violence in Senegal, West Africa." *PoLAR (Political and Legal Anthropology Review)* 20:83–91.

Loseke, Donileen R. 1992. *The Battered Woman and Shelters: The Social Construction of Wife Abuse.* Albany: State University of New York.

MacKinnon, Catherine A. 1979. *Sexual Harassment of Working Women: A Case Study of Sex Discrimination.* New Haven, Conn.: Yale University.

———. 1989. *Toward a Feminist Theory of the State.* Cambridge, Mass.: Harvard University.

Mahabir, Cynthia. 1996. "Rape Prosecution, Culture, and Inequality in Postcolonial Grenada." *Feminist Studies* 22(1):89–117.

———. 2001. "The Rise of Calypso Feminism: Gender and Musical Politics in the Calypso." *Popular Music* 20(3):409–30.

Mahabir, Kumar. 1996. "Whose Nation Is This? The Struggle over National and Ethnic Identity in Trinidad and Guyana." *Caribbean Studies* 29(2):283–302.

Mahoney, Martha R. 1991. "Legal Images of Battered Women: Redefining the Issue of Separation." *Michigan Law Review* 90(1):1–94.

———. 1994. "Victimization or Oppression? Women's Lives, Violence, and Agency." In *The Public Nature of Private Violence: The Discovery of Domestic Abuse.* Martha Albertson Fineman and Roxanne Mykitiuk, eds. Pp. 59–92. New York: Routledge.

Martin, Del. 1976. *Battered Wives.* San Francisco: Glide Publications.

Mather, Lynn, and Barbara Yngvesson. 1980/81. "Language, Audience, and the Transformation of Disputes." *Law & Society Review* 15:775–822.

Matoesian, Gregory M. 1993. *Reproducing Rape: Domination through Talk in the Courtroom.* Chicago: University of Chicago.

———. 1995. "Language, Law and Society: Policy Implications of the Kennedy Smith Rape Trial." *Law & Society Review* 29:669–701.

———. 2001. *Law and the Language of Identity: Discourse in the William Kennedy Smith Rape Trial.* Oxford: Oxford University.

Matthews, Nancy A. 1994. *Confronting Rape: The Feminist Anti-Rape Movement and the State.* London: Routledge.

Maurer, Bill. 1997. *Recharting the Caribbean: Land, Law, and Citizenship in the British Virgin Islands.* Ann Arbor: University of Michigan.

Maurer, Bill, and Sally Engle Merry. 1997. "From the Editors." *PoLAR (Political and Legal Anthropology Review)* 20(2):v-vii.

McLindon, James B. 1987. "Separate but Unequal: The Economic Disaster of Divorce for Women and Children." *Family Law Quarterly* 21:351-409.

Mehrotra, Aparna. 2002. *Gender and Legislation in Latin America and the Caribbean.* United Nations Development Programme (UNDP). http://www.undp.org/rblac/gender/legislation.

Mendes, John. 1986. *Cote ce Cote la: Trinidad and Tobago Dictionary.* Arima, Trinidad and Tobago: Privately published.

Merry, Sally Engle. 1990. *Getting Justice and Getting Even: Legal Consciousness among Working-Class Americans.* Chicago: University of Chicago.

———. 1994. "Court as Performances: Domestic Violence Hearings in a Hawai'i Family Court." In *Contested States: Law, Hegemony and Resistance.* Mindie Lazarus-Black and Susan F. Hirsch, eds. Pp. 35-58. New York: Routledge.

———. 1995a. "Gender Violence and Legally Engendered Selves." *Identities: Global Studies in Culture and Power* 2(1-2):49-73.

———. 1995b. "Resistance and the Cultural Power of Law." *Law & Society Review* 29(1):11-26.

———. 2000. *Colonizing Hawai'i: The Cultural Power of Law.* Princeton, N.J.: Princeton University.

———. 2001a. "Spatial Governmentality and the New Urban Social Order: Controlling Gender Violence through Law." *American Anthropologist* 103(1):16-29.

———. 2001b. "Rights, Religion, and Community: Approaches to Violence against Women in the Context of Globalization." *Law & Society Review* 35(1):39-88.

———. 2003. "Constructing a Global Law: Violence against Women and the Human Rights System." *Law & Social Inquiry* 28(4):941-77.

Mileski, Maureen. 1971. "Courtroom Encounters: An Observation Study of a Lower Criminal Court." *Law & Society Review* 5:473-538.

Miller, Daniel. 1994. *Modernity an Ethnographic Approach: Dualism and Mass Consumption in Trinidad.* Oxford: Berg.

———. 1997. *Capitalism: An Ethnographic Approach.* Oxford: Berg.

Miller, Susan L., and Rosemary Barberet. 1994. "A Cross-Cultural Comparison of Social Reform: The Growing Pains of the Battered Women's Movement in Washington, D.C., and Madrid, Spain." *Law & Social Inquiry* 19(4):923-66.

Millette, James. 2004. "Decolonization, Populist Movements and the Formation of New Nations, 1945-70." In *General History of the Caribbean. Volume 5: The Caribbean in the Twentieth Century.* Bridget Brereton, ed. Pp. 174-233. Paris and London: UNESCO and MacMillan.

Ministry of the Attorney General and Legal Affairs, Trinidad and Tobago. 2000. *Initial, Second and Third Periodic Report of the Republic of Trinidad and Tobago: The International Convention on the Elimination of Discrimination against Women.* New York: United Nations.

Minow, Martha. 1990. *Making All the Difference: Inclusion, Exclusion and American Law*. Ithaca, N.Y.: Cornell University.

Mohammed, Patricia. 1989. "Women's Responses to the 70s and 80s in Trinidad: A Country Report." *Caribbean Quarterly* 35(1/2):36–45.

———. 1991. "Reflections on the Women's Movement in Trinidad: Calypsos, Changes and Sexual Violence." *Feminist Review* 38:33–47.

———. 1998. "The Idea of Childhood and Age of Sexual Maturity among Indians in Trinidad: A Sociohistorical Scrutiny." Paper presented at the Annual Conference of the Association of Caribbean Historians, Suriname. April 17–22.

———. 2002a. *Gender Negotiations among Indians in Trinidad 1917–1947*. New York: Palgrave.

———, ed. 2002b. *Gendered Realities: Essays in Caribbean Feminist Thought*. Barbados, Jamaica, and Trinidad and Tobago: The Press University of the West Indies and Centre for Gender and Development Studies, Jamaica.

Momsen, Janet H., ed. 1993. *Women and Change in the Caribbean: A Pan-Caribbean Perspective*. Kingston, Jamaica: Ian Randle.

Moog, Robert S. 1997. *Whose Interests Are Supreme? Organizational Politics in the Civil Courts in India*. Ann Arbor, Mich.: Association for Asian Studies. Monograph and Occasional Papers Series. No. 54.

Moore, Brian. 1995. *Cultural Power, Resistance and Pluralism: Colonial Guyana 1838–1900*. Montreal: McGill-Queen's University.

Moore, Erin. 1994. "Law's Patriarchy in India." In *Contested States: Law, Hegemony and Resistance*. Mindie Lazarus-Black and Susan F. Hirsch, eds. Pp. 89–117. New York: Routledge.

Moore, Sally Falk. 1986. *Social Facts and Fabrications: Customary Law on Kilimanjaro, 1880–1980*. Cambridge: Cambridge University.

———. 1992. "Treating Law as Knowledge: Telling Colonial Officers What to Say to Africans about Running Their Own Native Courts." *Law & Society Review* 26:11–46.

———. 2001. "Certainties Undone: Fifty Turbulent Years of Legal Anthropology, 1949–1999." *Journal of the Royal Anthropological Institute* 7:95–116.

Morrow, Betty Hearn. 1994. "A Grass-Roots Feminist Response to Intimate Violence in the Caribbean." *Women's Studies International Forum* 17(6):579–92.

Munasinghe, Viranjini. 2001. *Callaloo or Tossed Salad? East Indians and the Cultural Politics of Identity in Trinidad*. Ithaca: Cornell University.

———. 2002. "Nationalism in Hybrid Spaces: The Production of Impurity out of Purity." *American Ethnologist* 29(3):663–92.

Munn, Nancy D. 1992. "The Cultural Anthropology of Time: A Critical Essay." *Annual Review of Anthropology* 21:93–123.

Nader, Laura. 1990. *Harmony Ideology: Justice and Control in a Zapotec Mountain Village*. Stanford: Stanford University.

———. 2002. *The Life of the Law: Anthropological Projects*. Berkeley: University of California.

Nimmer, Raymond T. 1978. *The Nature of System Change: Reform Impact on the Criminal Court*. Chicago: American Bar Foundation.

Nurse, Keith. 1999. "Globalization and Trinidad Carnival: Diaspora, Hybridity and Identity in Global Culture." In *Identity, Ethnicity and Culture in the Ca-*

ribbean. Ralph Premdas, ed. Pp. 80–114. St. Augustine, Trinidad and Tobago: University of the West Indies, School of Continuing Studies.

O'Barr, William M. 1982. *Linguistic Evidence: Language, Power, and Strategy in the Courtroom*. New York: Academic Press.

Pargass, Gaietry, and Roberta Clarke. 2003. "Violence against Women: A Human Rights Issue Post Beijing Five Year Review." In *Gender Equality in the Caribbean: Reality or Illusion*. Gemma Tang Nain and Barbara Bailey, eds. Pp. 39–72. Kingston, Jamaica: Ian Randle.

Parsad, Basmat Shiw. 1988. "Domestic Violence: A Study of Wife-Abuse among East Indians of Guyana." Paper presented at the 13th Annual Meeting of the Caribbean Studies Association, Guadeloupe. May 25–27.

———. 1999. "Marital Violence within East Indian Households in Guyana: A Cultural Explanation." In *Matikor: The Politics of Identity for Indo-Caribbean Women*. Rosanne Kanhai, ed. Pp. 40–61. St. Augustine, Trinidad and Tobago: University of the West Indies, School of Continuing Education.

Peterson del Mar, David. 1996. *What Trouble I Have Seen: A History of Violence against Wives*. Cambridge, Mass.: Harvard University.

Philips, Daphne. 2000. "Domestic Violence and Public Policy in Trinidad and Tobago." *Caribbean Journal of Criminology and Social Psychology* 5(1/2):181–88.

Philips, Susan U. 1994. "Local Legal Hegemony in the Tongan Magistrate's Court: How Sisters Fare Better Than Wives." In *Contested States: Law, Hegemony and Resistance*. Mindie Lazarus-Black and Susan F. Hirsch, eds. Pp. 59–88. New York: Routledge.

———. 1998. *Ideology in the Language of Judges: How Judges Practice Law, Politics, and Courtroom Control*. New York: Oxford University.

Pierce, Paulette. 1996. "Boudoir Politics and the Birthing of the Nation: Sex, Marriage and Structural Deflection in the National Black Independent Political Party." In *Women Out of Place: The Gender of Agency and the Race of Nationality*. Brackette F. Williams, ed. Pp. 216–44. New York: Routledge.

Pleck, Elizabeth. 1987. *Domestic Tyranny: The Making of Social Policy against Family Violence from Colonial Times to the Present*. New York: Oxford University.

Pratt, Christina. 2000. "Violence against Women: A Cross-National Study of Policy in Barbados and New York." *Caribbean Journal of Criminology and Social Psychology* 5(1/2):1–39.

Ptacek, James. 1999. *Battered Women in the Courtroom: The Power of Judicial Responses*. Boston: Northeastern University.

Purdy, Jeannine M. 1997. *Common Law and Colonized Peoples: Studies in Trinidad and Western Australia*. Brookfield, Vt.: Ashgate.

Ramkeesoon, Gema. 1988. "Early Women's Organizations in Trinidad: 1920s to 1950s." In *Gender in Caribbean Development*. Patricia Mohammed and Catherine Shepherd, eds. Pp. 353–56. Barbados, Jamaica, Trinidad and Tobago: The Press University of the West Indies and Women and Development Studies Project.

Rawlins, Joan M. 2000. "Domestic Violence in Trinidad: A Family and Public Health Problem." *Caribbean Journal of Criminology and Social Psychology* 5(1/2):165–80.

Razack, Sherene H. 1998. *Looking White People in the Eye: Gender, Race, and Culture in Courtrooms and Classrooms.* Toronto: University of Toronto.

———. 1999. "Images of Indian Women in the Law: What Gender Images in the Diaspora Can Tell Us about Indianness." In *Matikor: The Politics of Identity for Indo-Caribbean Women.* Rosanne Kanhai, ed. Pp. 155–71. St. Augustine, Trinidad and Tobago: University of the West Indies, School of Continuing Education.

———. 2002. "Gendered Racial Violence and Spatialized Justice: The Murder of Pamela George." In *Race, Space, and the Law: Unmapping a White Settler Society.* Sherene Razack, ed. Pp. 121–56. Toronto: Between the Lines.

Rebovich, Donald J. 1996. "Prosecution Response to Domestic Violence: Results of a Survey of Large Jurisdictions." In *Do Arrests and Restraining Orders Work?* Eve S. Buzawa and Carl G. Buzawa, eds. Pp. 176–91. Thousand Oaks, Calif.: Sage.

Reddock, Rhoda. 1991. "Social Mobility in Trinidad and Tobago 1960–1980." In *Social and Occupational Stratification in Contemporary Trinidad and Tobago.* Selwyn Ryan, ed. Pp. 210–33. St. Augustine, Trinidad and Tobago: University of the West Indies, Institute of Social and Economic Studies.

———. 1994. *Women, Labour and Politics in Trinidad and Tobago: A History.* Kingston, Jamaica: Ian Randle.

———, ed. 1995. "Women and Family in the Caribbean: Historical and Contemporary Considerations: With Special Reference to Jamaica and Trinidad and Tobago." Prepared for the CARICOM Secretariat for the International Year of the Family, 1994 by Women and Development Studies Group/Centre for Gender and Development Studies, University of the West Indies, St. Augustine, Trinidad and Tobago.

———. 1998a. "Gender Relations: A Changing Landscape." In *Caribbean Perspectives.* Frank Mills, ed. Pp. 9–17. Virgin Islands: Eastern Caribbean Center, University of the Virgin Islands.

———. 1998b. "Women, the Creole Nationalist Movement and the Rise of Eric Williams and the PNM in Mid 20th Century Trinidad and Tobago." *Caribbean Issues* 111(4):41–65.

———. 1998c. "Women's Organizations and Movements in the Commonwealth Caribbean: The Response to Global Economic Crisis in the 1980s." *Feminist Review* 59:57–73.

———. 1999. "Jahaji Bhai: The Emergence of a Dougla Poetics in Contemporary Trinidad and Tobago." In *Identity, Ethnicity and Culture in the Caribbean.* Ralph R. Premdas, ed. Pp. 185–210. St. Augustine, Trinidad and Tobago: University of the West Indies, School of Continuing Studies.

Red Thread. 2000. "Women Researching Women: Selected Findings from a Survey on Domestic Violence in Guyana." Georgetown, Guyana: Red Thread. http://www.sdnp.org.gy/hands/wom_surv.htm.

Republic of Trinidad and Tobago. 2002. *2000 Population and Housing Census: Community Register.* Port of Spain, Trinidad and Tobago: Central Statistical Office.

———. 2004. *Pocket Digest.* Port of Spain, Trinidad and Tobago: Central Statistical Office.

Rheinstein, Max, ed. 1954. *Max Weber on Law in Economy and Society.* New York: Clarion.

Richie, Beth. 1996. *Compelled to Crime: The Gender Entrapment of Battered Black Women.* New York: Routledge.

———. 2005. "Foreword." *Domestic Violence at the Margins: Readings on Race, Class, Gender, and Culture.* Natalie J. Sokoloff, ed. Pp. xv–xviii. New Brunswick, N.J.: Rutgers University.

Rivera, Jenny. 1995. "Puerto Rico's Domestic Violence Prevention and Intervention Law and the United States Violence against Women Act of 1994: The Limitations of Legislative Responses." *Columbia Journal of Gender and Law* 5(1):78–126.

Roberts, Dorothy E. 1993. "Motherhood and Crime." *Iowa Law Review* 79(1):95–141.

Robinson, Tracy S. 1999. "Changing Conceptions of Violence: The Impact of Domestic Violence Legislation in the Caribbean." *Caribbean Law Review* 9:113–35.

———. 2000. "New Directions in Family Law Reform in the Caribbean." *Caribbean Law Review* 10(1):101–31.

———. Forthcoming. "Transforming Conceptions of Violence: The Ideology of Domestic Violence Laws." In *Caribbean Criminology.* Maureen Cain, ed.

Romany, Celina. 1994. "Killing the Angel in the House: Digging for the Political Vortex of Male Violence against Women." In *The Public Nature of Private Violence: The Discovery of Domestic Abuse.* Martha Albertson Fineman and Roxanne Mykitiuk, eds. Pp. 285–302. New York: Routledge.

Rosen, Ruth. 2000. *The World Split Open: How the Modern Women's Movement Changed America.* New York: Penguin Books.

Ryan, Selwyn. 1972. *Race and Nationalism in Trinidad and Tobago: A Study of Decolonization in a Multiracial Society.* Toronto: University of Toronto.

———, ed. 1988. *Trinidad and Tobago: The Independence Experience 1962–1987.* St. Augustine, Trinidad and Tobago: University of the West Indies, Institute of Social and Economic Research.

———, ed. 1991. *Social and Occupational Stratification in Contemporary Trinidad and Tobago.* St. Augustine, Trinidad and Tobago: University of the West Indies, Institute of Social and Economic Research.

———. 1996. *Pathways to Power: Indians and the Politics of National Unity in Trinidad and Tobago.* St. Augustine, Trinidad and Tobago: University of the West Indies, Institute of Social and Economic Research.

———. 1999. *Winner Takes All: The Westminster Experience in the Anglophone Caribbean.* St. Augustine, Trinidad and Tobago: The University of the West Indies, Institute of Social and Economic Research.

———. 2001. *The Judiciary and Governance in the Caribbean.* St. Augustine, Trinidad and Tobago: University of the West Indies, Sir Arthur Lewis Institute of Social and Economic Studies.

Schneider, David M. 1980 [1968]. *American Kinship: A Cultural Account,* 2nd ed. Chicago: University of Chicago.

Schneider, Elizabeth M. 1999. "Engaging with the State about Domestic Violence: Continuing Dilemmas and Gender Equality." *Georgetown Journal of Gender and Law* Summer:173–84.

———. 2000. *Battered Women and Feminist Lawmaking.* New Haven, Conn.: Yale University.

Schutz, Alfred. 1962. *Collected Papers: I. The Problem of Social Reality.* Maurice Natanson, ed. The Hague: Martinus Nijhoff.

Scott, James C. 1985. *Weapons of the Weak: Everyday Forms of Peasant Resistance.* New Haven, Conn.: Yale University.

Seebaran-Suite, Lynette. 1991. "Gender among the Professions in Trinidad and Tobago." In *Social and Occupational Stratification in Contemporary Trinidad and Tobago.* Selwyn Ryan, ed. Pp. 239–49. St. Augustine, Trinidad and Tobago: University of the West Indies, Institute of Social and Economic Research.

Segal, Daniel A. 1987. "Nationalism in a Colonial State: A Study of Trinidad and Tobago." Ph.D. dissertation, University of Chicago, Chicago, Illinois.

———. 1993. "Race and Color in Pre-Independence Trinidad and Tobago." In *Trinidad Ethnicity.* Kevin A. Yelvington, ed. Pp. 81–115. Knoxville: University of Tennessee.

Seng, Yvonne. 1994. "Standing at the Gates of Justice: Women in the Law Courts of Early-Sixteenth-Century Uskudar, Istanbul." In *Contested States: Law, Hegemony and Resistance.* Mindie Lazarus-Black and Susan F. Hirsch, eds. Pp. 184–206. New York: Routledge.

Senior, Olive. 1991. *Working Miracles: Women's Lives in the English-Speaking Caribbean.* Bloomington: Indiana University.

Sewell, Jr., William H. 1992. "A Theory of Structure: Duality, Agency, and Transformation." *American Journal of Sociology* 98(1):1–29.

Shepherd, Cathy. 1991. "Debate on the Trinidad and Tobago Domestic Violence Bill, January–July, 1991." Newspaper files compiled for Caribbean Association for Feminist Research and Action (CAFRA). Tunapuna, Trinidad and Tobago.

Shepherd, Verene, Bridget Brereton, and Barbara Bailey, eds. 1995. *Engendering History: Caribbean Women in Historical Perspective.* New York: St. Martin's.

Singh, Kirti. 1994. "Obstacles to Women's Rights in India." In *Human Rights of Women: National and International Perspectives.* Rebecca J. Cook, ed. Pp. 375–96. Philadelphia: University of Pennsylvania.

Sitaraman, Bhavani. 2002. "Policing Poor Families: Domestic Dispute Resolution in All-Women Police Stations." Paper presented to the Law & Society Association, Vancouver, Canada. May 30–June 1.

Slocum, Karla, and Deborah A. Thomas. 2003. "Rethinking Global and Area Studies: Insights from Caribbeanist Anthropology." *American Anthropologist* 105(3):553–65.

Smith, Raymond T. 1987. "Hierarchy and the Dual Marriage System in West Indian Society." In *Gender and Kinship: Essays toward a Unified Analysis.* Jane Fishburne Collier and Sylvia Junko Yanagisako, eds. Pp. 163–96. Stanford: Stanford University.

———. 1996. *The Matrifocal Family: Power, Pluralism, and Politics.* New York: Routledge.

Smyth, Ailbhe. 1996. "Seeing Red: Men's Violence against Women in Ireland." In *Women in a Violent World: Feminist Analyses and Resistance across Europe.* Chris Corrin, ed. Pp. 53–76. Edinburgh: Edinburgh University.

Sokoloff, Natalie J. ed. (with Christina Pratt). 2005. *Domestic Violence at the Margins: Readings on Race, Class, Gender, and Culture.* New Brunswick, N.J.: Rutgers University.

Sokoloff, Natalie J., and Ida Dupont. 2005a. "Domestic Violence at the Intersections of Race, Class, and Gender." *Violence Against Women* 11(1):38–64.

———. 2005b. "Domestic Violence: Examining the Intersections of Race, Class, and Gender—An Introduction." In *Domestic Violence at the Margins: Readings on Race, Class, Gender, and Culture*. Natalie J. Sokoloff, ed. Pp. 1–13. New Brunswick, N.J.: Rutgers University.

Spohn, Cassia, and David Holleran. 2001. "Prosecuting Sexual Assault: A Comparison of Changing Decisions in Sexual Assault Cases Involving Strangers, Acquaintances, and Intimate Partners." *Justice Quarterly* 18(3):651–88.

Spooner, Mary. 2001. "Women under Subjection of the Law: A Study of the Legal Responses to Women's Abuse in the English-Speaking Caribbean." Ph.D. dissertation, University of Massachusetts, Boston.

———. 2004. "Protecting Victims of Domestic Violence in Caribbean Communities." *Journal of Immigrant & Refugee Services* 2(3/4):117–34.

Stanko, Elizabeth A. 1982. "Would You Believe This Woman? Prosecutorial Screening for Credible Witnesses and a Problem of Justice." In *Judge, Lawyer, Victim, Thief: Women, Gender Roles, and Criminal Justice*. Nicole Han Rafter and Elizabeth A. Stanko, eds. Pp. 63–82. Boston: Northeastern University.

———. 1990. *Everyday Violence: How Women and Men Experience Sexual and Physical Danger.* London: Pandora.

Starr, June. 1989. "The Role of Turkish Secular Law in Changing the Lives of Rural Muslim Women, 1950–1970." *Law & Society Review* 23:497–523.

———. 1992. *Law as Metaphor: From Islamic Courts to the Palace of Justice.* Albany: State University of New York.

Starr, June and Jane F. Collier, eds. 1989. *History and Power in the Study of Law: New Directions in Legal Anthropology.* Ithaca: Cornell University.

St. Bernard, Godfrey. 1998. *The Family and Society in Trinidad and Tobago: The Findings of the National Survey of Family Life.* Port of Spain, Trinidad and Tobago: Ministry of Social Development.

———. 1999. "Ethnicity and Attitudes towards Interracial Marriages in a Multiracial Society: The Case of Trinidad and Tobago." In *Identity, Ethnicity and Culture in the Caribbean*. Ralph R. Premdas, ed. Pp. 157–84. St. Augustine, Trinidad and Tobago: University of the West Indies, School of Continuing Studies.

Straus, Murray A., and Richard J. Gelles. 1986. "Societal Change and Change in Family Violence from 1975 to 1985 as Revealed by Two National Surveys." *Journal of Marriage and the Family* 48:465–79.

Sudnow, David. 1965. "Normal Crimes: Sociological Features of the Penal Code in a Public Defender's Office." *Social Problems* 12:255–76.

Sunder Rajan, Rajeswari. 1993. *Real and Imagined Women: Gender, Culture, and Postcolonialism.* London: Routledge.

Szalay, Kriszta. 1996. "Domestic Violence against Women in Hungary." In *Women in a Violent World: Feminist Analyses and Resistance across Europe*. Chris Corrin, ed. Pp. 41–52. Edinburgh: Edinburgh University.

Thomas, Dorothy Q., and Michele E. Beasley. 1993. "Domestic Violence as a Human Rights Issue." *Human Rights Quarterly* 15:36–62.

Thompson, John B. 1991. "Editor's Introduction." In *Language and Symbolic*

Power. Pierre Bourdieu and John B. Thompson, eds. Pp. 1–31. Gino Raymond and Matthew Adamson, trans. Cambridge, Mass.: Harvard University.

Thompson-Ahye, Hazel. 2002. *Women and Family Law and Related Issues: 229 Questions Answered*. St. Augustine, Trinidad and Tobago: Privately published.

———. 2004. "Domestic Violence and Legal Protection in the Bahamas: A Reality or an Illusion?" *The West Indian Law Journal* 29(1):73–85.

Tomlins, Christopher. 2001. "The Legal Cartography of Colonization, the Legal Polyphony of Settlement: English Intrusions on the American Mainland in the Seventeenth Century." *Law & Social Inquiry* 26(2):315–72.

Trinch, Shonna L. 2001. "The Advocate as Gatekeeper: The Limits of Politeness in Protective Order Interviews with Latina Survivors of Domestic Abuse." *Journal of Sociolinguistics* 5(4):475–506.

———. 2003. *Latinas' Narratives of Domestic Abuse: Discrepant Versions of Violence*. Amsterdam: John Benjamins.

Trinidad and Tobago Coalition Against Domestic Violence. 2005. *Domestic and Gender-Based Violence Judicial Training and Resource Manual*. Port of Spain, Trinidad and Tobago: Trinidad and Tobago Coalition Against Domestic Violence.

Trotman, David. 1986. *Crime in Trinidad: Conflict and Control in a Plantation Society 1838–1900*. Knoxville: University of Tennessee.

Trotz, D. Alissa. 2004. "Between Despair and Hope: Women and Violence in Contemporary Guyana." *Small Axe* 15:1–20.

Tsing, Anna Lowenhaupt. 1990. "Gender and Performance in Meratus Dispute Settlement." In *Power and Difference: Gender in Island Southeast Asia*. Jane Monnig Atkinson and Shelly Errington, eds. Pp. 95–125. Stanford: Stanford University.

Urla, Jacqueline. 1993. "Cultural Politics in an Age of Statistics: Numbers, Nations, and the Making of Basque Identity." *American Ethnologist* 20(4):818–43.

Valiente, Celia. 1996. "Partial Achievements of Central-State Public Policies against Violence against Women in Post-Authoritarian Spain (1975–1995)." In *Women in a Violent World: Feminist Analyses and Resistance across Europe*. Chris Corrin, ed. Pp. 166–85. Edinburgh: Edinburgh University.

Vatuk, Sylvia. 2000. "Domestic Violence in India: What Is the Law, How Effective Is it, and Why?" Paper presented at the 24th Annual Meeting of the Law & Society Association, Miami. May 26–29.

———. 2001. "Where Will She Go? What Will She Do? Paternalism toward Women in the Administration of Muslim Personal Law in Contemporary India." In *Religion and Personal Law in Secular India: A Call to Judgment*. Gerald James Larson, ed. Pp. 226–48. Bloomington: Indiana University.

———. 2003. "Muslim Women in the Indian Family Courts: A Report from Chennai." In *Divorce and Remarriage among Muslims in India*. Imtiaz Ahmad, ed. Pp. 137–60. New Delhi: Manohar Publishers.

Ventura, Lois A., and Gabrielle Davis. 2005. "Domestic Violence: Court Case Conviction and Recidivism." *Violence Against Women* 11(2):255–77.

Vertovec, Steven. 1992. *Hindu Trinidad: Religion, Ethnicity and Socio-Economic Change*. London: MacMillan Caribbean.

Volpp, Leti. 2005. "Feminism versus Multiculturalism." In *Domestic Violence at the Margins: Readings on Race, Class, Gender, and Culture.* Natalie J. Sokoloff, ed. Pp. 39–49. New Brunswick, N.J.: Rutgers University.

Walker, Gillian A. 1990. *Family Violence and the Women's Movement: The Conceptual Politics of Struggle.* Toronto: University of Toronto.

Walker, Lenore E. 1984. *The Battered Woman Syndrome.* New York: Springer.

Wan, Angela Moe. 2000. "Battered Women in the Restraining Order Process: Observations on a Court Advocacy Program." *Violence Against Women* 6(6):606–32.

Weber, Max. 1946. "Politics as a Vocation." In *From Max Weber: Essays in Sociology.* H. H. Gerth and C. Wright Mills, eds. Pp. 77–128. Oxford: Oxford University.

———. 1978. *Economy and Society.* 2 Vols. Guenther Roth and Claus Wittich, eds. Berkeley: University of California.

Websdale, Neil. 1998. *Rural Woman Battering and the Justice System: An Ethnography.* Thousand Oaks, Calif.: Sage.

Weitzman, Lenore J. 1985. *The Divorce Revolution: The Unexpected Social and Economic Consequences for Women and Children in America.* New York: Free Press.

———. 1987. "Judicial Perceptions and Perceptions of Judges: The Divorce Law Revolution in Practice." In *Women, The Courts, and Equality.* Laura L. Crites and Winnifred L. Hepperle, eds. Pp. 74–113. New York: Sage.

West, Carolyn M. 2005. "Domestic Violence in Ethnically and Racially Diverse Families: The 'Political Gag Order' Has Been Lifted." In *Domestic Violence at the Margins: Readings on Race, Class, Gender, and Culture.* Natalie J. Sokoloff ed. Pp. 157–73. New Brunswick, N.J.: Rutgers University.

White, Lucie E. 1991. "Subordination, Rhetorical Survival Skills, and Sunday Shoes: Notes on the Hearing of Mrs. G." In *At the Boundaries of Law: Feminism and Legal Theory.* Martha Albertson Fineman and Nancy Sweet Thomadsen, eds. Pp. 40–58. New York: Routledge.

Williams, Brackette F. 1991. *Stains on My Name, War in My Veins: Guyana and the Politics of Cultural Struggle.* Durham, N.C.: Duke University.

Williams, Eric. 1962. *History of the People of Trinidad and Tobago.* London: Andre Deutsch.

Wittner, Judith. 1998. "Reconceptualizing Agency in Domestic Violence Court." In *Community Activism and Feminist Politics: Organizing across Race, Class, and Gender.* Nancy A. Naples, ed. Pp. 81–104. New York: Routledge.

Women and Development Program. 1992. *Confronting Violence: A Manual for Commonwealth Action.* Human Resource Development Group. London: Commonwealth Secretariat.

Wood, Donald. 1968. *Trinidad in Transition: The Years after Slavery.* London: Oxford University.

Yelvington, Kevin A. 1995. *Producing Power: Ethnicity, Gender, and Class in a Caribbean Workplace.* Philadelphia: Temple University.

———. 1996. "Flirting in the Factory." *Journal of the Royal Anthropological Institute* 2:313–33.

Yngvesson, Barbara. 1988. "Making Law at the Doorway: The Clerk, the Court, and the Construction of Community in a New England Town." *Law & Society Review* 22:409–48.

———. 1993. *Virtuous Citizens, Disruptive Subjects: Order and Complaint in a New England Court.* New York: Routledge.

———. 1994. "Kidstuff and Complaint: Interpreting Resistance in a New England Court." In *Contested States: Law, Hegemony and Resistance.* Mindie Lazarus-Black and Susan F. Hirsch, eds. Pp. 138–50. New York: Routledge.

Trinidad and Tobago Newspaper Sources (from the West India Collection, University of the West Indies Library, St. Augustine, Trinidad and Tobago, and The Hugh Wooding School of Law Library, St. Augustine, Trinidad and Tobago)

The Independent, November 26, 1997.

Newsday, November 24, 26, 1997.

Sunday Guardian, March 10, 1991; April 21, 1991; November 23, 1997; January 25, 1998.

Trinidad Express, January 31, 1991; February 1, 20, 21, 28, 1991; March 6, 7, 8, 13, 14, 17, 1991; April 18, 1991; November 26, 1992; November 26, 1993; December 16, 23, 1994; December 3, 13, 1997.

Trinidad Guardian, March 10, 11, 12, 13, 1991.

INDEX

Page numbers in *italics* indicate
tables

abortion, 27
Abraham, Margaret, 23, 107, 181n17,
207n15
Abrams, Philip, 91
accusatory questions, 103
Adelman, Madelaine, 3, 6, 24, 122,
154, 156, 173, 208n2
adjournments, 40, 53, 54–55, 56, 66,
70, 95–96, 122, 127, 130, 137
adultery, 1–2, 177n1
Afro-Trinidadians, 9, 13, 25–26, 52,
142, 147, 194n16
age cohort of litigants, 51–52, 183n28
agency in law, 40, 89, 162; court rites
and, 7, 139–40; defined, 181n17; negotiated, 18, 140, 174; time deployment and, 137–38
Alcoholics Anonymous, 58
Alexander, M. Jacqui, 4, 5, 23, 24,
184n2, 208n2, 209n2
Alonso, Ana Marie, 184n1
Alternative Dispute Resolution
(ADR) movement, 167
Anglicanism, 9
Angrosino, Michael, 142
Appeals Court, 11
arrest warrants, 32, 70, 96, 112
assault and battery, 2, 23
attorneys: delegalizing rite, 170–71; erroneous or inadequate advice from,
108–9; fees of, 204n11; ineffective
assistance, 96–98, 109; mediation
by, 40, 41–42, 47, 58–59, 149–50;
objectification of clients, 107; time
deployment by, 18, 127–28

Babb, Cecilia, 4, 28, 186n6
Bailey, Barbara, 22
Bailey, Wilma, 4
Barberet, Rosemary, 24
Barriteau, Eudine, 5, 22, 26, 33, 34,
187n10
Barrow, Ayanna, 4
Barrow, Christine, 22, 142, 143, 144
Bartky, Sandra Lee, 7, 32, 89
battered woman designation, 117
battered woman syndrome, as legal
defense, 22
Battered Women's Working Group
(U.S.), 108–9
Baumgartner, M. P., 17, 166–67
Beasley, Michele E., 24, 161, 208n2
Belknap, Joanne, 16, 162, 192n6
Bell, 142
Biolsi, Thomas, 3
Birth, Kevin K., 5, 33
Bishop, Joan, 27, 28
Bissessar, Ann Marie, 5, 24, 25,
186n6, 208n2
Blankenhorn, David, 112
Blumberg, Abraham, 127, 130, 165
Bograd, Michelle, 15, 16
Boucaud, Donna, 175
Bourdieu, Pierre, 201n10
Boxill, Eileen, 4
Boychuk, Tascha, 164, 199n21
Boyle, Elizabeth Heger, 16, 24–25, 34,
160
Bradley, Christine, 4
Braithwaite, Farley, 4
Branche, Clement, 4
breach cases: criminal sanctions in,
178n5; disposition of, 49–50, *50*,
54, 55–56, 113; duration of, 50–51;

235

evidence in, 193n12; police role in, 38, 55, 193n12; undertakings, 32, 63, 71, 84, 86; unenforced enforcement of, 113

Breines, Wini, 23

Brereton, Bridget, 22, 25

Britain: common-law tradition of, 5, 22, 93, 162; domestic violence law in, 191n29; magistrates' courts in, 201n8

Brown, Judith, 5

Bumiller, Kristin, 16, 89

Burchell, Graham, 82

Burgess, Ann W., 5

Business and Professional Women's Club of South Trinidad, 28

Buzawa, Carl B., 16, 52, 61

Buzawa, Eve S., 16, 52, 61

Cain, Maureen, 4, 28, 33, 52, 185n4

Cameron-Padmore, Jacqueline, 145–46

Campbell, Carl C., 25, 26, 27

Campbell, Jacquelyn, 5

Caribbean Association for Feminist Research and Action (CAFRA), 28, 31, 185n4, 190n24, 195n24

CARICOM, 28, 32

Carlen, Pat, 100, 101, 103, 106, 107, 201n8

Carrillo, Ricardo, 53

Catholicism, 9, 147

Chevannes, Barry, 142, 143

child abuse, 28, 82, 197n12

children: family stability and, 146, 152, 165–66; legitimacy of, 142; man sharing relationships and, 106; paternity affiliation, 168–69, 172; visitation, 95, 96, 103, 104, 169, 172, 173

child support decision: culture of reconciliation and, 168–73; delegalizing rite, 102–3; legalizing rite, 113–14; second chances in, 111–12; unenforced enforcement rite, 112

Cicourel, Aaron, 104, 106

Clarke, Roberta, 3, 4, 28, 29, 32, 145, 179n11, 180n12, 186n6, 190n28, 209n2

class. *See* social class

Coalition Against Domestic Violence, 31, 59, 63

Cobb, Sara, 83, 166

Collier, Jane F., 3

Colón, Alice, 15, 24, 26, 29, 33, 146

colonialism, 9, 11, 25, 140

Comaroff, John L., 3, 5, 24, 25, 179n7

common-law tradition, English, 5, 22, 93, 162

Concerned Women for Progress (CWP), 27–28

Conley, John M., 3, 6, 17, 92, 99, 101, 110, 130, 179n8, 201n6, 202n12

Connell, Patricia, 3, 16, 156

Connors, Jane, 190–91n28

contact orders, 207n12

Corrin, Chris, 24

counseling: culture of reconciliation and, 148–49, 155; by religious community, 147; services for, 28, 82, 204n8; time deployment and, 128, 129, 132–33

Counts, Dorothy, 5

court orders, 48–49, 49, 62, 84, 87–88, 140

court personnel: culture of reconciliation and, 148–50, 155; delegalizing rite of, 102; misinformation from, 108–9; time deployment and, 123–24. *See also* probation officers

court rites, 14, 17; in case study, 95–98; class and gender hierarchies reinforced by, 7, 92, 111, 116–18; constraints on agency in, 7–8; culture of reconciliation and, 168–73; defined, 6, 92–93, 163; delegalizing, 102–3, 114, 171; disempowerment of complainant, 98; empowerment of complainant, 113–16; erroneous or inadequate advice, 108–9; euphemistic language, 6, 17, 105–7, 110, 114; humiliation, 104–5, 171; instructions to litigants, 99–100; intimidation, 6, 100, 101–102; judicial discretion, 99, 111, 198n16; legalizing, 103–4, 114; objectification of litigants, 107–8, 171; second chances, 111–12, 170; silencing, 6,

109–10, 170; time deployment and, 8, 169–70, 173, 204n9; types of, 6– 7, 163–64; unenforced enforcement, 112–13

courts: Appeals Court, 11; bureaucratic administration of, 92; delays in, 120; Family Court, 175; hierarchical structure of, 93, 182n24; High Court, 11, 29, 127, 175; implementation of legal reform, 91–92; public holidays, 195n2; rule-oriented vs. relational accounts in, 202n12; women judges, 188–89n17. *See also* court personnel; court rites; legal system; magistrates' courts

Coutin, Susan Bibler, 3, 6, 89, 92, 103, 107, 110, 173, 181n17, 203n5

creolization, 206n6

Creque, Merri, 4, 28, 59, 60

criminalization of non-heterosexual relationships, 184n2

Crocker, Diane, 89

cross-charges, 47, 47–48, 53, 169–70

Crowell, Nancy A., 5

culture, 205n2

cultures of reconciliation: Alternative Dispute Resolution (ADR) movement, 167; attorney mediation and, 40, 41–42, 47, 58–59, 149–50; as barrier to protection, 8–9, 18, 155–56, 167; court rites and, 168–73; cross-cultural comparisons, 141, 151–57, 166–67; in divorce process, 147, 166, 205n3; family stability and, 8, 141, 142–46, 151–52, 153–54, 165–66; historical tradition and, 140; magistrates and, 84, 148; probation officers and, 148–49; as reason for dismissed and withdrawn cases, 39, 61, 146, 150–51; religion and religious authorities in, 147, 152; silence about domestic violence and, 14–15; structural deflection and, 141; tenets of, 8, 141; undertakings and, 150

Daly, Stephanie, 23, 30

Daniel, Ramdaye, 1, 177n1

Daniel, Richard, 1, 177n1

Danns, George K., 4, 52, 122, 156, 180n15

defendants. *See* respondents

"degradation ceremony," 104

delegalizing, as court rite, 102–3, 114, 171

demographic characteristics, 9

Deosaran, Ramesh, 10

dismissed cases: for breach of protection, 49, 50, 54, 63; comparative data on, 54, 57, 60, 60; with cross-charges, 48; for fabricated claims, 83; with female complainant, 42, 61; incidence of, 36, 38–39, 39, 54, 61, 140; interim orders in, 42; with male complainant, 43, 44, 45; for non-appearance, 38, 53, 54, 61, 70, 83, 130, 169; reasons for, 39–40, 61, 83–84, 163, 192n6; with same-sex litigants, 44

disposition of cases: for breach, 37, 38, 49–51, 50, 54, 55–56, 63; comparative data on, 57–59, 60, 60, 63–64; court orders, 48–49, 49, 62, 84, 87–88, 140; cross-charges and, 47, 47–48; gender of litigants and, 42–43, 43, 62; interim orders, 41, 41–42, 48, 49, 62, 130, 140; peace bonds, 150; structural deflection and, 161–62; surname of litigants and, 193n9; types of, 38, 39. *See also* dismissed cases; undertakings; withdrawn cases

divorce: culture of reconciliation and, 147, 166, 205n3; reasons for, 206n7; stigma of, 2, 132, 144

Dobash, R. Emerson, 16, 23, 24, 26–27, 122, 125

Dobash, Russell P., 16, 23, 24, 26–27, 122, 125

domestic violence: adultery and, 2; conferences on, 27, 28; criminal statutes on, 178n5; deserved and undeserved, 195n1, 203n6; euphemisms for, 107; fabricated, 83, 198–99n17; forms of, 49, 63, 81–82; history of, 207n14; as "husband-wife business," 2, 12, 23, 30, 109,

151, 156; parent abuse, 38, 54, 67–73; patterns in abusive relationships, 93–95; public awareness of, 28, 88; reconciliation after, 39, 83; services to victims of, 28, 187–88n14; "sharing a man" and, 106–7; silencing of victim, 109, 117; social class and, 52–53; wife murder, 1–2, 177n1, 178n4

Domestic Violence Act of 1991: cultural practices reflected in, 160; in decolonization and nation building process, 185n4; effectiveness of, 87–90; ejectment under, 198–99n17; opponents of, 189n18; parliamentary debate over, 29–32, 34; passage of, 32; provisions of, 2, 12, 23, 29–30, 81, 82, 84, 162, 178–79n6; public awareness of, 65, 79, 88; spouse defined in, 29, 31

Domestic Violence Act of 1999: peace bonds under, 150; police power under, 190n27; provisions of, 14, 193n11

domestic violence cases. *See* protection orders, proceedings

Domestic Violence Hotline, 188n14

domestic violence law: in Caribbean nations, 179–80n12, 190–91n28, 194–95n23; English common law and, 5; equitable practice in, 160–61; eviction motives and, 198n17; historical background to, 184–85n3; international concerns in passage of, 24–25, 33–34; international influence on, 186n6; local ideology and practice in, 185–86n6; in nineteenth century, 184–85n3; precedent-setting nature of, 2, 5, 33; structural deflection and, 36, 64, 161–62; theoretical literature on, 3–5; women's movement in passage of, 23–24, 28, 31–32, 33; worthy and unworthy victims, 16–17, 88–89. *See also* Domestic Violence Act of 1991; Domestic Violence Act of 1999

domestic violence study methodology, 12–15

dress, in court appearances, 99–100

drug-addicted sons, in parent abuse cases, 67–73, 81, 82, 162

Dupont, Ida, 181n17

duration of case, 37, 44–46, *45, 46,* 48, 57, 62–63

East-Indians. *See* Indo-Trinidadians

Eaton, Mary, 99, 201n8

Economic Commission for Latin America and the Caribbean, 4, 194–95n23, 199n17

economic growth: as condition for regendering the state, 33; history of, 10; impact on women's movement, 26–27; oil industry and, 10, 27

education: colonial system of, 186n9; as condition for regendering the state, 33; nationalist commitment to, 26; of women, 23, 27, 33, 187n9, 187n12

education level: gender differences in, 27, 187n12; of litigants, 67, 78, 94

Eigenberg, Helen M., 198n16

Ekeh, Kaylene Richards, 3, 4

Emerson, Robert M., 6, 56–57, 99, 101, 104, 105, 106, 107, 130, 165, 173, 201n9

employment: entrepreneurship, 115; family assistance and, 143, 144–45, 166; gender inequity in, 10, 27; professional women, 33; social class and, 11

employment status of litigants, 52, 67, 77, 78, 135, 182n28

Engel, David M., 3, 17

Erez, Edna, 3

Escobar, Arturo, 82, 90

ethnicity, 9, 13; dispute resolution and, 180n15; geographic distribution, 194n16; incidence of domestic violence, 52; kinship patterns and, 142–43; nationalism and, 189–90n23

euphemism, as court rite, 6, 17, 105–7, 110, 114

Ewick, Patricia, 110, 126

exclusion orders, 198–99n17

Fagan, Jeffrey, 61
Family Court, 175, 210–11nn15–16
"Family Ideal," 151–52
family law, 185–86n6
family stability, culture of reconcili-
    ation and, 8, 141, 142–46, 151–52,
    153–54, 156, 165–66
family status of litigants, 38, 51, 67,
    81–82, 183n28
Federation of Women's Institutes
    (UWI), 186n7
Feeley, Malcolm, 6, 99, 101, 102, 106,
    108, 126, 127, 130, 173, 192n7,
    200n1
Ferraro, Kathleen J., 164, 199n21
Ffolkes, Suzanne, 3, 4
fieldwork, 12–15
financial abuse, 14
Fineman, Martha Albertson, 112, 166
fines and penalties, 14, 196n5
Fischer, Karla, 3, 61
Ford, David A., 3, 61, 89, 122, 197n15
Forde, Norma Monica, 4
Foucault, Michel, 18, 82, 89
Fraser, Arvonne, 209n3
French, Rebecca R., 17, 119, 137,
    202n1, 203n4
Frohmann, Lisa, 16, 23, 83, 89,
    207n12

Garfinkel, Harold, 104
Garland, David, 185n4
Gelles, Richard J., 24
gender inequality: court rites and,
    7, 92, 111, 116–18; dual-marriage
    system, 197n13; in education level,
    27, 187n12; in employment, 10,
    27; family patterns and, 8, 143–44;
    global and local pressure against,
    160–61; "regendering the state,"
    21–23, 26, 32–33, 161, 176; struc-
    tural deflection and, 36. *See also*
    women's movement
gender of litigants: cross-charges and,
    47, 47–48; disposition of case by,
    42–43, 43, 62; duration of case by,
    44–46, 45, 46; evasion of police by,
    39–40; female complainants, 38, 42,

43, 45, 62; male complainants, 38,
    43, 43–44, 45, 46, 53, 62; same-sex,
    38, 44, 45, 46; undertakings and, 62
Gittens, Eunice, 28
Goffman, Erving, 104
Gopaul, Roanna, 4
Gordon, Colin, 82
Gordon, Linda, 16, 23, 26
Gramsci, Antonio, 3, 91
Greenhouse, Carol J., 3, 17, 120, 137,
    181n17, 207n11

Hadeed, Linda, 4, 124, 147
Hagley, Lystra, 86
Hampton, Robert L., 53
Handwerker, W. Penn, 4, 197n12
Hann, Robert G., 175
Hanna, Cheryl, 193n13
harmony ideology, 167
Harney, Stefano, 5, 25, 27, 33
Harrell, Adele, 3, 16, 61, 162
Harriott, Anthony, 4
Hartley, Carolyn Copps, 16
Headley, Bernard, 43
hegemony, in legal system, 91, 94
Henderson, Thelma, 27, 33
Henriques, Zelma Weston, 3, 4
High Courts, 11, 29, 127, 175
Hinduism, 9, 147, 208n17
Hirsch, Susan F., 3, 6, 24, 91, 92, 98,
    112, 117, 201n7
Hirschel, David, 16, 153, 162
Hodge, Merle, 144
Holstein, James A., 201n9
homosexuality, 23
Horney, Julie, 183n29
Hosein, Emmanuel, 29
Housewives Association of Trinidad
    and Tobago (HATT), 27
human rights, women's, 209n3
humiliation, as court rite, 6, 104–5, 171
"husband-wife business," 2, 12, 23,
    30, 109, 151, 156
Hutchison, Ira W., 16, 153, 162

independence movement, 25–26
India, culture of reconciliation in,
    154–55, 166

Indo-Trinidadians, 9, 13, 25–26, 52, 142, 143, 145, 184–85n3, 194n16, 206n8
instructions to litigants, 99–100
interim orders, 38, *41*, 41–42, 48, 49, 62, 130, 140
intimidation of litigants, 6, 100, 101–2
Islam, 9
Israel, culture of reconciliation in, 154

Jackson, Jean, 102, 112
Jamaica, court rites, in, 100, 101
James-Sebro, Meryl, 4, 24, 28, 33, 208n2
Joseph, Janice, 3, 4
judicial discretion, 99, 111, 198n16, 200n1
judicial style, 58, 63
judicial system. *See* legal system
Just, Peter, 3
justice of the peace: as gatekeeper, 123; misinformation from, 108

Kabeer, Naila, 7
Kanhai, Rosanne, 143–44
Kelkar, Govind, 208n17
Khan, Aisha, 182n21
Kiely, Ray, 10
Kim, Joan, 53
Klein, Dorie, 16
"knowing the man," police and, 124–25
Kuper, Adam, 140, 205n1

labor force. *See* employment
LaFont, Suzanne, 99, 100, 101, 102, 105, 112, 122, 123, 124, 173
Lamb, Sharon, 16
lawyers. *See* attorneys
Lazarus-Black, Mindie, 3, 5, 12, 16, 21, 22, 24, 25, 28, 34, 37, 52, 56, 57, 61, 83, 91, 92, 94, 104, 105, 112, 114, 145, 161
LeFranc, Elsie, 4
legalizing, as court rite, 103–4, 114
legal system: agency and structure in (*see* agency in law; structural constraints); common-law tradition, 5,

22, 93; hegemony in, 91, 94; regendering the state, 21–23, 176; time deployment in, 119–21. *See also* court personnel; court rites; courts; domestic violence law; magistrates' courts
Leo-Rhynie, Elsa, 22
Levinson, David, 179n10
Loseke, Donileen R., 17, 23, 89, 197n14, 199n18

MacKinnon, Catherine A., 22
magistrates: culture of reconciliation and, 84, 148; judicial discretion of, 198n16; judicial style of, 58, 63, 195–96n3; qualifications of, 182n24; time deployment of, 129–30; women as, 188–89n17
magistrates' courts: behavior and dress in, 99–100; comparative data on domestic violence cases, 51–61, 247; court records on domestic violence cases, 37–51; family cases in, 11–12, 66; fieldwork in, 12–14, 35; number of domestic violence cases, 66; police screening in, 56; time deployment in, 123–24, 129–30; workloads of, 56–57, 66. *See also* court personnel; court rites; protection orders, proceedings
Mahabir, Cynthia, 4, 28
Mahoney, Martha R., 4, 7, 17, 126
Maintenance Act, 29
making a living, 143–45, 166, 205n1
Manning, Patrick, 182n22
manslaughter charges, 2
marriage patterns, 142–43
Martin, Del., 4, 122, 153
Mather, Lynn, 84
Matoesian, Gregory M., 3, 6, 17, 89, 92, 110, 202n12
Matrimonial Proceedings and Property Amendment Act, 29
Matthews, Nancy A., 21, 23
Maurer, Bill, 3, 5, 17, 30
McCall, Patricia L., 16, 35, 37, 56, 57, 191nn2–3
McLindon, James B., 112

mediation by attorney, 40, 41–42, 47, 58–59, 149–50

Mehrotra, Aparna, 4, 32

men: education level of, 27; "sharing a man" relationships, 106. *See also* domestic violence; gender of litigants; respondents

Mendes, John, 11

Merry, Sally Engle, 3, 4, 6, 16, 17, 22, 25, 34, 84, 88, 92, 99, 102, 110, 111, 122, 123, 130, 136, 152, 156, 161, 203n6, 204n9, 207–8n16

Mertz, Elizabeth, 23, 83

middle class: court personnel, 123; in independence movement, 25; shift in class boundaries, 11; victims, 12, 17, 53, 110, 131–32, 201n7

Mileski, Maureen, 101, 105

Miller, Daniel, 2, 5, 26, 27, 33, 143, 186n8

Miller, Peter, 82

Miller, Susan L., 24

Millette, James, 25

Minow, Martha, 7, 180–81n16

Mohammed, Patricia, 22, 23, 24, 27, 28, 33, 88, 142, 156, 186n9, 187n13, 197n13, 208n18

Momsen, Janet H., 143

Moog, Robert S., 202–3n3

Moore, Brian, 183n26

Moore, Sally Falk, 3

Morrow, Betty Hearn, 4, 24

Munasinghe, Viranjini, 5, 143, 182n21, 190n23, 206n6

Munn, Nancy D., 17

Murrell, Franklyn, 175

Muslim community, 147

Nader, Laura, 3, 167

National Alliance for Reconstruction (NAR), 28, 186n7

National Commission on the Status of Women, 27

National Family Services, 128

nationalism, Trinidadian, 25, 26, 33

Newmark, Lisa, 16, 61, 162

Nimmer, Raymond T., 17

Noaks, Lesley, 16

nongovernmental associations (NGOs), women in, 29

Nurse, Keith, 27

O'Barr, William M., 3, 6, 17, 92, 99, 101, 109–10, 130, 179n8, 201n6, 202n12

objectification, as court rite, 6, 107–8, 171

obsessed partners, abuse by, 73–80, 82

occupational status of litigants, 52, 77, 78

oil industry, 10, 27

orders of protection. *See* protection orders

parent abuse, 38, 54, 67–73, 81, 149

Pargass, Gaietry, 4, 179nn11–12, 209n2

Parliament, 10; Domestic Violence Act of 1991 in, 29–32, 34; women in, 29

Parsad, Basmat Shiw, 4, 52, 122, 144, 145, 156, 180n15, 182n26, 206n8

participant observation, 12–13

paternity affiliation, 168–69, 172

peace bonds, 14, 150

Pentecostals, 147

People's Education Group (PEG), 186n7

People's Education Movement (PEM), 186n7

People's Nationalist Movement (PNM) party, 25, 26, 186n7

Peterson del Mar, David, 207n14

Philips, Daphne, 2, 61, 178n4

Philips, Susan U., 3

Pierce, Paulette, 36, 64, 141, 161

Pleck, Elizabeth, 4, 23, 188n15

police: arrest warrants, 32, 70, 96, 112; in breach cases, 38, 55, 193n12; bureaucratic incompetence of, 80; changing attitudes toward litigants, 88; community police, 197n11; courthouse screening by, 56; delegalizing of complaints, 103; under Domestic Violence Act of 1999, 190n27; erroneous or inadequate advice from, 69–70; instructions to litigants, 99, 100, 125; "knowing the man," 124–25; meting out justice, 204n10; as respondent, 124, 125–26; respondents' evasion of, 39–40, 126; respondents' fear of, 86, 132, 146; serving of summons, 66, 70, 96, 112–13, 124, 132; silencing of victims, 109; time deployment of, 17–18, 124–25; training in domestic violence, 188n14

political participation of women, 28–29, 188–89n17

political system, 10

postcolonial state, 5, 22, 24, 25–29

"powerless" speech, 110

Pratt, Christina, 153–54, 156

Presbyterianism, 9

Preves, Sharon E., 16, 24–25, 34, 160

Privy Council (England), 11

probation officers: as advocate for complainant, 136; culture of reconciliation and, 148–49; magistrates' use of, 86; time deployment by, 18, 128–29

protection orders: ancillary orders, 14; comparative data, 51–61; contents of, 198n17; court data, 15, 16, 37–38; court rites as constraint on, 6–8; cultures of reconciliation as constraint on, 8–9; under Domestic Violence Act of 1991, 2, 12, 23, 190n25; under Domestic Violence Act of 1999, 14, 190n27; status of applicants, 183n28

protection orders, proceedings: adjournments of, 40, 53, 54–55, 56, 66, 70, 95–96, 122, 127, 137; of breach cases (*see* breach cases); criteria for success in, 84, 86–87; duration of, 37, 44–46, *45, 46, 48*, 57, 62–63, 130; improvement of, 196n4; number of filings, *60, 60*, 66; self-representation in, 73, 134, 184n31; successful cases, 67–80, 84–87, 162; time in (*see* time, deployment of); types of applicants, 81–82; unsuc-

cessful cases, 95–98. *See also* dismissed cases; disposition of cases; gender of litigants; undertakings; withdrawn cases

Ptacek, James, 4, 23, 52, 58, 64, 89, 99, 100, 103, 104, 108, 109, 122, 125, 151–52, 153, 156, 198n16

Purdy, Jeannine M., 99

Rahamut, Tara, 27, 28

Ramkeesoon, Gema, 33

rape crisis center, 28

Rape Crisis Society, 28, 31

Rawlins, Joan M., 4, 52, 61, 180n15

Razack, Sherene H., 4, 7, 82, 89, 92, 195n1, 197n14

reconciliation. *See* cultures of reconciliation

Reddock, Rhoda, 4, 10, 15, 24, 26, 27, 29, 33, 146, 182n21, 186n7

Red Thread, 4

regendering the state, 21–23, 26, 32–33, 161, 176, 184n1

Regoli, Mary Jean, 3, 61

religious groups, 9; culture of reconciliation and, 147, 152, 154

respondents: cross-charges, 47, 47–48, 53, 169–70; evasion of police, 39–40, 126; fear of police, 86, 132, 146; non-appearance of, 38, 53, 54, 61, 70, 83, 126, 130, 169, 192–93n7; in parent abuse cases, 38, 54, 67–73, 81, 149; police officer as, 124, 125–26; time deployment of, 125–26; women as, 38, *43*, 43–44, 45, 46, 53, 62, 82. *See also* breach cases; court rites; domestic violence; gender of litigants; undertakings

Rheinstein, Max, 200n1

Richards, George Maxwell, 182n22

Richie, Beth, 181n17

Rivera, Jenny, 24, 208n2

Roberts, Simon, 3, 179n7

Robinson, Tracy S., 4, 14, 185–86n6, 190n26, 190n28

Rock, Letnie, 4

Romany, Celina, 24, 208n2

Rose, Mary, 3, 61

Rosen, Ruth, 24
Ryan, Selwyn, 15, 26

Saith, Radica, 28
same-sex litigants, 38, 44, 45, 46, 53
Schneider, David M., 165
Schneider, Elizabeth M., 24, 109, 110, 152, 202n13
Schutz, Alfred, 174
Scott, James C., 111
second chances, 111–12, 141, 170
Seebaran-Suite, Lynette, 27, 190n24
Segal, Daniel A., 182n21
Senior, Olive, 27, 105, 106
Sewell, William H., 181n17, 181n19
sexual harassment, 22, 187n13
Sexual Offenses Act of 1986, 22–23, 28, 187n13
Shallhoup-Kevorkian, Nadera, 3
sharing relationships, 106
Shelter for Battered Women, 59, 63
Shepherd, Cathy, 28, 160, 190n24
Shepherd, Verene, 22
Silbey, Susan S., 110, 126
silencing, 6, 109–10, 117, 170
Sitaraman, Bhavani, 122, 154–55, 156, 195n1
Smith, Barbara E., 3, 16, 61, 162
Smith, Raymond T., 190n23, 197n13
Smyth, Ailbhe, 24
social class: court personnel/litigant interactions and, 102, 123; court rites and, 7, 92, 111, 116–18; of litigants, 12, 17, 52–53; structure of, 10–11
Sokoloff, Natalie J., 52, 180n15, 181n17
Spohn, Cassia, 183n29
Spooner, Mary, 4, 24, 122, 123, 125, 144, 156, 198n15, 206n9, 209n2
spouse: de facto, 189n20; defined, 29, 31
Stanko, Elizabeth A., 14, 17, 89
Starr, June, 3
St. Bernard, Godfrey, 143, 144
Straus, Murray A., 24
structural constraints, 89, 140, 162; defined, 181n19; forms of, 7–8; in-

terpreted, 18–19, 174–75; and legal processes, 18
structural deflection, 36, 64, 141, 161–62, 164
suicide attempts, in wife murders, 2
summons, serving, 66, 70, 96, 112–13, 124, 132, 134
Sunder Rajan, Rajeswari, 24
Szalay, Kriszta, 24

Teachers' Education and Cultural Association (TECA), 186n7
telephone harassment, 49, 75, 76, 77, 78, 133
temporary restraining orders, 209n10
Thomas, Dorothy Q., 24, 161, 208n2
Thompson, John B., 105
Thompson-Ahye, Hazel, 31, 178n5
time: by applicant, 122, 131; by attorneys, 18, 127–28; case studies, 131–37; as constraint on agency and entitlement, 137–38; in courthouse, 123–24; court rites and, 8, 169–70, 173; deployment of, 164–65; functions in legal process, 119–21; as instrument of power, 17; by magistrate, 129–30; by police, 17–18, 124–25; by probation officers, 18, 128–29; by respondent, 125–26
Tomlins, Christopher, 22
Trinch, Shonna L., 7, 92, 107, 162, 181n18
Trinidad Express, 28, 29, 30, 31, 145–46
Trinidad Guardian, 28, 30, 31, 32
Trinidad and Tobago: class system in, 10–11; colonial heritage of, 9, 11, 24; cultural identification in, 186n8; demographic characteristics of, 9, 194n16; government of, 10; independence movement in, 25–26
Trinidad and Tobago Coalition Against Domestic Violence, 28
Trotz, D. Alissa, 24

UN Decade for Women, 27
undertakings: breach of, 32, 63, 71, 84, 86; culture of reconciliation

and, 146, 150; defined, 84; effectiveness of, 85–86; by female respondents, 44, 62; as final disposition,
38, 41, 46, 48, 49, 57, 58, 61, 71, 85,
140; in parent abuse case, 71; priori-
tized cases with, 130; respondents'
reasons for, 85; as second chance,
112
unemployment, gender differences
in, 10
unemployment status of respondents,
68, 70
unenforced enforcement, 112–13
United States: court rites in, 101,
102–3, 104, 107, 108–9, 164, 173,
204n9; culture of reconciliation
in, 151–54; disposition of cases,
199n21; domestic violence law in,
178n5, 183n29, 188n15, 191n29;
temporary restraining orders,
209n10; time and legal process in,
122, 123–24, 125, 126, 164–65; wife
abuse, defined, 199n18; withdrawn
cases in, 197–98n15
University of the West Indies, 27
Urla, Jacqueline, 15, 35, 191n1

Valiente, Celia, 24
Vatuk, Sylvia, 4, 8, 122, 124, 154, 155,
156, 166, 173, 195n1, 204n10
Vertovic, Steven, 143
visitation arrangements, 95, 96, 103,
104, 169, 172, 173

Walker, Gillian A., 24
Walker, Lenore E., 22
Wan, Angela Moe, 105, 153
warrants, arrest, 32, 70, 96, 112
Weber, Max, 6, 8, 21, 92, 200n1
Websdale, Neil, 124, 125, 156, 183n30
Weitzman, Lenore J., 112
well-being, socioeconomic, 205n1
West, Carolyn M., 53
White, Lucie E., 92, 101
wife murder, 1–2, 177nn1–2

Williams, Brackette F., 205n1
Williams, Eric, 25, 26
withdrawn cases: for breach of protection, 49–50, 50, 63; with cross-
charges, 47; incidence of, 36, 38, 39,
55, 140; interim orders in, 42; with
male complainant, 43–44, 45, 62;
reasons for, 40–41, 83, 131–35, 146,
163, 192n6, 197–98n15; with same-
sex litigants, 44
witness testimony, 73, 76–77
Wittner, Judith, 4, 100, 101, 110, 122,
126, 156, 197–98n15
women: education of, 23, 27, 33,
187n9, 187n12; family stability as
responsibility of, 146, 152, 165–66;
in labor force, 10, 27, 33; political
participation of, 28–29, 188–89n17;
in sharing relationships, 106. *See
also* domestic violence; gender
inequality; gender of litigants;
women's movement
women's movement: economic
growth in development of, 26–27;
education and, 27; mobilization
of, 27–28; in passage of domestic
violence law, 23–24, 28, 31–32,
188n15; in postcolonial states, 24;
in regendering the state, 33
working class: employment patterns
of, 11; litigants from, 12, 67–73
Working Women, 31, 190n24
Working Women for Social Progress,
28
workplace: harassment in, 52, 75, 76,
77, 78–79, 133; protection orders
in, 48
worthy and unworthy victims, 16–17,
88–89, 162
Wortley, Scot, 4

Yelvington, Kevin A., 5, 10, 27, 30,
33, 142, 190n23, 197n13
Yngvesson, Barbara, 3, 6, 17, 84, 92,
102, 103, 105, 110, 123, 124, 204n9

MINDIE LAZARUS-BLACK is a professor in the
Department of Criminal Justice and an affiliate
professor of anthropology at the University of Illinois
at Chicago. She teaches classes in law and society,
violence, and surveillance. Dr. Lazarus-Black is the
author of *Legitimate Acts and Illegal Encounters:
Law and Society in Antigua and Barbuda* and
coeditor of *Contested States: Law, Hegemony and
Resistance.* She was a Fulbright Senior Scholar to the
University of the West Indies, Trinidad and Tobago.

The University of Illinois Press
is a founding member of the
Association of American University Presses.

Composed in 9.5/12.5 Trump Mediaeval
by Jim Proefrock
at the University of Illinois Press
Manufactured by Sheridan Books, Inc.

University of Illinois Press
1325 South Oak Street
Champaign, IL 61820-6903
www.press.uillinois.edu